Around and About Abuja

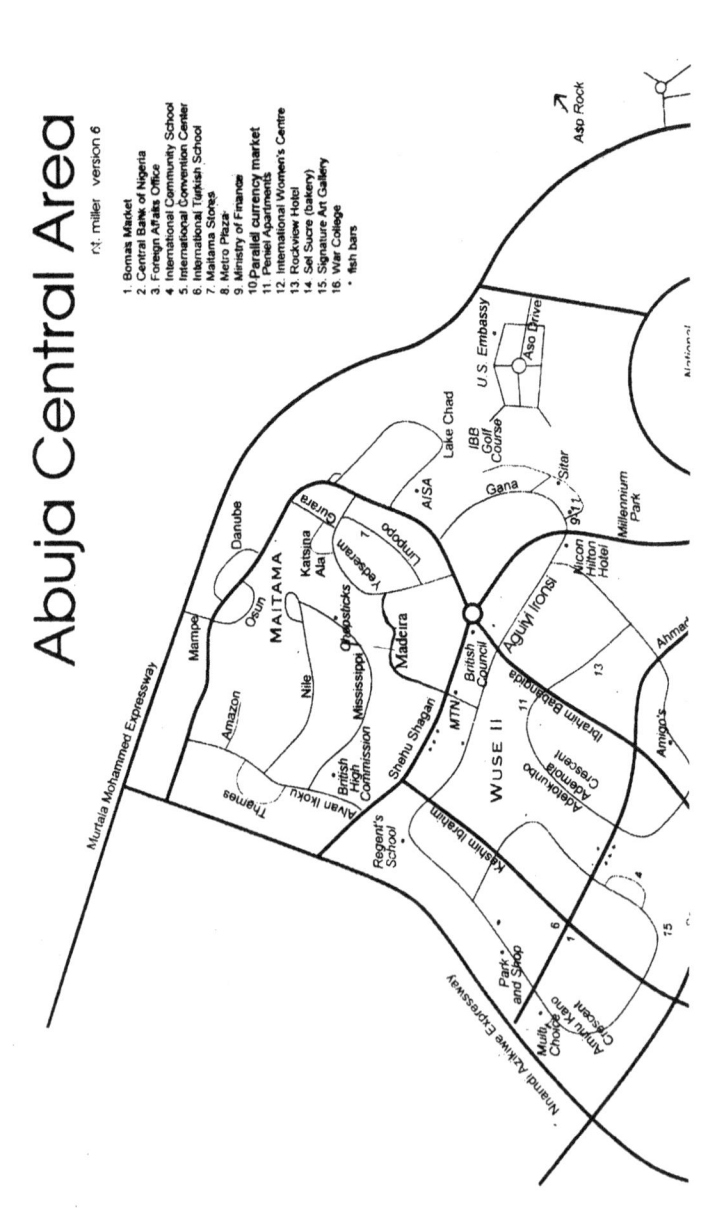

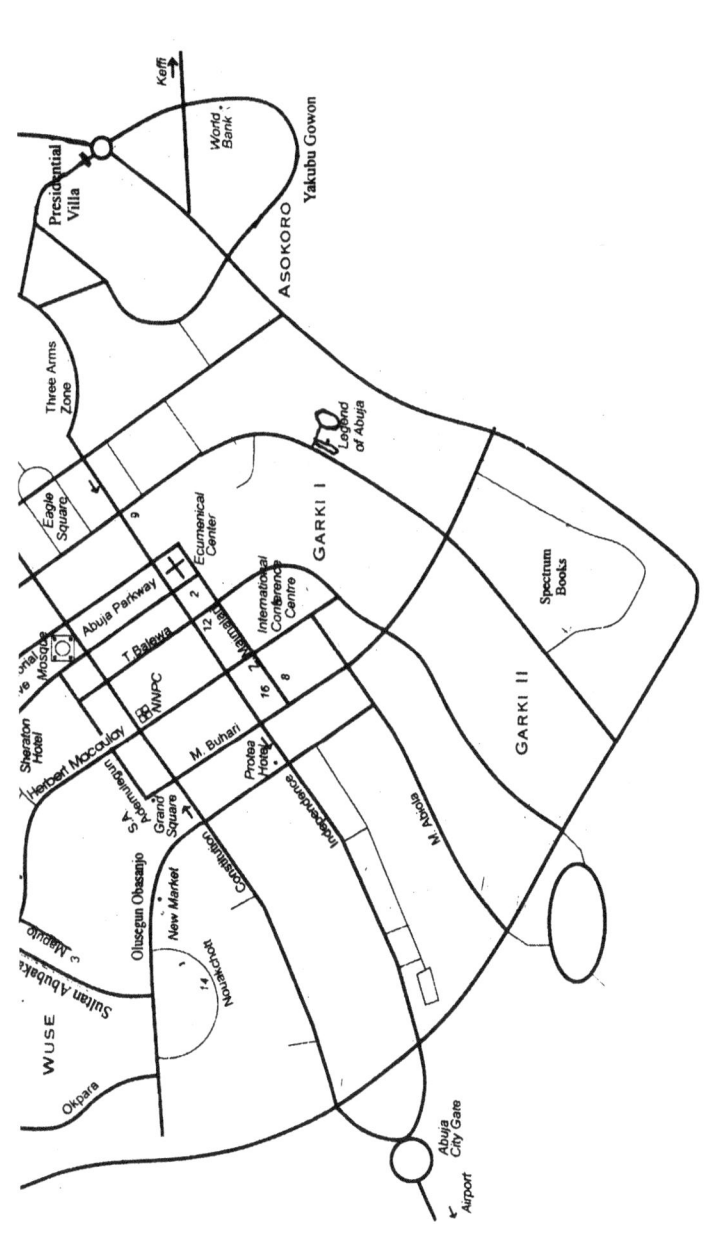

Around and About Abuja

Francine Rodd
Jewell Kidd
Willie Cohen
Taniko Noda

Spectrum Books Limited
Ibadan
Abuja •Benin City •Lagos •Owerri

Spectrum titles can be purchased on line at
<u>www.spectrumbooksonline.com</u>

Published by
Spectrum Books Limited
Spectrum House
Ring Road
PMB 5612
Ibadan, Nigeria
e-mail:admin1@spectrumbooksonline.com

in association with
Safari Books (Export) Limited
1st Floor
17 Bond Street
St Helier
Jersey JE2 3NP
Channel Islands
United Kingdom

Europe and USA Distributor
African Books Collective Ltd
The Jam Factory
27 Park End Street
Oxford OX1, 1HU, UK

© Francine Rodd, Jewell Kidd, Willie Cohen & Taniko Noda

First published, 2005

All rights reserved. This book is copyright and so no part of it may be reproduced, stored in a retrieval system, or transmitted, in any form or by any means, electronic, mechanical, electrostatic, magnetic tape, photocopying, recording or otherwise, without the prior written permission of the copyright owners.

ISBN: 978-029-525-9

Contents

Foreword   xiii
Acknowledgements   xv

Chapter 1
You Are Welcome!   1
How the Book Was Developed   1
How the Book Should Be Used   2
An Excellent Companion   2
Caveats on the Information Included   2
Our Favourites   3

Chapter 2
Introduction to Abuja   4
Background   5
History   7
Abuja FCT Administration   9
The Three Arms Zone   9
Nigeria   9
Climate   10
The People and Culture   11
The Languages   13

Chapter 3
Hints to Foreigners   16
Before You Come   16
On Arrival   23
Dress and Social Etiquette   24
Life Events   26
The Food   29
High Commission/Embassy Contact Information   32
International Organisations   58

Chapter 4
Getting Here   62
Travelling to Abuja   62

Shipping to Abuja	63
Import Allowances	64
Prohibited Items	65
Airlines and Travel Agencies	66

Chapter 5
Getting Settled — 74

Real Estate	75
Water Service	80
Electricity Hook-up and Payment	82
Fuel Purchases and Delivery	86
Cooking Fuel	86
Television and Satellite TV Hook-up	87
Telephone Connection and Telephone Payment	89
Prepaid Calling Cards	91
Street-side Calling	91
Mobile Phone Options	91
Refuse	93
Landscaping	94
Fumigation (Pest Control)	95
Post Offices	98
Security Services	99
Personal Effects Insurance	100
Home Repairs (Plumbers and Electricians)	101
Swimming Pool Maintenance	102
Hiring Domestic Help	102

Chapter 6
Getting Around — 106

Taxis and Motorcycles	106
Importing Vehicles	107
Car Hires	108
Car Purchases	109
Fuel Servicing	110
Car Servicing	111
Driver's Licence	113
Car Insurance	113

Chapter 7
Minding the Children — **115**
Schools — 116
Recreation Options — 128
Outings — 129
Kid Friendly Places to Eat — 134
Party and Function Organisers — 135
Toys and Children's Clothes — 136
Travelling with Children — 138

Chapter 8
Going Out — **139**
Service Symbol Keys — 140
Going-out Notes — 141
Bakeries — 143
Cafes — 146
Fast Food and Take-away — 146
Restaurants — 152
Fish Bars — 162
Bars — 163
Disco/Night Clubs — 167
Casinos — 170

Chapter 9
Stocking-up — **171**
Appliances and Electronics — 172
Arts and Crafts — 173
Butchers — 173
Drinks — 174
Florists — 174
Fish: Fresh and Frozen — 175
Furniture and Furnishings — 176
Green Grocers — 179
Interiors and Household Accessories — 181
Local Nigerian Markets — 182

Supermarkets	184
Toys, Clothes and Shoes	189

Chapter 10
Getting Rest — 193

Hotels and Service Apartments	193
Getting Rest Symbol Keys	194
Getting Rest Notes	195
Hotels	196
Service Apartments	212

Chapter 11
Getting Down to Business — 215

Public Holidays	215
Business Hours	216
Business and Investment Information	216
Banks and Banking	217
Money Changing	218
Courier Services	218
Office Supplies	219
Computer/Office Equipment Repairs/IT Consulting	220
Graphic Design/Website Development Companies	221
Printing Companies	222
Corporate Image Promotion Materials	222
Photocopies/Photocopiers	223
Furniture Rentals	223
Sound/Lights	223
Film Developing	224

Chapter 12
Staying in Touch — 225

Internet Hook-ups	225
Satellite Internet	228
Television	228
Radio	229
Newspapers	229
Websites	230

Libraries	230
Bookstores and Stationers	231
Cyber Cafes	233

Chapter 13
Staying Healthy — 236

Prevention	237
Evacuation Insurance	241
When You are Ill	241
Health Hazards	242
Seeking Medical Advice	258
Drugs	258
Maternity Facilities	260
Hospitals and Medical Clinics: In Case of Emergency	260
Dental Care	264
Laboratories	265
Pharmacies	266
Keeping Your Pet Healthy	267

Chapter 14
Staying Safe — 270

Know the Situation	270
Driving in Abuja	271
Driving Outside of Abuja	273
The "Dash"	273
Fraud and Scams — 419	274
Some Stay Safe Rules in Nigeria	275
In Case of Emergency	276

Chapter 15
Staying Fit and Beautiful — 279

Sports and Recreation Centres	279
Salons	282
Clothing and Shoes	285
Dressmakers/Tailors	285
Dry Cleaners	287

Chapter 16
Staying Active — 288
Churches — 289
Charitable Organisations (volunteer opportunities) — 291
Cultural Activities — 291
Sports — 293
Annual International Social Events — 294

Chapter 17
Enjoying the Culture — 296
Annual Festivals — 296
Music — 300
Literature — 301
Clothing — 301
Art and Crafts Work — 302
Tourist Spots around Abuja — 306
Markets in Outlying Villages — 306
Pottery — 307
Guided Tours — 307
Further Afield — 309
Mileage Guide — 309

Chapter 18
Additional Resources — 316
Abuja Specific Resources — 316
Other Non-fiction — 317
Fiction — 318
Quotes — 319
Travel Books — 319
Websites — 319

Appendix — **323**

Foreword

Around and About Abuja, written by four expatriate ladies, is a welcome important contribution to the literature on Abuja. It provides in great detail where to eat, where to shop, where to sleep and how to enjoy the beautiful scenery of Abuja and its surroundings. It is an excellent companion and one of the most in-depth and complete books ever written about the Nigerian Federal Capital. It represents a well-researched, descriptive, illustrated and richly informative piece of work.

The book provides rare details of many nooks and crannies in the city. Reading the book will make visitors and residents proud and happy to visit, live and work in Abuja. It is very relevant, comprehensive and educative.

I congratulate the authors, for doing a good job by painstakingly highlighting Abuja positively, and the publishers, for making the book available.

I recommend *Around and About Abuja* to everybody.

Nasir Ahmad el-Rufai, OFR

Minister of Federal Capital Territory

Acknowledgements

As with most such endeavours, there are many people to thank for the production of this book: from the hundreds of people who filled in questionnaires on restaurants, stores and services, to the friends who loaned us existing resources. We are indebted to them all.

Collectively, we have never worked on a project with as much energy and momentum as this one. Families, friends and colleagues were unanimous in their support of such a guide. They had no idea how much that meant we were going to be bothering them for information and ideas. Our families have been particularly supportive, especially when deadlines were approaching.

Special thanks go to Helene Poletti for her wonderful artwork throughout the book, and Millie Bowie, who gave us permission to use edited excerpts of her travelogue, "Travels with Millie". Mrs. Teresita Villapando, wife of the Consul - General of the Philippine Embassy, graciously allowed us to use her "Basic Guide to Make Your Move to Abuja Easier" as a resource. Rob Miller spent countless hours developing the overview map, currently accurate with this city's ever-changing streets. Tamara Rusinow, Julie Fischer, Roger Gillespie, Laurie Palmetier, Roger Blench and Catherine Chatham spent countless hours reading and editing the text before we sent it to the publisher. The following people also helped by either providing recommendations, information or constructive criticism: Theresa Ford, Pooja Keswani, Lyn Kingsmill, Simona Noca, Lola and Francis Odubekun, Tamar Pesti, May-Britt Searty, John Ella, Cecil Qadri and Jolene Van Wyk. We thank them for their support and openness. John Chisholm pitched in at the last minute to assist with "fact-checking". Friends like these are hard to find.

We found the American Women's Club guide to Lagos — *Lagos: Easy Access* — late in our planning stage and were amazed at how similar our topics and ideas were. The excellent work done there helped us to hone some of our own thinking.

Finally, we are grateful to Chief Joop Berkhout of Spectrum Books Limited for his immediate and eager support for our work.

He took the daunting tasks of publishing, marketing and sales off our backs and eased our minds so that we could provide the best product within the shortest possible period of time.

We decided to donate our share of the proceeds from the sale of this book to the Abuja office of Family Care International. There is a Nigerian proverb that says, "*Hope makes a good breakfast but a bad supper*". Our hope is that this book will not only help make your stay in Abuja more enjoyable, it will also help to ensure a brighter future for those in need of a good supper.

Francine Rodd
Jewell Kidd
Willie Cohen
Taniko Noda

CHAPTER 1

You Are Welcome!

The water that you will drink from the river will not flow past you.

(Nigerian Proverb)

"You are Welcome!" will likely be the first words you will hear upon setting foot in the airport in Abuja, the new Federal Capital of Nigeria. They are words that will often be spoken and (for the most part) heartily felt.

This book has been written by a group of women who have genuinely felt welcome and so want to make it easier for others to also feel at home in Abuja. There is a great deal to appreciate about Abuja and we want to make sure that visitors and long-term residents find out the best about Abuja in one easy-to-read and easy-to-use guide.

How the book was developed

We wanted to take a "client-centred" approach in developing this guide. First, we conducted a survey to ascertain what people thought should be included in the guide. Then we used questionnaires with vendors and customers to solicit the most useful information possible.

How the book should be used

This book should be viewed as a **guide** — it gives advice and help on how to make the best of your stay in Abuja. For long-term residents, we recommend you read it from cover to cover as there are bound to be pieces of information that you did not know but which can make your life here a bit easier. Short-term visitors will obviously want to skim through the contents and go directly to specific areas of interest. We have made it a portable reference book that can easily be carried.

An excellent companion

An excellent resource companion for this guide is the *Abuja City Guide Map.* It contains a well-indexed map of streets and businesses. Published by MDZ Multimedia, it is sold at hotels, shops or contact MDZ office at 08037874835 or *mdzmulti@aol.com*.

Caveats on the information included

We have done our best to ensure that the addresses, telephone numbers and information in this book are accurate and up-to-date. However, anyone who has lived in Abuja for more than a week would tell you that what is true today, may not be so tomorrow. Businesses relocate, telephone numbers go temporarily and permanently "out of service" and the nice woman behind the counter could easily be a relative on holiday from school. Therefore, we cannot be held responsible or accountable for any of the information found within the guide more than one minute after press time. Seriously, this information was gathered from foreign and Nigerian residents in Abuja in 2003. (At that time the exchange rate ranged between 135-149 Naira per $1.) Reach out to current residents to ensure that the information found within this guide is still accurate.

The best advice we can give you on your stay in Abuja is to take life slowly and not to be in a hurry. If taken to heart, that advice will prevent frustrations when for example, it takes an entire day to accomplish one task; it will, instead, allow you to think of it as time well-spent soaking in the sights, sounds and cultures of Abuja.

Our favourites

An image of the heart (♥) near an entry in the book indicates that we had personal experience with that vendor or activity and can recommend it to you.

CHAPTER 2

Introduction to Abuja

Unity among the cattle makes the lion lie down hungry.

(Nigerian Proverb)

Interesting Facts about Nigeria	
Federal Capital	Abuja
Country Population	Approximately 150 million
Population Growth Rate	3.4%
Country Area	924,000 sq. km
Official Language	English
Predominant Religions	Christianity, Islam and Traditional
Time	GMT/UTC +1
Voltage	220/240 Volts; British 3-pin square plugs
Weights and Measures	Metric
Country Telephone Code	234
Seasons	Winter/Dry (October to March); Summer/Rainy (April to October)
Climate	Humid Sub-Tropical
Legal Law /Tax System	British-oriented; Sharia Law in the North

Currency	Naira
Per Capita GDP	U.S. $314
VAT (Value Added Tax)	5% usually included in prices quoted
Major Export Earner	Crude Oil
Major Agricultural Products	Cocoa, Groundnut, Palm Produces, Rubber
Abuja Population	6,000,000
Abuja Area	7,315 sq. km
Abuja Main Local Languages	Hausa, Igbo and Yoruba (over 500 different languages exist in Nigeria)
Abuja City Telephone Code	09

Background

The Federal Republic of Nigeria is bordered on the west by Benin Republic, on the north by Niger, on the east by Cameroon and on the South by the Atlantic Ocean. Named after the great River Niger, it came into existence in 1914 with the amalgamation of the Northern and Southern British protectorates. On October 1, 1960 Nigeria became a fully independent country. It is the 14th largest country in the world in terms of area and has the largest population in Africa with approximately 150 million people. There are 36 states and the Federal Capital Territory (FCT) of Abuja. There are at least 10 cities with a population of over one million. Lagos, the former capital, has a population in excess of ten million. For a comprehensive review of Nigerian history, politics and economics, please refer to the books noted in the "Additional Resources" section.

Like Brasilia, the capital of Brazil, Abuja was selected as the new capital of Nigeria when it was obvious that population pressures and political and ethnic divisions necessitated a move from Lagos. On February 4, 1976, a decree was signed establishing the Federal Capital Territory of Abuja and setting up the Federal Capital Development Authority (FCDA), the organisation tasked with developing the new capital. Abuja began to operate officially as the new capital in 1991. Physically located in the centre of the country and viewed as neutral ethnically and religionwise, it is where culture and religion meet. The vehicle license plate for the FCT serves as a constant reminder that Abuja was selected in the hope of creating a "Centre of Unity".

The FCT is bordered on the north by Kaduna State, on the east and south-east by Nassarawa State, on the south-west by Kogi State and on the west by Niger State.

As a new capital, Abuja has an advantage of being well-planned over many capital cities. Visitors and arriving residents will be greeted by wide, well-designed and maintained roads and clean streets. Abuja also has excellent access to the wider road network to the rest of the country. It is built on a pre-Cambrian basement (granite) rock complex of distinctive domes and hills, the most striking of which is called Aso Rock.

The 1979 master plan called for Abuja to be developed in four phases. It estimated a population of about 1.6 million by the year 2000 and a maximum population of 3 million well into the 21st century. Nearly the entire Phase 1 development has been completed and it includes the following: the central business district, the Three Arms Zone (Presidency, National Assembly and Supreme Court) as well as the Maitama, Wuse, Garki and Asokoro residential and business districts. Most of the diplomatic missions have relocated to Abuja from Lagos; some are using temporary buildings and residences while their permanent structures are being built. The Gwarinpa District, where many of the construction companies' "Life Camps" are located, has also been developed but lies outside the Phase 1 area. Construction of service companies and enterprises continues at a fast pace in Abuja and new places open weekly. Phase 2, under development currently, involves the integration of the surrounding Katampe, Mabushi, Otako, Wuye, Durumi, Gudu, Jabi, Dutse and Gaduwa areas into the city. Phases 3 and 4 have not yet been fully planned.

Unfortunately, some of the initial infrastructural facilities are now being overstretched. The government is aware of this challenge and is working to rectify the disparity. The main source of water for Abuja is the Usman Dam. The digital telecommunications system is maintained by Nigeria Telecommunications Limited (NITEL). There are also a number of other privately owned satellite and mobile cellular telephone systems (see the "Getting Settled" section).

Both international and domestic flights arrive at the Dr Nnamdi Azikiwe International Airport. It is named after the first President of Nigeria and is about 40 km from the centre of Abuja.

History

The land now called Abuja was originally the south-western part of the ancient Habe (Hausa) kingdom of Zazzau (Zaria). It was populated for centuries by several semi-independent tribes. The largest of those tribes was the Gbagyi (Gwari), followed by the Koro and a few other smaller tribes. In the early 1800s, when Zaria fell to Fulani invaders, Muhammadu Makau, fled south with some followers and his brothers - Abu Ja and Abu Kwaka. Abu Ja succeeded Makau in 1825.

The full name of the king was Abubakar; Abu was his nickname. By some accounts his fair complexion earned him the nickname "Ja" which means "red" or "fair-skinned" in Hausa. He became known as "Abu-Ja" meaning "Abu the red" or "Abubakar the fair one." Other sources say that the "Ja" is a shortened form of Ishaku Jatau, his father's name. King Abubakar founded the kingdom of Abuja.

Abuja became a major commercial centre from which goods were exchanged by long distance traders. The inhabitants successfully fought off the Fulani and were not conquered as the surrounding lands were. In 1902, Abuja was occupied by the British colonial army. The British reorganised the kingdoms and called them "emirates" which means "kingdoms" in Arabic. Until 1975, it remained the relatively quiet emirate of Abuja.

The persistent problems associated with the capital being in Lagos, as mentioned earlier, led to the search for a new capital that year. Abuja was selected from amongst 33 possible sites. The criteria used for selection included: centrality, health, climate, land availability and use, water supply, multi-access possibilities, security, existence of resources, drainage, good soil, physical planning convenience and ethnic accord. The Emir of Abuja at the time, Alhaji Suleiman Barau, was asked to meet with his Emirate Council to approve contributing four of the five districts of Abuja to become the new capital. The council was divided as some districts considered it too much of a sacrifice; but at the end, they approved the request from the Federal Government. Thus, the Abuja Emirate in Niger State contributed 80% of the land of the territory, Plateau

State (now Nassarawa State) contributed 16 percent of the Southeast territory and Kwara State (now Kogi State) contributed about four percent of the South-west territory.

The Emirate was then asked to give up the name Abuja for the Federal Capital Territory. Again the council was divided. In the end, they agreed believing that the name of the emirate would become famous throughout the world. The previous town of Abuja was renamed Suleja after the then Emir Suleiman Barau and "Ja," the last syllable of the first emir's name.

Another interesting historical fact is that in the Gbagyi (or Gwari) language, the word "Aso" means "success" or "victory." According to tradition, the original inhabitants of the region lived at the base of the rock for centuries without being conquered. The rock was a refuge as well as a mystical source of strength. Asokoro ("Aso Koro"), the name of one of the local areas, therefore, means "people of victory." In addition, the term "Aso Rock" is increasingly being used to refer not only to the physical structure of the most imposing rock in the area, but also as a symbol of government power and national unity.

The View of Aso Rock from the Zoo

Abuja FCT Administration

There are six Area Councils in the Federal Capital Territory, each subdivided into wards headed by local councils. The Minister of the Federal Capital Territory is the overall leader and is appointed by the President of Nigeria.

The Three Arms Zone

The "Three Arms Zone" or TAZ is fashioned after Capitol Hill in Washington D.C. where the U.S. Congress, the Supreme Court and the White House are within a short distance of each other. In Abuja, the TAZ consists of the Presidential Villa, the National Assembly and the Supreme Court, all surrounded by a ring road.

National Assembly with Aso Rock at the Background

Nigeria

Agriculture was the mainstay of the Nigerian economy at the time of independence, but this changed with the discovery of oil in the Niger Delta in the 1960s. Today, Nigeria is the world's sixth largest producer of oil and the largest in Africa. Oil provides 20% of GDP, 95% of foreign exchange earnings and about 65% of budgetary revenues. Overdependence on oil continues to pose a problem for the Nigerian economy and the country is especially vulnerable to fluctuations in international crude oil prices. The country's gas industry has also witnessed tremendous development in recent years and continues to grow in importance.

Despite a wealth of natural resources, economic growth has been erratic since the 1970s. Hampered by the fluctuation of international oil prices, a number of missteps in macroeconomic planning and widespread corruption, Nigeria is among the world's poorest countries with per capita income significantly lower in real terms than at the time of independence.

The growing oil industry has resulted in substantial urban migration, to the detriment of the agricultural sector, and this phenomenon continues to persist.

The largely subsistence agricultural sector has failed to keep up with rapid population growth, and Nigeria - once a large net exporter of food - now imports food to feed a rapidly increasing population.

Economic growth for 2002 was 3.3%, with industrial output running at 21% of capacity. The GDP was ₦5,726 billion ($49 billion) at current prices, out of which oil makes up 85%. The GDP per capita is approximately $314. Currency conversion rates as of 28/11/04 were $1.00/₦132 at the weekly government auctions and $1.00 / ₦148 on the parallel market. The country's foreign exchange reserve balance averaged $8 billion in 2004.

In terms of investment, Nigeria offers potentially Africa's largest domestic market, relatively low-cost labour and substantial natural resources. Restrictions on foreign currency conversions were removed following the Foreign Exchange Decree of 1995, as a result of which foreign investors are now allowed to bring capital into the country without requiring prior government approval.

Climate

In the summer/rainy season (April to October), hot humid air from the Atlantic drifts into Nigeria from the south-west. By July, the entire country is covered in humid air. The rains fall from about mid-March until about mid-October. The average rainfall is 60-70 inches. Heavy rain storms are frequent, especially in the early evening hours. The winds are normally gentle except during thunderstorms when they can reach 40 miles an hour. During the rainy season, houses can feel damp and mildew on clothes is not uncommon.

In the winter, the harmattan, a mass of cold dry air from the desert, crosses the country. The thick dusty haze that the harmattan brings can last for weeks or months. This can affect people who suffer from hay fever or chest infections. Eye irritations are also common; so those who wear contact lenses often use their glasses during this period. Mornings (especially in the North) and nights can be cold enough to warrant a light sweater during this period. The harmattan winds die down by the end of January and the dry season finishes around the end of March or the middle of April.

The People and Culture

Nigerians are generally warm, friendly, intelligent and courteous people. In general, they are hardworking and kind to strangers and have a good sense of humour. People who travel internationally know that cultural values and norms are different in each country and sometimes within regions of the same country. It is a good idea to find out about them and to listen, watch and learn for a while upon entering a new country.

Nigerians have had a great impact in the fields of politics, science, arts and literature, music and sports. In sports, Nigerian basketball player Hakeem Olajuwon and footballers Nwankwo Kanu and Austin 'Jay-Jay' Okocha are some of the most legendary. Some of the more notable literary and musical artists are discussed in greater length in the "Enjoying the Culture" section and they include Nobel Prize winner Wole Soyinka, writer Chinua Achebe and musicians King Sunny Ade and Fela Anikulapo-Kuti.

There are over 500 different ethnic groups, each with its own language. Three, however, constitute half of the country's population – the Hausa in the north, the Yoruba in the west and the Igbo in the "east." The "east" Igboland refers to what is actually geographically the centre of the country. Hausa is the dominant native language spoken in Abuja. It is a good idea to learn a few words in Hausa, Igbo, Yoruba and Pidgin. You will have fun and Nigerians will appreciate it. At the end of this section is a list of basic greetings in the three languages and pidgin.

For the most part, dominant religions follow geographical lines. The Muslims dominate the north, the Christians the east and the west, with traditionalists throughout the regions. There are also a number of other cults and syncretic religions that combine Christianity with local spirits and guardians.

A large percentage of the population is Muslim. Muslims uphold the five pillars of Islam and pray five times a day (5.30 a.m., 1.30 p.m., 3.30 p.m., 6.30 p.m. and 7.30 p.m. – these times are approximate and depend upon the rising and setting of the sun). The holy day is Friday and around 1.30 p.m., most Muslim men (and some women) will travel to mosques to pray. Non-believers and women are not allowed into the mosque unaccompanied. Unless one is attending services, it is best to avoid travelling near any mosque areas between 1.30 p.m-4.00 p.m. on Fridays due to the dense traffic surrounding them. The Central Mosque in Abuja is an amazingly beautiful sight.

The other large percentage of the population is Christian. In many cases, Catholics and Protestants and other Christian sects have mixed Christianity with traditional beliefs. The Aladura Church is a unique result and an original religion.

A smaller portion of the population are traditionalists. The commonality that unites traditionalists is the belief that there is a supreme being who created everything and that there is a spiritual nature to every entity. There is also a strong belief that ancestors can influence the spirit world and bring luck or illness on the living. Therefore, ancestor worship is strong. The use of objects and words to cast spells and the sacrifice of animals to appease various spirits, deities or ancestors is common. The term used for these practices is juju. It would not be unusual to find materials, such as animal skulls, dried insects, bones, etc., used in juju ceremonies in markets.

The Languages

There are over 500 different languages found in Nigeria. The most prominent languages in Abuja are Igbo, Hausa and Yoruba. Most Nigerians speak at least three languages: their local language; English and Pidgin English. The tables below translate some commonly used phrases.

Commonly Used Phrases

English	Pidgin English	Igbo	Hausa	Yoruba
Hello	Well done! (How now?)	Ndeewo (Kedu?)	Sannu (when used in the north this can also be taken as "sorry")	E n le (Bawo ni?)
Good morning	Good Morning	I saala (I boola) chi	Barka da ina kwana	E kaaro
Welcome	Welcome	Nnoo	Barka da zuwa; Sannu da zuwa	E kaabo
Goodbye	Bye bye	Ka e mesia	Sai an jima	Oda bo
Please	Abeg	Biko	Don Allah	Jowo
Thank you	Thank you	I meela (Daalu)	Na gode	Ese/Ese gan
How was the night?	You sleep well?	I rahukwara nke oma	Yaya Dare	E karo. Se dada loji?
Excuse me please	Sorrio, I beggo	Biko nye m efe	Bani hanya	E jowo
Right	Right	Aka nri	Dama	Otun
Left	Left Aka ekpe	Hagu		Osi
Done	E don do	Meela	Ka tsaya	Se
In the middle of	For middle	N'etiti	Tsakiya	Aarin
Opposite	For other side	Nke chere ihu	Gaba	Idakeji

Introduction to Abuja 13

English	Pidgin English	Igbo	Hausa	Yoruba
I am looking for	I de find	Ana m acho	Nna nema	Mo nwa
Yes	Ehn/Yes/Thank you	Ee (Eee ya)	E	Beni
No	No/ M-m	Mba	Aa A'a	Rara/Bee Ko
Please speak slowly	Talk small small	Were nwayo	Magana a hankali	Soro die die
Which is the road to?		Kedu uzo e si eje…	Wache hanya che na zuwa	Ona wo lo ja si
How much does this cost?	How much be dis?	O bu ego ole?	Nawa yeke	Eelo ni e nta
It is too expensive	E too cost	O galara onu, o di oni	Yana da tsada	O ti won ju
Lower the price	Reduce price	Wetuo onu ya	Rage kudi	Din ku die
It is not expensive	E no cost	O di onu ala	Ba tsada	Ko won
Give me	Gimme	Nye m	Ba ni	Fun mi
Show me	Make I see	Gosi m	Nuna mi ni	Fi han mi
He is here	E de	O no n'ebe a	•Yana nan	O wa nibi
He is not here	E no de	O noghi n'ebe a	•Yana baya nan	Ko si nibi
Stop	Wait	Kwusi	Ka tsaya	Duro

New arrivals might also be interested in some localised usage of English terms.

American English	Nigerian English
Oven	Cooker
Pop, soda, soft drink	Mineral
Turn on	On it
Turn off	Off it
Power	Light or Nepa (e.g., "there has been no Nepa for hours")
In the office	On seat
Out of stock	Finished
Living quarters for domestic staff	Boys quarters or "BQ"
Lady of the house	Madame, Auntie
Man of the house	Master; Oga (Oga also used as a sign of respect for a person in power)
To give a tip or gift	Dash
Flashlight	torch
Motorcycle taxi	Okada
Bus taxi	Danfo bus

CHAPTER 3

Hints to Foreigners

He who wants to fly must first learn to stand.

(Nigerian Proverb)

Before You Come

Immigration Procedures
Visas are required for entry into Nigeria. Visitor and business visas are available in single or multiple entry form. There are several different types of visas: 1) tourist 2) visitor 3) business and 4) subject to regularisation (STR).
(See www.nigeria.embassyhomepage.com; or
www.nigeriaembassyusa.org)

The procedure for each is as follows:
Tourist Visa requires
- One completed application form
- Passport (ensure it is valid for at least 6 months)
- One passport-size photo
- Fee
- Onward or return ticket. May also need hotel reservations

Visitor Visa (valid for 3 months and one cannot work)
Provide the nearest Nigerian consulate with:
- Passport (ensure it is valid for at least 6 months)
- Two passport size photos
- A copy of your round-trip airline ticket (or ticket with onward destination)
- A letter of invitation from someone in Nigeria (or a letter from your travel agent)
- An official bank account statement showing sufficient funds
- Proof of vaccination for yellow fever
- Confirmation of a reservation from a hotel in Nigeria.

Persons entering Nigeria on a tourist or visitors visa are not allowed to work or conduct business.

Business Visa (valid for up to 12 months, multiple entry)
- Passport (ensure it is valid for at least 6 months)
- Two passport size photos
- A copy of your round-trip airline ticket (or ticket with onward destination)
- A letter of invitation from someone in Nigeria inviting you to come for business and assuming full financial responsibility for you during your stay
- An official bank account statement showing sufficient funds
- Proof of vaccination for yellow fever
- Confirmation of a reservation from a hotel in Nigeria.

Subject to Regularisation (valid for 3 months for people coming to work)
Applicants need the following to receive an STR visa:

- Passport (ensure it is valid for at least 6 months)
- A letter of appointment from your organisation
- A letter of acceptance of appointment signed by you
- A copy of your CV/Resume
- Credentials
- Three passport size photos.

This visa allows the recipient to work for three months while his/her resident status is being regularised.

TWP (Temporary Work Permit – valid for 3 months)
A TWP can be issued to expatriates coming to Nigeria for a brief specialised job.

Cerpack (Combined Expatriate Residence Permit)
This is the equivalent of a resident permit or an alien card. It allows the recipient to live and work in Nigeria. It is a plastic card that replaces the old paper residence permit and is renewable yearly. You need this as well as a visa unless the Nigerian government has given your organisation an exemption.

Applications for visas and inquiries are handled by:

The Comptroller General of Immigration,
Nigeria Immigration Service,
Old Secretariat, Block E,
Garki,
Abuja.

Nigerian embassies are beginning to restrict the issue of visas. If you are a foreigner residing in a country other than that of your national origin, it may be difficult to obtain a visa from the Nigerian Embassy there. Depending on where you are applying and the time of the year, it could take from two days to two weeks to receive a visa. The rules and requirements are subject to change, so check with the local Nigerian Embassy as early as possible.

Please, remember that it is illegal and unwise to engage in any business activity in Nigeria on a tourist visa.

Residence Permits

Non-ECOWAS foreigners working in Nigeria require a Form A residence permit. It is issued for up to two years on the basis that the employer has a valid expatriate quota. Foreigners holding STR visas issued by Nigerian diplomatic missions overseas need to apply to the Nigerian Immigration Service for a residence permit within three months of arrival.

Dependants need a Form B residence permit. It is also issued for up to two years. Required documentation includes copies of birth and marriage certificates. Form B residence permit holders may not automatically begin work. In most cases, a change of residence status will be required. Children may attend school without specific permission or change in status.

Personal Effects (Household Goods)

All imported items are expensive as they must undergo various forms of taxation and "dash"* to get into the country. You will pay about 50-100% more for items here than you would in your own country. If you have a preference for any particular brand items, it is recommended that you bring a good quantity with you. Although there is a wide range of cosmetics and toiletries, your specific brand preference is not guaranteed. Be sure also to read the "Staying Healthy" section to get an idea of the immunisations needed prior to arrival. Because of the large amount of fake drugs on the market, it is recommended that you bring many medicines and personal care items with you. Recommended items include:

Anti-malarial tablets
Intestinal antiseptics (Ercefurryl, Intetrix)
Anti-diarrhoea tablets (Imodium)
Anti-spasmodic (Spasfon, Buscopan)
Skin antiseptics
Sterile dressings
Ointments and antibiotic eye-washes

---

* See page 15

Antibiotics
Antihistamine
Ibuprofen and or Paracetamol
Cold syrup for adults and children
Multivitamins
Sunscreen
Mosquito repellent
Contact lens solution
Hearing aid batteries

Clothes

The dress code of Nigeria's Civil Service and business community is relatively formal. Therefore businessmen should bring plenty of lightweight suits and ties. Out of office hours dress is mostly casual. Slacks with open neck shirts and T-shirts are appropriate. Shorts are essentially reserved for sporting events. Evening events can range from casual (no jacket) to formal (National Dress and black tie – although black tie is rare). Lightweight leather shoes are normally worn in the office. Trainers, sandals or flip-flops (called 'slippers') are worn for casual wear. Flip-flops are widely available.

For women, office wear includes suits, cotton dresses, blouses and skirts. Tights/stockings are not usually worn. Trousers are becoming more common, but are still the exception. Out of the office lightweight slacks, T-shirts and tops are worn. Again, shorts are generally reserved for sporting occasions. It is also advisable to bring extra swim suits as they do not last long with frequent use and exposure to the sun and chlorine. Sandals or light shoes are commonly worn. For more information, see "Dress and Social Etiquette" and "Life Events" later in this section.

Other Items

Other suggested items include:
- at least 20 passport-sized photographs of each family member for various uses (I.D. cards, drivers' licenses, visa renewals, etc.)
- a European style GSM cell phone that is 'unlocked' (SIM cards can be purchased here from several service providers – see the "Getting Settled" section)

- a large sturdy umbrella for the rainy season and to protect against the sun on outings.

Medical Insurance

Visitors and residents are strongly urged to make sure they have medical insurance and evacuation coverage valid for Nigeria. Many travel agents and private companies offer insurance plans that will cover health care expenses incurred overseas including emergency services such as medical evacuation.

Export/Import Requirements for Pets

Parrots and other exotic animals are prohibited. Export/Import Licenses are required for other domestic pets entering and leaving Nigeria. Allow at least three months for the application process to be completed. If you can visit the office, you can obtain a permit on the same day. Remember also to follow the airline's requirements for paperwork, cages, food and watering of the animal en-route.

Application for the Export/Import licenses should be sent to:

The Director, Federal Department of Livestock and Pest Control Service
Area 11
Garki, Abuja
Attn: Dr S.A. Anzaku
☎ 09 523-1376; 0803-314-4549

To apply, send a letter with the following information:

Species, name, age, sex, colour, breed, country of origin, proposed date of travel (entry/exit), port of embarkation/ disembarkation, final destination (for export), means of transportation (e.g., air, sea, etc.) and any distinguishing features of the animal.

The applicant will also need to attach:
- a vaccination certificate for Rabies (good for one year)
- a current health certificate issued by a registered veterinary

surgeon of the country of origin of the animal (valid for two weeks).

The Export/Import License will then need to be added to the vaccination certificate and the health certificate for the airlines to accept the animal. Upon arrival in Abuja, you will also need to pay a small clearance fee.

Similar procedures are necessary to export the pet. Allow at least three weeks for the paperwork and physical examinations to be completed. In addition, be sure to make a reservation for the animal via the airline. There are different requirements and charges depending upon whether the animal is shipped as excess baggage accompanying the passenger on the flight or as unaccompanied baggage/cargo. The weight of the animal and the dimensions of the cage (height, length, width) will be needed when making the reservation. Travellers are reminded that several countries (U.K., Ireland, New Zealand and Australia) require lengthy and stringent quarantine procedures upon the arrival of the animal. In addition, it is also extremely difficult to export pets that are on the endangered species list. Specific permits are needed in these cases and some airlines will not carry them.

Bringing Money

Nigeria is a cash-based society. Traveller's cheques are not easily accepted in Nigeria. Some establishments (international hotels for example) accept credit cards; however, due to the scale of financial fraud in the country, it is not recommended to use credit cards. This causes quite a dilemma for visitors who should also be wary of carrying large amounts of cash. (Some international visitors do use credit cards at the Hilton and Sheraton hotels without problem.) Amounts of more than $5,000 are to be declared on the immigration and customs forms. Many local banks now offer debit schemes where you can deposit a sum of money and use their "Value Card" to pay for goods.

If you decide to bring cash, you will receive the best rate for $100 bills (only the new ones with the big heads are accepted). The denomination of the notes for the Pound and the Euro do not

Hints to Foreigners 23

matter and are also commonly exchanged.

The basic currency unit is the Naira (₦). 1 Naira = 100 Kobo (K). There are ₦1 and 50K coins, but they are rarely used. Change is usually made to the nearest 5 Naira. Paper notes can be obtained in 500, 200, 100, 50, 20, 10 and 5 Naira denominations. The exchange rate on the parallel market has varied over 2002-2004 from $1 = ₦125-₦152; £1=₦158-₦254.

Photography

If you have come to Abuja as a tourist and wish to take pictures, please be aware that some people may be offended at being photographed. Even when witnessing crowd scenes, you should ask around for permission before taking the photo. Sensitivity and understanding are needed as the photograph is viewed as providing a service and a "tip" or "dash" may be requested as payment for providing the service. As with many countries, it is prohibited to take photographs of bridges, airports, military personnel and installations, harbours and government buildings without permission from Nigerian security personnel.

On Arrival

Arrival Day

On the plane, you will be required to fill in an immigration form that will be kept by the immigration officials. You will need to show your valid passport with a visa for Nigeria upon entering the country. There are free trolleys at the baggage claim area and baggage handlers available to assist you with your baggage. Be prepared to tip them about ₦100 for a trolley.

Employment Opportunities for Spouses

Spouses are technically allowed to work only if they are issued a work permit from the Ministry of Internal Affairs. To get a work permit, spouses will need a letter of invitation from the company hiring them. They will also need to provide verification that the employer has agreed to add them to their official quota for foreign employees. The most opportunities exist for technical jobs such as doctors, engineers, nurses and teachers. Occasionally, job opportunities with diplomatic missions and other international organisations arise. These are mostly clerical or secretarial work.

Embassy/High Commission Registration

It is important for foreigners who plan to spend more than just a few weeks in Nigeria to register with their Embassies and/or High Commissions. Registration is good for both social and safety reasons. Some Embassies invite their nationals to attend special events (national day, visit of dignitaries, etc.) and they need to know how to contact you to let you know about these opportunities. Likewise, some Embassies have a "warden" system established to alert their citizens on general safety issues. The warden system can also be used to contact you in the event of a personal emergency. Registration is a simple process that should not take more than a few minutes. Be sure to bring your passport and local contact information, including contact information via a neighbour and/or friend who might be able to help reach you in an emergency. The locations and phone numbers of the High Commissions and Embassies in Nigeria are located at the end of this section.

Dress and Social Etiquette

Foreigners living in Nigeria for any length of time (three months or more) would do well to quickly identify a Nigerian as their cultural mentor. This person should be someone who is knowledgeable and tolerant of the different religions and cultures. He should be consulted when special dates (Muslim holidays, the Christmas season, etc.) approach and when foreigners are invited to special occasions (weddings, funerals, etc.).

Clothing

In general, dress in Nigeria is conservative. Women wear clothing that covers their arms and legs and some cover their heads. Trousers on women are being seen more and more. Nigerian women wear shorts only for sporting events. Men also dress casually-conservative, meaning that trousers and short or long sleeved shirts are the norm. For important business meetings suits and the national dress are worn. Foreigners who wish to be easily accepted would be wise to follow suit, especially if on their first visit to the country and trying to make acquaintances and friends. Nigerians providing cultural training for foreigners put it clearly and succinctly by saying, "we do not want to see the geography of your body."

Begging

Begging is an acceptable part of life in the Muslim religion. The more believers give to those in need, the higher place they attain in the afterlife. It is important to determine what feels right for you; some people provide ₦5 or ₦10 to beggars as they approach the vehicle. Others select a charity organisation to which to give. In any case, a polite acknowledgement by bowing your head and smiling is essential.

Social Conventions

It is important not to give or receive items with your left hand. This hand is normally reserved for personal hygiene. This is particularly important when eating with your hands. It is, however, acceptable to use knives and forks with both hands.

Greetings are extremely important in every situation – whether passing someone on the street, walking into an office or meeting someone at a party. While walking in the street, it is important at a minimum to simply nod your head and say good morning, good afternoon or good evening as you pass. At the office, the greeting should be more elaborate. "Hello, how are you? How was the night? How is the family?" are commonly heard. When you arrive at a party, you should acknowledge the others present either by shaking hands all around, or nodding, smiling and murmuring greetings, if the crowd is too large. It is important that the person who issued you the invitation knows that you attended the event. Be sure to greet that person even if you do not stay the entire time.

The word "sorry" is used often in Nigeria and has a variety of useful meanings. Nigerians often say it when they see someone sneeze, cough, trip (or have a different type of accident), or if they hear bad news about something that happened to someone (losing their job, getting ill, having a bad day). It is not meant as an apology but to share sympathy or to say, 'I feel sorry for you.'

Social Misconceptions

The concept of "personal space" is different for Nigerians. Foreigners may feel Nigerians are standing "too close" to them in lines or at public events. No offence is intended; foreigners simply feel the need for more personal space. Likewise, no offence is intended if you feel you are being "stared at". Although this happens less in Abuja and Lagos than in the provinces, there are still quite a good number of Nigerians that are not used to being around foreigners and natural human curiosity takes over. There is also the common misconception that because some Nigerians do not look you in the eye when they speak, they must be lying or hiding something. It is actually being done out of respect.

Life Events

Social relationships are extremely important in Nigeria. "Life Events" are marked by the gathering of family friends, work colleagues, primary school friends and in smaller areas – the entire village. It is not unusual for there to be several thousand people at major social occasions. Nigerians appreciate those who share in their joy and sorrow. Personal visits before or after the large social occasion are very meaningful.

Many occasions are held in public buildings because of large attendance. Evening parties are often held under canopies in the yard or on the street. There is often more than one band – which may make conversation difficult. Men and women often sit separately, although it is acceptable for foreigners to sit together regardless of gender.

Most social occasions begin later than scheduled and last several hours. Invitations to several occasions on the same day are common because there are so many and they tend to last a long time. It is socially acceptable to arrive late, stay long enough to greet the key people and leave. Guests staying for the entire event will see a large turnover of visitors. Nigerian social occasions are very expensive. Friends and relatives assist each other with substantial donations. For example, a man who buries his father will receive envelopes of money from his friends. He then contributes when his friend's daughter gets married, names a baby or has a death in the family. Foreigners invited to such occasions should take gifts or money along. The amount of money will depend upon your position and relationship to the family. It is wise to consult cultural mentors to determine what is appropriate for each occasion.

Nigerians are usually very well dressed for such occasions. Foreigners who attend should be formally dressed, e.g., dark suits and tie for men and formal dress, hat and heels for women. At many churches, women are expected to cover their heads. It is often appreciated if a foreigner wears Nigerian dress. However, it is necessary to check with the cultural mentor to make sure that what you are planning is appropriate for the occasion (e.g., formal enough, from the right region, for the right gender and worn properly).

Weddings

A wedding is the union of two families, not two individuals. After letters are sent from the groom's family to the bride's and back again, there is an "introduction and engagement" ceremony – what Westerners would consider as the traditional wedding. There are extensive introductions of family members, speeches, various rituals and the exchange of gifts. This event usually takes place in the house of the bride and is a relatively small gathering of people (about 100). The formal church, mosque or registry wedding, including formal receptions and night parties follow. There may be thousands of guests, elaborate clothes and long speeches. Light refreshments will be served at the reception. There will be a band and a full meal at the evening party.

Friends of specific participants in the wedding will often wear the same type and/or design of cloth, e.g., friends of the bride's mother may wear one type of cloth and the friends of the groom's mother may wear another. If you are very close to a key participant, they may ask you to wear the cloth too. For women who prefer not to cut it and have it made into a dress, there are ways that it can be wrapped to resemble a dress. It shows your support and friendship to get the cloth, even if you are unable to attend the wedding.

If you are not wearing the choice cloth of one of the participants, your dressing should be formal. Women may wear long dresses that cover their arms and a hat, while men could wear suits. For gifts, you can ask the family what they would like. Money, traditional fabrics and kitchenware are always appreciated. Bring wads of crisp bank notes/currencies with you as there will also be plenty of opportunities to give donations to the families, the mosque and/or church, etc. Some cultures also have the custom of a 'money dance' where currency notes are tossed or plastered on the bride and/or groom during a dance (popularly called "spraying"). As with other Nigerian events, weddings tend to start late and last very long. So if you arrive on time, be patient, the experience will be worth the wait.

Funerals

Funerals are here viewed from two different perspectives -- one for an elderly person and another a young person. The funeral of an elderly person who has lived a full life is cause for celebration. In Christian families, the deceased is often not buried until weeks after their death so that family members can travel back home and adequate funds for a proper burial ceremony can be gathered. There is likely to be a wake in the evening/night prior to the funeral, then a church funeral, followed by the burial. Guests go to the home of the deceased for a party, complete with full meal, band, dancing and "spraying" (putting money on the forehead of significant members of the family or of anyone who is dancing particularly well). However, in the Islamic religion where strict conventions on burials are observed, the deceased needs to be buried within 24 hours after death. Then there is a party eight days later and again forty days later. Dress for both occasions is formal.

The funeral of a young person whose life has been cut short is much more sombre. The ceremonies are usually the same, but are not accompanied by eating, drinking and dancing. Likewise, dress is sombre. An 'outing' ceremony takes place after a funeral when families put on bright clothes and go to church together.

Naming Ceremonies

In most cultures in Nigeria a baby is named on the seventh or eighth day after birth. The ceremony is usually done in the early morning and may have Christian or Muslim prayers.

Birthdays
Certain birthdays have great meaning and are often accompanied by big parties, e.g. ages 1, 2, 10, 21, 40, 50 and 60. But ages 70 and 80 have the greatest meaning and attract the highest esteem.

Chieftaincy Ceremonies
Chieftaincy titles are still highly valued and sought after by many Nigerians. Titles are based on personal achievement, inherited positions or wealth. Foreigners who have lived in the country for a long time and/or made substantial contributions to a community or culture may sometimes be made ceremonial chiefs. Often, several chiefs are installed during the same ceremony.

'Washing'
This is a celebration of a new prestigious acquisition such as a car or a house. The 'washing' of a house is similar to the western house-warming celebration where friends come to help and rejoice in good fortune.

The Food
In general, Nigerians like spicy food. Each ethnic group has its own diet, which is largely determined by the geography and agricultural production available in the area. Because Abuja now has such a mix of cultures, most staples can be found here. Meals often consist of a large portion of carbohydrates such as yam, *gari* (cassava), rice, sorghum, corn or millet, with a stew and some cooked vegetables. For an interesting discussion of the various merits and deficiencies of these carbohydrates, see *The Vegetarian Food Book*.

The carbohydrate eaten defines the meal, e.g., "I ate pounded yam," not "I ate chicken with vegetables." The carbohydrate is accompanied by some stew or soup, which is usually made up of tomatoes, onion and hot pepper ground together. It may also include ground seeds, nuts or cut vegetables. For example, egusi soup contains ground melon seeds, dried fish, efon (spinach), vegetables and palm oil. The pounded staple accompanies the soup; rice also goes with stew.

Vegetables are usually cooked either inside the stew or as a side accompaniment. Starter courses such as raw vegetables and desserts are not part of the normal diet. Fruits are often eaten as snacks in between meals and can be purchased on the street. Street vendors often sell oranges, pineapples, bananas, apples, groundnuts (peanuts), popcorn, corn fritters, puff-puff (similar to doughnuts), roasted plantain or maize, raw garden eggs (eggplant), carrots, meat pastries, suya meat, akara (a puffy deep-fried cake made with black-eyed beans accompanied by chilli dip) and kulikuli (small peanut paste balls).

The term "tea" refers to any hot beverage. It is usually served with bread, preferably the sweet Nigerian-type or cakes.

Bukutu or little "restaurants" with local foods can also be found on almost every street. However, the sanitation arrangements in these places are not the same as in other more established places where running water can be used to clean the dishes, etc. Local food is featured at some of the restaurants included in the "Going Out" section. This is a safer choice.

Local Foods/Dishes

Name	Description
Akara, Kose	Bean fritters; best when eaten fresh and hot
Amala	Dry yam puree
Bitter leaf soup	A spinach stew
Eba	Cassava semolina
Edikang-ikong	A type of stew
Efon	A type of spinach
Egusi soup	Fiery hot stew made with meat/fish and ground melon seeds, and ed peppers, dried prawns and efon (a type of spinach)
Fufu	Pounded tubers of cassava
Gari	Cassava flour; served with main meal as an accompaniment to the soups/stews

Gombo okro	Okra, gumbo, ladies finger
Groundnut stew	Vegetables, meat and ground peanuts
Iyan	Pounded tubers of yam, cocoyam
Kilishi	Dried, seasoned meat
Kosam	Yoghurt sold by Fulani
Kulikuli	Deep-fried peanut paste balls
Kunnu	Drink made from guinea corn
Nono da fura	Porridge derived from a mixture of guinea-corn. Paste in milk.
Masa	Small fried cake
Moin-moin (Moyin-moyin)	Steamed bean flour cake with fish, liver or boiled egg
Palm nut soup	Meat, peppers, tomatoes, onions and palm nut oil
Pepper soup	Fiery hot soup served with entrails, unless prepared as "fish pepper soup, goat head pepper soup or chicken pepper soup"
Pottage	Bean paste and yam
Puff-puff	Doughnuts
Shinkafa da wake	A dish of rice and beans
Suya	Small pieces of charcoal-grilled, skewered meat, very spicy
Tuwon shinkafa	Pounded rice (tuwo [food], shinkafa [rice])
Ukwaka	Steamed pudding based on corn and ripe plantain
Yazhi	Pepper mixed-salad sold by suya sellers

High Commissions and Embassies

Please note that a number of Embassies are in temporary locations until their permanent offices are built. As a result some of these addresses and phone numbers are subject to change.

High Commissions

Australia

Chancery:	Plot 2940
	Aguiyi Ironsi Road
	Maitama
	Abuja
Telephone:	09 413 5226
Admin:	09 413 5227
Policy:	09 413 5228
Office Hours:	Monday – Thursday: 0800 - 1630 hours
	Friday: 0800 - 1300 hours

British

Chancery:	Mississippi Street, Shehu Shagari Way (North), Maitama, Abuja
Telephone:	09 4132010, 4132011, 4132796, 4132880, 4132883, 4132887, 4139817
Fax:	09 4133552
Office Hours:	Monday – Friday: 0800-1500 hours

Management, Commercial, Visa & Consular Sections

Address:	Dangote House, Aguiyi Ironsi Street, Maitama, Abuja
Telephone:	09 4134559-64, 4133885-7
Management Fax:	09 4133888
Visa Fax:	09 4134565
Hours of Duty	Monday – Friday: 0800-1500 hours

Canada

Chancery:	3A Bobo Street
	Off Gana Street, Maitama, Abuja
Telephone:	09 4139910, 4139931, 4139933, 4139953, 4139956
Fax:	09 413 9911
Hours of Duty:	Monday – Friday: 0800-1600 hours

The Gambia

Chancery:	Plot 1304 Yankari Street,
	Parakou Crescent
	P.O. Box 5058 Wuse II
Telephone:	09 523, 1224, 523 1225
Fax:	09 524 1228
Email:	*gamhicom@micro.commg*
Chancery:	Plot 25, Ontario Crescent,
	Off Mississippi Street Maitama, Abuja
Telephone:	234 9 4138545, 4138546
Fax:	234 9 4138548
Lagos Liaison Office:	162 Awolowo Road, S.W. Ikoyi, Lagos
	P.O. Box 8073
Fax/Telephone:	01 2695558, 2670829
Hours of Duty:	Monday –Thursday: 0900-1600 hours
	Friday: 0900-1300 hours

The Republic of Ghana

Chancery:	Plot 301, Olusegun Obasanjo Way
	Area 10, Garki, Abuja
	P.O. Box 2025
Telephone:	09 234 5184, 234 5193

Around and About Abuja

Fax:	09 234 5192
Email:	*Ghana h@hotmail.com*
Hours of Duty:	Monday – Friday: 0830-1500 hours

India

Lagos office (Chancery):	8A Walter Carrington Crescent, Victoria Island P.M.B. 80128, Lagos
Telephone:	01 616604, 615905, 615078
After Work Hours:	01 615905
Telex No.:	090-28969 HCI- NG
Email Address:	*hindlos@hyperia.com*
Hours of Duty:	Monday – Friday: 0830 -1700 hours
Visa Section:	Collection of Visa/Passport Forms Monday – Friday: 0900-1100 hours Delivery of Passports: 1630-1700 hours
Abuja Office:	Plot 684B, Agadez Crescent, Off Aminu Kano Crescent, Wuse II, Abuja
Telephone:	09 5236099, 523 6078, 671 2577
Fax:	09 5236088

Jamaica

Chancery:	NICON Plaza, Plot 242 Muhammadu Crescent, Central District, Abuja
Telephone:	09-234 5107
Fax:	09-234 2726
Hours of Duty:	Mon –Thurs: 0900-1700 hours Friday: 0900-1600 hours
Visa:	Tue, Wed &Thurs: 0900-1200 hours

Kenya

Chancery:	52 Oyinkan Abayomi Drive P.O. Box 6464, Ikoyi, Lagos
Telephone:	01-2670221, 2670537
Fax:	01-2670686

Telex: 21124
Email: kenyahi@alpha.linkserve.com
Answer-back: KEREP NG
Hours of Duty: Monday – Friday: 0800-1500 hours
Visa Section: Tuesday – Thursday: 1000-1400 hours

Malaysia

Chancery: Plot 205, Abiola Segun Ajayi Street, Victoria Island
P.O. Box 3729, Lagos
Telephone: 01 612710, 619415
Fax: 612741
Hours of Duty: Monday – Friday: 0800-1615 hours

The Republic of Namibia

Chancery: Plot 1738 T.Y. Danjuma Street
Cadastral Zone A4, Asokoro District
P.O. Box 5097 Wuse Abuja
Telephone: 09 3142741, 3142742, 3142744
Fax: 09-3142743
Hours of Duty: Monday – Friday: 0800-1300 hours
1400-1600 hours
Visa Section: Tuesday – Thursday: 1000-1200 hours

The Islamic Republic of Pakistan

Chancery: 1805 Samora Machel Street
Off Yakubu Gowon Crescent, Asokoro, Abuja
Telephone: 09-314 1650, 314 1651, 314 1660
Fax: 09-3141652
Telex No: 99007 PHC ABJ NG
Email: pahicabuja@yahoo.com
Hours of Duty: Monday – Thursday: 0800-1400 hours
1500-1600 hours
Friday: 0800-1300 hours

Sierra Leone

Chancery:	Plot 308 Mission Road (Opp. Ministry of Defence - Shiphouse) Diplomatic Zone Central Business District- Abuja
Lagos Liaison Office:	Plot 148 Younis Bashorun Street, Victoria Island, Lagos.
Telephone/Fax:	012613151

The Republic of South Africa

Chancery:	Plot 676 Vaal Street, Off Rhine Street Off IBB Way, Maitama District, Abuja
Telephone:	09 -4133776, 4133862, 4133574
Fax:	4133829
Email:	sahcniga@rosecome.net
Office Hours	Monday –Thursday: 0800-1700 hours
	Friday: 0800-1430 hours

The United Republic of Tanzania

Chancery:	No. 15, Yedsaram Street Maitama District, Abuja
Postal Address:	P.M.B. 5125 Wuse, Abuja
Telephone:	09-4132313
Fax:	09-4132314
Hours of Duty:	Monday – Friday: 0800-1500 hours
Consular Section:	Monday – Friday: 1000-1500 hours

Trinidad & Tobago

Chancery:	Plot 130, Senator Kura Mohammed Street, Parakou Crescent Off Aminu Kano Crescent, Wuse II, Abuja
Telephone:	09-5237534, 5236417
Fax:	09-5237684
Email:	trinidadtobago@linkserve.com; trinitobagoabi@yahoo.com
Hours of Duty:	Monday – Friday: 0800-1600 hours

Uganda

Chancery:	Plot 44 Ontario Crescent, Off Mississippi Street, Ministers' Hill, Maitama
	P.M.B. 223, Abuja
Telephone:	09-4138069
Fax:	09-4138070
Office Hours:	Monday –Thursday: 0900-1600 hours
	Friday: 0900-1400 hours

Zambia

Chancery:	Plot 351 Mission Road, Central Area District, Abuja.
Telephone:	09-2347060, 2348855, 4131925
Tel/Fax:	09-413 1925
Hours of Duty:	Monday – Friday: 0830-1500 hours

Chancery:	Plot 767, Off Panama Street, Ministers Hill Maitama, Abuja
Telephone:	09-4131925
Tel/Fax:	09-4131925
Hours of Duty:	Monday – Friday: 0800-1500 hours
	Wednesday: 0830-1300 hours

Embassies

People's Democratic Republic of Algeria

Chancery:	Plot No. 1398, Honourable Justice Mamman Nasir Street, Cadastral Zone A4, Asokoro District, Abuja
Telephone:	09-3142840, 3142841
Fax:	09-3142842
Email:	*ambalg abuja@hotmail.com;www.mae.dz*
Hours of Duty:	Monday – Friday: 0900-1600 hours
Visa Hours:	Monday – Friday: 1000-1300 hours

The Republic of Angola

Chancery:	5, Kasumu Ekemode Street, Victoria Island, Lagos
	P.O. Box 50437 Falomo, Lagos
Telephone:	01-611135, 611702
Fax:	01-618675
Telex:	097428974 EMBRAL NG
Email:	angolaembassy@yahoo.com.br
Hours of Duty:	Monday – Friday: 0830-1430 hours
Visa Hours:	Mon, Wed & Friday: 0900-1230 hours
Abuja Office:	9 Pope John Paul II Street, Maitama, Abuja
Telephone:	09-413 5121
Fax:	09-413 5121

Argentina

Chancery:	Plot 1161, Yusuf Maitama Sule Street Asokoro District, Abuja
Telephone:	
Fax:	
Telex:	28271EVBARG NG
Email:	emargen@infoweb.abs.net
Hours of Duty:	Monday – Friday: 0900-1500 hours
Consular section	Monday – Friday: 0930-1300 hours

Austria

Chancery:	Fabac Centre (Behind the Mobil House)
	3b Ligali Ayorinde Avenue, Victoria Island
	P.O. Box 1914 Lagos
Telephone:	01-2616081, 2616286
Fax:	01-2617639
Hours of Duty:	Monday – Friday: 0900-1600 hours
Visiting hours:	Tue, Wed. & Fri. 1000-1200 hours

Commercial Section:	65 AL Oyinkan Abayomi Drive, Ikoyi P.O. Box 1217, Lagos
Telephone:	01-2636827, 2696212, 2696213
Fax:	01-2694229
Hours of Duty:	Monday – Friday: 0730-1530 hours
Visiting hours:	Tuesday – Friday: 1000-1200 hours

Belgium

Chancery:	No 67, Mississippi Street, Maitama, Abuja
Telephone:	09-4137930, 4137943, 4133796, 4133743
Fax:	09-4133797
Email:	ambabelab@premiernetng.net

Republic of Benin

Chancery:	Plot No. 2579 A6 (near Algon Guest House) Yedseram Street, Maitama District, Abuja
Telephone:	09-4138424
Fax:	09-4138425
Hours of Duty:	Monday – Friday: 0900-1600 hours

The Federative Republic of Brazil

Chancery:	257 Kofo Abayomi Street, Victoria Island P.O. Box 72802, Victoria Island
Telephone:	01-2610135, 2610136, 2610177
Telex:	23347
Hours of Duty:	Monday-Friday: 0830-1430 hours
Visa Section:	Monday-Friday: 0830-1400 hours
Abuja Office:	Plot 173, Mississippi Street, Maitama, Abuja
Telephone:	09-413 4066, 413 4067
Fax:	09-413 4066

The Republic of Bulgaria

Chancery:	3 Walter Carrington Crescent, Victoria Island P.O. Box 4441, Lagos
Telephone:	01-2611931, 611932
Fax:	01-2619879
Hours of Duty:	Monday – Friday: 0900-1500 hours
Abuja Office:	Europe House, Plot 533 Usuma Street, Maitama, Abuja.

Burkina Faso

Chancery:	4, Freetown Street, Off Ademola Adetokunbo Crescent Wuse II, Abuja
Telephone:	09-4130491
Fax:	09-4130492
Email:	ebfn@nova.net.ng
Hours of Duty:	Monday – Friday: 0900-1700 hours

The Republic of Chad

Chancery:	10, Mississippi Street (Off Shehu Shagari Way-North) Plot 152, Maitama District P.M.B. 488 Garki, Abuja
Telephone:	09-4130751, 08033222556
Hours of Duty:	Monday – Friday: 0800-1600 hours

The People's Republic of China

Chancery:	Plot 343 Bamako Street, Zone 1, Wuse, Abuja P.M.B. 327, Garki, Abuja
Telephone:	09-5236105, 5236106, 5238330
Fax:	09-5236107, 5236023, 5236476
Hours of Duty:	Monday – Friday: 0900-1400 hours

Commercial office
(*Chancery*): Plot 2232A, Yedseram Street,
              Maitama, Abuja
Telephone: 09-41337993, 4137994, 4137995, 4137950
Fax: 09-4137949

The Democratic Republic of Congo (Republique Du Congo)
Chancery: Plot 940, Azores Street
             Off Aminu Kano Crescent
             Wuse II, Abuja
             Telephone: 09-4131105, 4131107
             Fax: 09-4132311
Hours of Duty: Monday – Friday: 0900-1500 hours
Fax: 314-2157

2nd Chancery: Plot 447, Lobito Crescent
                 Wuse II,
                 P.M.B. 540 Garki-Abuja
Telephone: 09 4137407
Fax: 234 94130 157

The Republic of Cote d'Ivoire
Chancery: Plot 2630, Gurara Street
             Off Ibrahim Babangida Way
             Maitama, Abuja
Telephone: 09-4133087, 413 3687, 413 2724
Fax: 09-4133137
Hours of Duty Monday – Friday: 0830-1500 hours

The Republic of Cuba
Chancery: 42 Usuma Street, Maitama District, Abuja
Telephone: 09-4130380, 4130270
Fax: 09-4134971
Email: *consulcuba_abuja@linkserve.com*
Hours of Duty: Monday – Friday: 0900-1200 hours

The Czech Republic

Chancery:	Plot No. 1223 Zone A4, Asokoro District
	Gnassigbe Eyadema Street, Zone A4
	Asokoro District Abuja
	P.O. Box 4628
Telephone:	09-3141245, 3141247
Fax:	09-3141248
Hours of Duty:	Monday – Friday: 0800-1200 hours
	1300-1600 hours
Consular and Visa:	Tuesday & Thurs. 0930-1130 hours

The Arab Republic of Egypt

Chancery:	Plot 3319, Barada Close, Off Amazon Street,
	Maitama District, Abuja
	P.M.B. Wuse Abuja
Telephone:	09-4132679, 4136091, 4136092
Fax:	09-4132602
Hours of Duty:	Monday – Friday: 0900-1600 hours
Consular section:	Monday – Friday: 0900-1200 hours

The Republic of Equatorial Guinea

Chancery:	7 Murtala Mohammed Drive, Ikoyi
	P.O. Box 4162, Lagos
Telephone:	01-2691211
Fax:	01-2618194
Hours of Duty:	Monday-Friday: 0900-1500 hours

The State of Eritrea

Chancery:	Plot 1510 Yedseram Street
	Maitama (Beside Maitama Guest House)
Telephone:	09-4136086
Fax:	09-4136085
Email:	algen23@operamail.com

The Federal Democratic Republic of Ethiopia

Chancery:	No. 19 Ona Crescent, Off Lake Chad Crescent Maitama District, Abuja
Telephone:	09-4131691
Fax:	09-4131692
Email:	etabuja@primair.net; ethiopiaemb@hotmail.com
Hours of Duty:	Monday – Friday: 0830-1230 hours
	1330-1600 hours
Visa Section:	Tuesday –Thursday: 0900-1200 hours

Finland

Chancery:	Plot 1597, Iro Dan Musa Street, Asokoro
	P.O. Box 5140 Maputo Street, Zone 3 Wuse,
Telephone:	09-314 7256, 314 7257
Fax:	09-314 7252
Email:	sanomat.aba@formin.fi
Hours of Duty:	Monday – Thursday: 0900-1600 hours
	Friday: 0900-1300 hours
Visa Hours:	Monday & Thursday: 0900-1100 hours

Lagos office (Chancery):	Plot 13, Walter Carrington Crescent, Victoria Island, Lagos
	P.O. Box 4433, Lagos
Telephone:	01-2610916, 2610528
Fax:	01-2613158
Email:	finemb@infoweb.abs.net
Hours of Duty:	Monday – Friday: 0800-1615 hours
Visiting hours:	Monday – Friday: 0800-1100 hours
Visa Hours:	Monday – Thursday: 0900-1200 hours

Abuja office:	Europe House: Plot 533 St Maitama District
Telephone:	09-4133144

France

Chancery:	32 Udi Street, (Off Aso Drive) Maitama, Abuja
Telephone:	09-5235506, 5235510
Fax:	09-5235362, 5235482
Email:	*Abuja@dree.org*
Hours of Duty:	Monday – Friday: 0900-1800 hours

Gabon

Chancery:	8 Norman Williams Street, S.W. Ikoyi P.O. Box 5989 Lagos
Telephone:	01-2690692
Fax:	01-7595928
Email:	*huguesdavin@hotmail.com*
Hours of Duty:	Monday – Friday: 0900-1500 hours

The Federal Republic of Germany

*Chancery:	Plot 3323, Barada Close Off Amazon Street Maitama Abuja, F.C.T
Telephone:	09 4130961, 4130962, 4130965
Fax:	09 413 0949

Greece

Chancery:	No. 71, Usuma Street, Maitama District P.O. Box 11525 Garki, Abuja
Telephone:	09-4135611, 4135511
Fax:	09-4135566
Email:	*greekemb.ng@cybaaspace.net*
Hours of Duty:	Monday – Friday: 0830-1500 hours

---

*To move to EU House with effect from 2005

The Republic of Guinea

Chancery:	Plot No. 349, Central Area District
	Cadastral Zone
	A.O. Opposite United Nations Common Premises
	P.M.B. 591 Garki, Abuja
Telephone:	09-5233495, 234 9144, 234 7277
Fax:	09-413 3407
Hours of Duty:	Monday – Thursday: 0900-1530 hours
	Friday: 0900-1300 hours
Visa:	Mon, Wed, Friday: 0930-1300 hours
Lagos office:	8, Abudu Smith Street
	Victoria Island
Telephone:	01-616961
Visa Section:	Mon, Wed & -Fri: 0930-1400 hours

Holy See

Chancery:	Pope John Paul II Crescent, Plot 3133, Maitama
	P.M.B. 541 Garki, Abuja
Telephone:	09-4138381, 413 8382, 413 8384, 413 8383
Fax:	09-413 6653
Email:	*nuntius2linkserve.com; nuntius@linkserve.com.*
Hours of Duty:	Monday – Friday: 0600-1400 hours

The Republic of Hungary

Chancery:	Plot 1585 Jose Marti Crescent,
	Cadastral Zone A4
	Asokoro Extension, Abuja
Telephone:	09-3141180, 3141181
Fax:	09-3141177
Email:	*hungembabv@hotmail.com; huemblgs@nova.net.ng.*
Hours of Duty:	Monday – Friday: 0800-1400 hours
Visa Section:	Tuesday – Thursday: 0800-1100 hours

The Republic of Indonesia

Chancery:	5B Anifowoshe Street, Victoria Island
	P.O. Box 3473, Lagos
Telephone:	01-2614601, 2612873
Fax:	01-2613301
Email:	*unitkomiga@hyperia.com*
Hours of Duty:	Monday – Thursday: 0800-1230 hours
	1400-1600 hours
Friday:	0800-1230 hours
Visa Section:	Monday – Thursday: 0800-1230 hours
	1400-1600 hours

Abuja office:	Plot 683 A5 Barawa Street, Off Gana Street, Maitama District, Abuja
Telephone:	09-4138626
Fax:	09-4138625
Hours of Duty:	Monday – Thursday : 0800-1230 hours
	1400-1600 hours
Friday:	0800-1330 hours

The Islamic Republic of Iran

Chancery:	No. 2 Udi Street, Off Aso Drive, Maitama District, Abuja
Telephone:	09-5238048, 5238049
Fax:	09-5237785
Email:	*embiri abuja@yahoo.com.*
Hours of Duty:	Monday-Friday: 0800-1500 hours
	Saturday: 0900-1200 hours

The Republic of Iraq

Chancery:	23 Plot 710 Kainji Crescent Ogg, Lake Chad Crescent
	Cadastral Zone A5
	Maitama District, Abuja
	P.M.B. 481 Abuja

Telephone: 09-4139256
Fax: 09-4139524
Hours of Duty: Monday – Friday: 0900-1300 hours

Ireland

Chancery: Plot 415 Negro Crescent Maitama District, Abuja
Telephone: 09-413 1751, 413 1752, 413 1753
Fax: 09-4131805
Email: irlembng@infoweb.abs.net
Hours of Duty: Monday – Friday: 0800-1500 hours
Visa Hours: Monday – Wed: 0900-1100 hours

The State of Israel

Chancery: Plot 1317 A&B Udo Udoma Crescent, Zone 4A Asokoro, Abuja
Telephone: 09-3143170, 3143176, 3143178, 3143179
Fax: 09-3143177
Hours of Duty: Monday – Thurs: 0900-1700 hours
Friday: 0900-1430 hours

Italy

*Chancery: Plot 1611, Yusuf Maitama Sule Street, Asokoro District, Abuja
Telephone: 09-3142985, 3142986
Fax: 09-3142987
Email: itabuja@bete.linkserve.com;itabuja@beta.linkserve.com
Hours of Duty: Monday – Friday: 0800-1400 hours

Japan

Chancery: Plot 585, Bobo Street, Off Gana Street Maitama, Abuja

*To move to EU House with effect from 2005

Telephone:	09-4138898, 4139718, 4139719, 4139258
Fax:	09-4137667
Hours of Duty:	Monday – Thurs: 0800-1645 hours
	Friday: 0800-1300 hours

The Democratic People's Republic Korea

Chancery:	Plot No.350, Central Area District, Cadastral Zone A.
	P.M.B. 407, Garki, Abuja
Telephone:	09-523 9480
Fax:	09-523 9766
Hours of Duty:	Monday – Friday: 0830-1230 hours
	1330-1730 hours

The Republic of Korea

Chancery:	Plot 934, Idejo Street, Victoria Island, Lagos
	G.P.O. Box 4668 Lagos
Telephone:	01-2615353 2615420
Fax:	01-2612342
Hours of Duty:	Monday – Friday(except Thursday):
	0800-1600 hours
	Thursday: 0800-1200 hours

Abuja office:	Plot 654, Off Usuma Street Cadastral Zone A5
	Maitama District, Abuja
Telephone:	09-4136524, 413 8065
Fax:	09-4136525
Hours of Duty:	Monday – Friday (except Thursday):
	0900-1700 hours
	Thursday: 0900-1200 hours

Lebanon

Chancery:	Lot 18, Walter Carrington Crescent, Lagos
	P.O. Box 651, Lagos
Telephone:	01-2610129, 2612011

Fax:	01-2614511
Email:	*emblebanon@hyperia.com*
Hours of Duty:	Monday – Friday: 0900-1400 hours

The Republic of Liberia

Chancery:	3, Idejo Street, Off Adeola Odeku Street P.O. Box 7084, Victoria Island, Lagos
Telephone:	01-618899, 611294
Fax:	01-611853
Hours of Duty:	Monday – Friday: 0900-1200 hours 0200-1600 hours

The Great Socialist People's Libyan Arab Jamahiraya

Chancery:	Plot 1591 Mike Okoye Close, Off George Sowemimo Street, Asokoro Extension P.M.B. 435, Garki, Abuja
Telephone:	09-3148356, 3148357
Fax:	09-3148354
Telex:	906 99004
Hours of Duty:	Monday – Friday: 0800-1500 hours

The Republic of Mali

Chancery:	Plot 465, Wuse Zone I, Nouakchott Street Off Olusegun Obasanjo Way, Abuja P.M.B 5082 Wuse, Abuja
Telephone:	09-5230494
Fax:	09-5238546
Email:	*ambamaliabuja@yahoo.com.*

The Kingdom of Morocco

Chancery:	Plot 1306, Udo Udoma Crescent Asokoro, Abuja
Telephone:	09-3141961, 3141962
Fax:	09-3141959

Hours of Duty: Monday – Friday: 0900-1600 hours
Visa and Visiting: Monday – Friday: 1000-1300 hours

Royal Netherlands Embassy

Consulate: Plot 622, 1 Gana Street Maitama District, Abuja
*Chancery: Embassy at EU House
Telephone: 09-4133789, 4135434, 4135436
Fax: 09-4133791
Email: ABJ@minbuza.nl
Hours of Duty: Monday – Thurs. 0800-1700 hours
Friday: 0800-1500 hours
Public Hours: Monday – Friday: 0900-1200 hours

Niger Republic

Chancery: 7, Sangha Street, Off Mississipi Street, Maitama District
P.O. Box 4251, Abuja
Telephone: 09-4136205, 413 6206
Fax: 09-4136205
Email: embniger@yahoo.fr
Hours of Duty: Monday – Friday: 0900-1500 hours

Royal Norwegian Embassy

Chancery: Plot 1529 T.Y. Danjuma Street
P.O. Box 5136 Wuse, Abuja
Asokoro District, Abuja.
Telephone: 09-314 9127, 314 9128,
Fax: 09-314 9130
Email: emb.lagos@mfa.no
Hours of Duty: Monday – Friday: 0800-1500 hours
Public Hours: Monday – Friday: 1000-13:00 hours
Visa: Wednesday – Fri. 0900-1200 hours

---

*To move to EU House with effect from 2005

The State Palestine

Chancery:	Plot 445, Lobito Crescent, Wuse II
	P.M.B. 429, Garki, Abuja
Telephone:	09-4135311, 4135058, 4135059
Fax:	09-4135308
Hours of Duty:	Monday – Friday: 0830-1500 hours

The Republic of the Philippines

Chancery:	16, Lake Chad Crescent, Corner Kainji Street
	Maitama District, Abuja
	P.O. Box 5122 Wuse, Abuja
Telephone:	09-4137981, 4137982
Fax:	09-4137650 (Temporary 4137829)
Hours of Duty:	Monday – Friday: 0800-1700 hours

The Republic of Poland

Chancery:	16, Ona Crescent (Off Lake Chad) Plot 775A
	Maitama District, Abuja
Telephone:	09-4138280, 4138283
Fax:	09-4138281
Hours of Duty:	Monday – Friday: 0730-1530 hours
Public Hours:	Monday – Friday: 0800-1200 hours
Visa:	Mon, Tues & Thurs. 1000-1300 hours

Portugal

Chancery:	Plot 27A Gana Street, Maitama
	P.M.B 539, Area 10 Garki, Abuja
Telephone:	09-4137211, 4137212
Fax:	09-4137214
Email:	portemb@rosecom.ne
Hours of Duty:	Monday – Friday: 0900-1500 hours

Romania

Chancery:	Plot 498, Nelson Mandela Street, Asokoro, Abuja
	P.O. Box 10376, Garki Abuja
Telephone:	09-3142304, 3142305
Fax:	09-3142306
Email:	romnig@nigtel.com
Hours of Duty:	Monday – Friday: 0830-1430 hours
Visa:	Monday –Thurs: 1000-1200 hours

The Russian Federation

Chancery:	5, Walter Carrington Crescent, Victoria Island
	P.O. Box 2723, Lagos
Telephone:	01-2613359, 2615022, 22612267
Fax:	01-4619994
Email:	*rusemlagos@vgccl.net*
Hours of Duty:	Monday – Friday: 0900-1300 hours
Visa:	Tuesday – Thurs. 0900-1100 hours
Abuja Liaison Office:	Plot 715, Panama Crescent, Zone A6, Maitama, Abuja
Telephone:	09-4134951
Fax:	09-4135374
Hours of Duty:	Monday – Friday: 0900-1300 hours

Sahrawi Arab Democratic Republic

Chancery:	No.4 Niger Street Off Suez Crescent,
	Off Ladi Kwali Street
	Ibrahim Sani Abacha Estate, Wuse, Abuja
Telephone:	09-5240936
Fax:	09-5240937
Email:	*embsahrawi@hotmail.com*
Hours of Duty:	Monday – Friday: 0830-1530 hours

The Royal Embassy of Saudi Arabia

Chancery: Plot 2666 Volta Close, Off Thames Street,
Off Alvan Ikoku Street
Ministers Hill, Maitama
P.M.B 5073, Wuse, Abuja
Telephone: 09-4131880, 4134143
Fax: 09-4134906
Hours of Duty: Monday – Thurs: 0900-1500 hours
Friday: 0900-1500 hours

The Republic of Senegal

Chancery: 12,14, Kofo Abayomi Road, Victoria Island
P. O. Box 2197 Lagos
Telephone: 01-611722
Fax: 01-611722
Hours of Duty: Monday – Thurs: 0830-1530 hours
Friday: 0830-1330 hours

Serbia and Montenegro

Chancery: 7 Maitama Sule Street, S.W. Ikoyi, Lagos
P.O. Box 978, Marina, Lagos
Telephone: 01-2690912, 2694202
Fax: 01-2691889
Hours of Duty: Monday-Friday: 0830-1530 hours
Monday-Friday: 1000-1400 hours

The Slovak Republic

Chancery: Plot 187, Deeper Life Street,
Asokoro District, Abuja
P.M.B. 582
Telephone: 09-3143731, 3143732, 670 5746, 3143374. 314 3371
Fax: 09-3143730

Email: *zulagos@yahoo.com*
Hours of Duty: Monday – Friday: 0900-1500 hours
Public Hours: Monday – Friday: 1000-1200 hours

Spain

Chancery: Plot 611 Bobo Close, Off Gana Street
Maitama District, Abuja
Telephone: 09-4137091, 4137092, 4137093
Fax: 09-4137095
Email: *embespng@mail.mae.es*
Hours of Duty: Monday – Thurs: 0800-1645 hours
Friday: 0800-1500 hours

The Republic of the Sudan

Chancery: Plot 337, Zone AO, Mission Road,
Central District Area, Abuja
Telephone: 09-2346266, 6700668
Fax: 09-2346265
Email: *sudaniabj@hotmail.com*
Hours of Duty: Monday – Friday: 0900-1600 hours

Sweden

Chancery: Plot 1520, T.Y. Danjuma Street, Off Jose Marti Street Asokoro, Abuja
P.M.B 569 Garki
Telephone: 09-3143392, 3143393, 3143394, 3143395, 3143396, 3143399
Fax: 09-3143398
Email: *swedenemb.abuja@foreign.ministry.se*
Hours of Duty: Monday – Thurs: 0800-1230 hours
1330-1600 hours
Visa: Monday – Thurs: 1000-1200 hours

Switzerland

Chancery:	Plot 1098, Kwame Nkrumah Crescent, Asokoro Abuja
Telephone:	09-3147263, 3142307, 3142308
Fax:	09-3148364
Email:	vetretung@abu.rep.admin.ch
Hours of Duty:	Monday – Friday: 0900-1600 hours
Public Hours:	Monday – Friday: 0900-1100 hours

The Syria Arab Republic

Chancery:	Plot 2420, Area A6, Maitama District, off Amazon Street P.M.B. 393, Garki, Abuja
Telephone:	09-4138334, 4138335, 5238335
Fax:	09-4138337
Hours of Duty:	Monday – Friday: 0830-1530 hours

The Republic of Togo

Chancery:	Plot 976, Oju Olobun Close, Victoria Island P. O. Box 1435, Lagos
Telephone:	01-617449
Hours of Duty:	Monday – Friday: 0800-1500 hours

The Republic of Tunisia

Chancery:	No 9 Usuma Street, Off Gana Street, Maitama 1, Abuja
Telephone:	09-4132966, 4132967
Telex:	28237
Fax:	09-4132968
Email:	emb.Tunisia.nig@micro.com.ng
Hours of Duty:	Monday – Friday: 0830-1500 hours

The Republic of Turkey

Chancery: Plot 2894, Amazon Street, Maitama A6, Abuja
Telephone: 09-4139787, 4138795, 4138692, 4138693
Fax: 09-4139457
Email: *turkishembassy@rosecom.net*
Hours of Duty: Monday – Friday: 0900-1700 hours

Ukraine

Chancery: Plot 1273, Parakou Crescent, Off Nairobi Street, Wuse II, Abuja
Telephone: 09-5239577, 5240087, 5240088
Fax: 09-5239578
Hours of Duty: Monday – Friday: 0900-1400 hours
Visa: Monday – Thurs. 0930-1230 hours

The United States of America

Chancery: 9 Mambilla Street, Maitama District, Abuja
Telephone: 09-5230916, 5230960, 5235857, 523-2205/2239/2235
Fax: 09-5230353, 5232083, 5238002, 5230353
Hours of Duty: Monday – Thurs. 0730-1630 hours
Friday: 0730-1330 hours

Venezuela

Chancery: No. 1361 Honourable Justice Sowemimo Street Asokoro, Abuja
Telephone: 09-3140900, 3140902
Fax: 09-3140901
Hours of Duty: Monday – Friday: 0900-1500 hours
Visa: Monday – Friday: 0900-1300 hours

The Republic of Zimbabwe

Chancery:	Plot 2908 Euphrates Street
	Off Aminu Kano Crescent, Wuse II
	P.O. Box 8214 Wuse, Abuja
Telephone:	09-4137996
Fax:	09-4137644
Email:	zimabuja@linserve.com
Hours of Duty:	Monday – Friday: 0800-1300 hours
	1400-1630 hours
Visa Section:	Monday – Friday: 1100-1300 hours

International Organisations

African Development Bank Group, Nigeria
Plot 819
Lake Chad Crescent
Maitama District, Abuja - FCT
Tel: 09 4133 261, 09 4133 262, 00 1321 956 3851
Fax: 09 4133 260
     00 1321 956 3851
Mobile Tel: 08036670043

Canadian International Development Agency (CIDA)
3A Bobo Street, Maitama, Abuja
Tel: 09-413-9910
Fax: 09-413-9911
Contact: Andrew Spezowka, *andrew.spezowka@international.gc.ca.*

Canada-Nigeria Cooperation Office
CIDA Program Support Unit (PSU)
89, Atbara Street
Off Cairo
Wuse II, Abuja
Tel: 09-413-0283

Fax: 09-413-0284
Contact: Kenna Owoh. kowoh@cidapsu-ng.org.

Department for International Development (DFID)
Plot 607, Bobo Street,
Off Gana Street, Maitama, Abuja.
09-413 7710-10,
www.dfid.gov.uk

Economic Community of West African States (ECOWAS)
60 Yakubu Gowon Crescent,
Asokoro District,
P.B. 401 Abuja,
Tel:09-3147647-9, 314 7427-9
Fax: 09-314 3005, 314 3006

European Union
Europe House,
Plot 63, Usuma Street,
Maitama District,
P.B. 280, Garki, Abuja.
09-4133145-8, 413 3792-3
Fax: 09-4133147
Email:delegation-nigeria@cec.eu.int

Food & Agriculture Organisation of the United Nations (FAO)
3 Oguda Close, Off Lake Chad Crescent
Maitama, Abuja.
P.B. 396, Garki, Abuja.
Tel:09-413 7546, 413 7545
Fax: 09-413 7544
Email: fao nga@field.fao.org.

German Technical (GTZ)
No 40, Julius Nyerere Street,
Asokoro
Tel: 09-314 9010, 314 3978

International Red Cross
Plot 436 Kumasi Crescent
Off Aminu Kano Crescent
Wuse II, Abuja
Tel: 09-413 3683, 413 5947, 671 1288/9
Fax:09-413 5948
Email: Abuja.abuj@icrc.org

International Monetary Fund (IMF)
Plot 1708
Hon Justice Mohammed Bello Street
Asokoro, Abuja
Tel:09-314 0329, 314 0385
Fax: 09-314 0383

Japan International Cooperation Agency (JICA)
AP Plaza
Wuse Zone II
Tel: 09-523 2869, 413 8898, 413 9258
Fax: 09-413 7667

National Centre for Women Development
Better Life Street
5th Street,
Central Area, Abuja
Tel: 09 234-0961-7; 234-0607
Fax: 09 234 0978

The Nigeria-Sao Tome and Principe Joint Development Authority
Headquarters
Plot 1101
Aminu Crescent
Wuse 11, Abuja.

*United Nations Educational Scientific and Cultural Organisation (UNESCO)
www.unesco.org
Email: Abuja@unesco.org.

*United Nations Children Fund (UNICEF)

*United Nations Development Programme (UNDP)

* United Nations Industrial Development Organisation (UNIDO)

UN House, Abuja
UNICEF Nigeria Country Office,
United Nations House
Central Area
Diplomatic Zone
Garki Abuja.
Fax: 234-9-4618578
Web:www.Unicef.Org.

United States Agency for International Development (USAID)
992 Metro Plaza
1st Avenue Off Herbert Macaulay Way
Central Area, Abuja.

World Bank
Plot 433, Yakubu Gowon Crescent
Asokoro
P.O. Box 2826, Garki
Tel: 09-314 5259, 314 5261/62/64/65/74/75
Fax: 09-314 5267, 314 5268

---
*All major UN organisations are now located in the UN House, Abuja

World Health Organisation (WHO)
Plot 1620, Yusuf Maitama,
Off Yakubu Gowon Crescent,
Asokoro District,
Abuja.
Tel:09-314 8776-7, 314 0578-9
Fax: 09-314 8778, 314 0578
Email:whoabuja@who-nigeria.org.

---

*All major UN organisations are now located in the UN House

CHAPTER 4

Getting Here

To learn to fly, a bird must first learn to leave the nest.
(Zambian Proverb)

Travelling to Abuja

There are several options for arrival in Abuja: British Airways, KLM and Lufthansa offer direct flights from Europe. There are also several domestic airlines that can transfer passengers from Lagos to Abuja. AeroContractors, however, is the only airline that is FAA (U.S. Federal Aviation Association) approved. For those travelling with a great deal of luggage, direct flights to Abuja are recommended.

The flights from Lagos to Abuja depart from the domestic airport, which necessitates a transfer by car from the Murtala Mohammed International Airport in Lagos to the local domestic airport 10 kms away. Due to security concerns, it is not recommended to travel to Lagos after dark. A complete list of international and domestic airlines is included in this section. Some travel agencies are also listed.

Shipping to Abuja

Freight Forwarders and Shipping Services can now send items by air directly to Abuja. For items travelling by sea, freight must be cleared in Lagos and sent by land to Abuja. This can be a time-consuming process. Be prepared to wait because a policy to inspect 100% of the shipments – the Lagos clearance process – can take up to four months. Therefore, if possible, it is recommended that the shipment go by air to Abuja.

Also, be sure that the shipper is aware of the clearance process. Duty should not have to be paid on personal items sent to Abuja provided they have been owned for a minimum of six months, or are not for resale, or are intended for the owner's continued use. Have a good itemised list of the contents of the shipment in addition to the routine packing list. It may be necessary to open a bank account and then request the bank to complete a "Form M" before goods can be sent to Nigeria (and certainly before they are cleared). This procedure varies depending upon the work/diplomatic status of the person shipping the goods. Make sure the entire shipping process is clear before sending goods to Nigeria to avoid any problems. Also, check the references of the customs clearing company to make sure they are clear and efficient with their customers.

IAL Nigeria Limited
Abuja Office:
Plot 74, Ralph Sodeinde Street
Off Ahmadu Bello Way
Central Business District, Abuja

Fax: 09 234-8853; 0803-304-5218; 0803-396-4661
M-F: 0800-1700
Sat.   0800-1300
Email: abuja@ialnigeria.com
Full service company that can handle the packing, shipping, customs clearing of sea and air freight, unpacking and storage of items. They also have offices in Lagos, Ikeja, Port Harcourt and Warri.

SDV

Total House Plot 247 Herbert Macaulay Way
(Opposite NNPC HQ)
Central District, Abuja
P.O. Box 8570 Wuse
☎   09 234-6798; 234-9701; 0803-334-3642
Fax: 09 234-8179
International transport and logistic company that provides packing, shipping, customs clearing of sea and air freight and unpacking of items.

In general, the documents required to clear personal effects out of customs include: passport (original); visa, work permit; full and detailed inventory (in English); Customs and Excise Unaccompanied Baggage Declaration; verification of residence change; a letter authorising the clearing company to clear the shipment; and a residence permit. It is strongly recommended that the person shipping the goods be present personally to supervise the clearing and unloading of the goods to ensure they are handled with care.

Import Allowances

In addition to the restriction on the importation of new items of personal effects, other limits per adult include:
Alcohol   – 1 litre of spirits (importation of sparkling wine is prohibited)
Tobacco   – 200 cigarettes; 50 cigars or 200g of tobacco
Perfumes – a small quantity of perfume

Getting Here 65

Prohibited Items

Imports

The following items are prohibited from importation into Nigeria.
- Arms and ammunition;
- Fireworks;
- Drugs and narcotics. Private individuals may bring drugs prescribed by a licensed medical doctor;
- Jewellery (other than for personal use), precious metals, raw textile material, alcoholic beverages (outside the limit mentioned above), soft drinks, beverages, fruits, vegetables and products made with rice, maize, or wheat.

Exports

Antiquities may not be bought or sold except with the permission of the Director of Antiquities (National Museum, Lagos) or an accredited agent. Benin bronzes are often considered to be antiquities and are subject to seizure by customs officials. Departing persons are, therefore, advised to obtain an export permit from the Director of Antiquities or his designated agents before attempting to depart Nigeria.

Zuma Rock

Airlines and Travel Agencies

In addition to purchasing tickets for domestic flights from the airline offices in hotels, they can also be purchased at the ticket counter in the airport. Travellers will often head directly for the airport and take the next available flight to their destination as the scheduled flights often do not leave on time.

International Airlines

Flights in and out of Abuja

British Airways
NICON Hilton Hotel
(Aguiyi Ironsi and Shehu Shagari Way)
Lower Lobby Area
☎ 09-413-9608; 413-9610 ext.6388
Fax: 09 413-9609
🕘 M-F: 0900 - 1700 Hours
Saturday: 0900 - 1300 Hours
5 times a week
London - Abuja - London
www.britishairways.com

KLM
Sheraton Hotel
Ladi Kwali Way
☎ 09 523-9966; 523-9965
☎ Airport 09 810-0034/39
🕘 M-F: 0830 - 1700 hours
Saturday: 0830 - 1200 hours
4 times a week
Amsterdam - Abuja - Kano - Amsterdam
www.klm.ng

Getting Here   67

Lufthansa
Nicon Hilton
(Aguiyi Ironsi and Shehu Shagari Way)
Congress Hall
☎ 09 413-3001
⏰ M-F: 0900 - 1300 hours
Saturday: 1400 - 1700 hours
Reservation: 0803-747-7474
Reconfirmation: 09 413-3002
2 times a week
Frankfurt-Lagos-Abuja-Lagos-Frankfurt
www.lufthansa.com.ng

Overland Airways
Domestic Terminal Building
Abuja.
☎ 08035717017, 08035351159, 0803700720

Flights in and out of Lagos

Air France
Plot 1264, Muhammadu Buhari Way
Off Ahmadu Bello Way, by CBN Junction
Garki II, Shopping Centre
Garki - Abuja
P.M.B. Box 9424, Abuja
☎ 09 234-0920-1
Fax: 09 234-0920; 080-331-16042
Email: waajayi@yahoo.com
⏰ M-F: 0800- 1700 Hours

Alitalia
Nicon Plaza
Plot 242 Muhammadu Buhari Way
Central Business District, 3rd Floor
☎ 09 234-8433
⏰ M-F: 0830 - 1700 hours
Saturday: 0900 - 1230 hours

Egypt Air
Engineering Close Street,
Lagos
☎   01 2619233, 2620087, 2661974, 2661102, 2613329

Emirates Airline
☎   01 2617738, 2617752, 2618025

Ethiopian Airline
Karimu-Kotun Street
Victoria Island,
Lagos
☎   01 7755723, 2626688-90, 2636663

Iberia Airlines
Sanusi Fafunwa Street,
Lagos
☎   01 7746615

South Africa Airlines
28 C Adetokunbo Ademola Street
Victoria Island, Lagos
☎   01 262-0607-9; 262-5921-5
Fax: 01 262-5929
🕘 M-F: 0830 - 1700 hours
Saturday: 0900 - 1230 hours

Virgin Atlantic
The Ark Towers,
Plot 17 Ligali Ayorinde Street
Victoria Island, Lagos
(ex-Airport Road)
☎   01 320-2747; 461-2747
🕘 M-Sat: 0900 - 1800 hours
Email: Lagos.Reservation.Request@ fly.vigin.com

Internal-Domestic Airlines

In addition to Lagos, some domestic airlines fly from Abuja to Kano, Port Harcourt, Enugu and Maiduguri. Some desks/offices may be unmanned even during posted office hours

ADC Airlines
Sheraton Hotel
Ladi Kwali Way
Near pool
☎ 09 523-0225 ext. 8723; 671-1536; fax 810-0142
🕘 M-Sat: 0800 - 1800 hours

AERO Contractors
Nicon Hilton Hotel
(Aguiyi Ironsi and Shehu Shagari Way)
Floor 01
☎ (airport) 09 810-0197; 413-8710
🕘 M-F: 0730 - 1800
Email: operations.fw@acn.aero
www.acn.aero

Albarka Air PLC
Nicon Hilton Hotel
(Aguiyi Ironsi and Shehu Shagari Way)
Floor 01
☎ 09 413-0322
🕘 M-F: 0730 - 1800 hours
Saturday: 0730 - 1300 hours

Bellview
Location 1: Nicon Hilton Hotel
(Aguiyi Ironsi and Shehu Shagari Way)
Floor 01
☎ 09 413-1811 ext 6371
Location 2: Sheraton Hotel
Ladi Kwali Way
Near pool

☎   09 523-0225 ext. 8177
⏱ 7 days: 0800 - 1700 Hours

Chanchangi
Location 1: Nicon Hilton Hotel
 (Aguiyi Ironsi and Shehu Shagari Way)
 Floor 01
☎   09 413-4301
Location 2: Sheraton Hotel
 Ladi Kwali Way
 Near pool
☎   09 523-0225 ext. 8343; 523-0011
⏱ M-F: 0800 - 1900 Hours
Saturday: 0800 - 1700 Hours

IRS Airlines
Location 1: Nicon Hilton Hotel
 (Aguiyi Ironsi and Shehu Shagari Way)
 Floor 01
☎   09 413 1811
Location 2: Sheraton Hotel
 Ladi Kwali Way
 Near pool
☎   09 523-0225; 08035960991
⏱ M-F: 0800 - 1900
Saturday: 0800 - 1700
Email: irsairlines2002@yahoo.co.uk
www.irsairlines.com

Overland Airways & Travel Centre
Terminal Building
Nnamdi Azikiwe International Airport
Abuja
☎   09 8100223, 08035717017
Fax: 01 4937699 (Lagos)
Email: cspd@overland.aero
www.overland.aero

Sosoliso Airlines

Location 1: Nicon Hilton Hotel
(Aguiyi Ironsi and Shehu Shagari Way)
Floor 01
☎ 09 413-3573; 0802-302-1968; 810-0122 (airport)
Location 2: Sheraton Hotel
Ladi Kwali Way
Near pool

Space World Airline

Sheraton Hotel
☎ 09 523-0225 ext. 8345
🕐 M-F: 0730 - 1800 hours
Saturday: 0730 - 1400 hours
Sunday: 0730-1600 hours
Email: fly@*sosolisoairline.com*

Travel Agencies

Most travellers purchase tickets directly through the airlines as the systems used by the travel agents can be cumbersome. A couple of agents recommended by users are noted below.

*Air Transvapid Travel Agency, Ltd ***

Agura Hotel
#10 Moshood Abiola Road
Area 10, Garki
☎ 09 234-2671
🕐 M-F: 0900-1700

*All States Travel and Tours**

Nicon Hilton Hotel
(Aguiyi Ironsi and Shehu Shagari Way)
Ground Floor
☎ 09 413 0405, 413 1811
Fax: 09 413-1941

---

* Licensed by the International Air Travel Association (IATA)

72   Around and About Abuja

Email: allstatesng@yahoo.com
🕓 M-F: 0900-1700 hours
Saturday: 0900-1300 hours

Habis Travel Ltd*
Nicon Hilton Hotel
(Aguiyi Ironsi and Shehu Shagari Way)
☎   09 523-2301
🕓 M-F: 0800-1800

Mayfair Travel Agent (Lagos)
Manager: Anshu
They will deliver tickets by DHL and purchase domestic tickets and provide airport transfer between the international and domestic airport. Mayfair Travel Agent (Lagos)
Email: anshu@mayfairtravel.net
☎   01 775-2277; 261-8326
🕓 M-F: 0800-1800

Intourist Nigeria, Ltd,
(Oluwole Adebayo)
17A Maitama Corner shop,
Aminu Kano Crescent
By old National Assembly Quarters road
Near the Regent School
☎   09 670-7351; 0804-418-7007, 0803-312-0444
🕓 M-F: 0800-1800
Sat: 0800-1300

Bensan Int. Travel and Tours
Suit B2
Zuma Shopping Mall
Ndora Square
Off Mike Okpara Street
Wuse Zone 5

---
* Licensed by the International Air Travel Association (IATA)

DISCOVER NIGERIA
SPECTRUM ROAD MAP

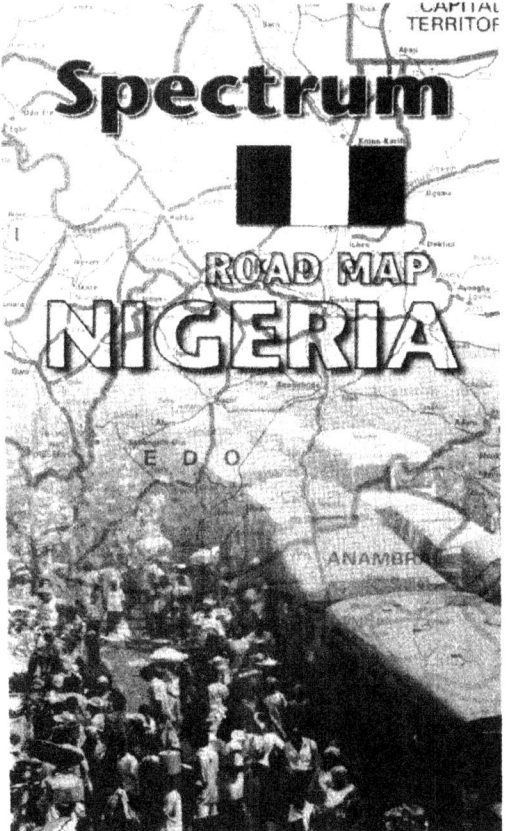

SPECTRUM BOOKS LIMITED
SPECTRUM HOUSE: RING ROAD, P.M.B. 5612, IBADAN
Tel: 02-2310145, 2311215, 2310058
Tel/Fax: 02-2318502, 2312705
e-mail:admin1@spectrumbooksonline.com
www.spectrumbooksonline.com
Hotline:08033842114

We still maintain our century-Long leadership in Bookselling, Printing and Publishing

CSS Bookshops Limited

For:

- Bibles, Hymn and Prayer Books and other Christian Literature
- Educational Books (All levels) and General Titles.
- Commercial printing of Books, Diaries, Posters, Calendars, Annual Reports, Etc.
- Publishing of Christian, Educational, Children and general Titles

For more information, please contact us at

Head Office:
BOOKSHOP HOUSE,
50/52, BROAD STREET, LAGOS.
☎01-2633010, 2633081, 2637009, 2637023
FAX: 2637089
E-MAIL: cssbookshops@skennet.com.ng
WEBSITE: www.cssbookshops.com

CSS Bookshops,
Bamenda Street,
Beside All Saints Nursery/Primary School
Behinde Abuja Shopping Mall
Wuse Zone 3
Abuja
☎/ Fax: 09-5233551

CSS Bookshops,
Ambeez Plaza,
Ndola Care,
Off Michael Okpara Way,
Wuse Zone 5,
Abuja.

Apapa
CSS Bookshops,
10/12, Warehouse Road,
Apapa.
☎ 01-5877732.

Kaduna
CSS Bookshops,
26, Ahmadu Bello Way,
Kaduna.
☎ 062-211601.

Port Harcourt
CSS Bookshops,
50, Hospital Road,
Port Harcourt.
☎ 084-233633, 0805-604-9783.

Akure
CSS Bookshops
69, Oba Adesida Road,
Akure.
☎ 034-244005..

... Serving you with dedication and trust since 1869

☎ 09 523-5592; 523-5748
⏲M-F: 0800-1800
Sat: 0800-1300

BTI Nigeria
28C Adetokunbo Ademola Street Victoria,
P.O. Box 50431, Ikoyi
Lagos Nigeria
☎ 012625920
Fax: 012625929

CHAPTER 5

Getting Settled

Nwayo, nwayo, ka mbe ji aracha ofe di oku
(Igbo Proverb)
Slow and steady wins the race

Caveat
While we have done our best to recommend only people that have received positive feedback from our readers, it is always possible that services and stores that are good today are not good (or even gone!) tomorrow. Please note that there is a general Value Added Tax (VAT) of 5% that is already included in the purchase price of goods.

Real Estate

Types of Accommodation
There are several different types of accommodation available in Abuja.
- Detached house or bungalow – a separate dwelling surrounded by a walled garden. It provides privacy, but also includes more responsibility as the tenant is responsible for all upkeep in the garden and most house repairs, the main exception being structural repairs.
- Apartment or duplex – joined dwellings in which people share access to the building with other tenants. The cost of electricity, generator and water is usually included in the price of the rent. Responsibility for the maintenance of the dwelling and its surroundings falls more on the landlord. However, tenants will have less control as to the speed with which repairs and payments are made and, therefore, will be more dependent upon the landlord.
- Houses in a complex or Life Camp. Some houses built by companies in a complex may be available for rent to people outside of the company on a space available basis. The Shell compound off Shehu Shagari in Maitama is one example of such a complex. The construction company camps of Dantata and Sawoe (German) and Bouygues (French) are examples of some of the Life Camps that sometimes rent to outside customers. In the case of the Life Camps, they cover the cost of electricity, running water and repairs.

Most accommodations are rented unfurnished. Unfurnished in Nigeria means without generator, stoves, refrigerators, washers/dryers, cookers (ovens) or air-conditioners. Therefore, be prepared to include the purchase of those items in a housing budget. In addition, renters are normally required to pay two years minimum rent in advance, so be prepared to take time and find the best accommodation. It can take up to two months to find the appropriate property. Some options for hotels and fully-serviced apartments during the search are included in the "Getting Rest" section of this book.

Location

As in other parts of the world, location plays a key role in the cost of the real estate. Houses and apartments in Asokoro, Maitama (including Ministers' Hill) are usually the most expensive followed by Wuse and Garki. A number of "bedroom" communities have developed around the outskirts of the city in communities such as Gwarinpa, Mabushi, Jabi, Kubwa, etc., to provide more affordable housing for government employees and some business persons. Due to security concerns, most foreigners live in Maitama, Asokoro or Wuse.

House Hunting Tips

Check the Construction
Unfortunately, many of the houses were put together quickly using poor quality materials. It is wise to take someone who has a basic knowledge of building construction along when looking at accommodation.

Check for Security Upgrades
Although Abuja is a relatively safe city as compared to Lagos, it is wise to make sure the home has basic security features. Such features include:
- a strong metal gate with a security peep hole.
- razor wire along the top of the wall.
- grilled doors and windows or metal doors with strong locks and additional security latches

General Tips
- Be sure that crime prevention measures do not prevent an easy and quick escape for your family in case of fire.
- If noise is an issue, avoid houses near heavy traffic flows, but, for security reasons, do not select a house that is too isolated.
- Get to know the neighbours. Select accommodation near neighbours who also have good security as they will likely keep an eye on your property, as well.

- Keep in mind that Abuja is situated between the Equator and the Tropic of Cancer, so all parts of the house will receive strong sunshine at some point during the day. Therefore, facilities for cooling (fans, air conditioners) are important. Fans are good even if there is air conditioning as power can often be too low to run the air conditioning.
- Make sure the doors and windows close without a gap, otherwise rain will enter during the rainy season and dust during the dry season.
- Check the wood and the lawn for termite infestation. Certain parts of Abuja have terrible termite problems. Take a close look at the doors and closets.
- Test the water in each room to make sure the hot water heaters are working and the water is indeed flowing. Some houses are not hooked up to the city water source and have their water delivered. Be sure to ask the landlord and the neighbours about the reliability of the source. Even houses that supposedly have reliable city water should have an underground, ground-level, tower or rooftop water storage tank to ensure water storage and constant water flow.
- If an apartment is preferred, ask the neighbours about the condition of the apartment and the reliability of the landlord. Also, make sure there are enough rooms for any domestic workers.
- Make sure the previous tenant of the house did not leave any unpaid bills as you may be held responsible for phone, electricity, water, etc. Ask for the payment receipts in order to prove past payment. It is also a good idea to save the old payment slips to prove payment and to pass them on to the next tenant.
- Ask about the presence and the functioning of a generator. Make sure it is clear who is responsible for the purchase, maintenance and functioning of the generator and fuel.
- Check for a working telephone line. In some areas, the telephone exchanges are full and it is difficult to obtain a landline.

Occupancy Tax

In 2001, the Nigerian government established a tenement rate tax. The primary liability for the tax lies on the occupier, except in multi-tenant properties in which case the owner is liable. Therefore, renters of single dwelling homes should be prepared to receive a tenement rate demand notice at their home. The tax bill will be payable within 21 days of receipt and must be paid to:

> AMAC Tenement Rate Account No. 091023912
> Lion Bank of Nigeria
> Dambata Close
> Area 7, Garki.

Real Estate Agents

Most landlords will not rent a property for less than two years. Payment is required in full (usually in cash) upon the signing of the lease. The standard commission for the real estate agent that recommends the selected house and assists in brokering a deal is 10% of the total rent. Before looking at houses with an agent, ensure that the services to be provided are clear (who drives and/or pays for taxis, helps negotiate a price, etc.) It is not wise to use too many different real estate agents to prevent problems caused when two or more agents show the same house. If you were shown a house by a previous agent, be sure to tell the other agent right away so that he/she knows that the commission might need to be shared.

Some agents used by our readers include:

Abishai Properties, Ltd.
Suite C14 Bobsar Complex
Michika Street
(Off Ahmadu Bello Way)
Garki II, Abuja
P.O. Box 10584

Garki, Abuja
☎ 09 314-2649; 0803-322-3559
✉ *abishai_ppty@yahoo.com*
Property managers, developers, builders and maintainers.
Ken U. Ndieli: Director of Projects

Cachez Ltd.
Plot 913 Alexander Crescent, Wuse II, Abuja
(Beside Whiz filling station, Off Aminu Kano Crescent)
☎ 09 413-8992; 413-8993; 413-4450
Fax: 09 413-4451
🕘 M-F: 0900-1700

C.E Nwogbo and Associates
Suite B27 Emab Plaza
Aminu Kano Crescent
Wuse II
☎ 670 8010, 08023087995

Danladi Bamaiyi and Co
Bamcar Complex
Plot 1935
Ndola Square
Zone 5 Wuse
☎ 523 9738, 523 9739

Diran Adetunji and Associates
Plot 495
Mambolo Street
Zone 2
Wuse
☎ 523 2615, 523 1823

Divention Properties Ltd.
Plot 740
Aminu Kano Crescent, Wuse II, Abuja
☎ 09 423-9564; 413-5214; 413-9795

Fax: 09 413-5214
Email: sanusialiyu@hotmail.com
◷M-F: 0830-1730

Penthouse Properties, Ltd.
Plot 12 Senanga Street, Suite 1, Zone 5, Wuse, Abuja
(Off Accra Street)
☎ 09 523-3111; 523-4289
Fax: 09 523-4289
www.penthousepropertiesng.com

Urban Shelter Ltd.
1st Floor, Shipper's Plaza
Plot 438 Michael Okpara Way, Zone 5, Wuse, Abuja
☎ 09 523-4147, 523-9862
Fax: 09 523-6922
Email: urbanshelter@yahoo.com

Mento Investment Nig.
Plot 102, Shop B42
Area 11 Corner shop
Garki
☎ 09 6701752, 314 8264, 314 0412, 08037002493

Sitar Services & Industries Ltd
Plot 664
Usuma Street
Maitama
☎ 4139833, 413 9834 0803787 6345

Water Service

City water is supplied by two dams and is assisted by several boreholes. The main dam is Usman dam (see "Staying Active" for information on how to visit the dam). Built in 1987, Usman dam has a reservoir of 120 million cubic meters of water and the capacity to treat 5,000 cubic meters of water per hour. Jabi Dam is a smaller

PATED MARBLE
ITALIAN QUALITY BUILDING MATERIALS

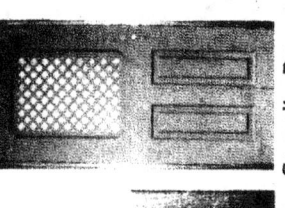

Security Doors

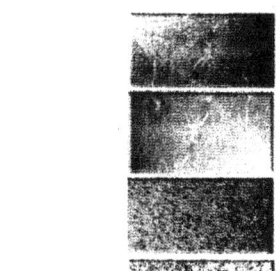

Marbles/Granite

Sanitary Ware

ABUJA
Sheraton Junction
Tel: 09-5238507, 5234653, 520591
Cell: 08033203663, 09 6709446
Email: patedmarmi@yahoo.com

LAGOS
13, Karimu Kotun St, Victoria Island
Tel: 01-610735, 2611704; Fax: 01 -2646788
Email: tluttwak@hotmail.com

All Building Materials At
VERY VERY VERY VERY COMPETITIVE PRICES

LOW PRICE

HIGH QUALITY

WAKKIS

...Just the way you want

The most popular Indian restaurant in town

No. 56, Zone 4 Shopping Centre, (Opposite Sheraton Hotel)
P. O. Box 8098, Wuse, Abuja. ☎: 234-9-5235436

dam built in 1982. The FCT Water Board is the parastatal that manages the water resources for the territory.

For home water service, payment and connection, contact the FCT Water Board located on Orlu St, Area 3, Garki, ☎09 234-1559; 234-2937; 234-2662; 234-1085. Water bills are sometimes delivered to homes. If they are not, customers need to go to the water office to collect and pay them.

There are different types of fees depending upon the service required. The fees change often, those noted as a guide below are from 2003 ($1 = ₦135).

Categories	Charge
Commercial, metered	₦60/m3
Commercial, flat rate	₦20,000/month
Domestic, metered	₦21/m3
Domestic, flat rate	₦2,800/month
Connection fee, domestic (25mm)	₦21,600
Connection fee, domestic (50mm)	₦33,600
Other charges:	consult the Water Board

Disconnection

When buying or moving to a house, make sure that the previous owner/tenant has paid any bills owed. The Water Board may disconnect the house from the water supply when the debt becomes large, no matter who was responsible.

Supply Reliability

Good water pressure is an indication that the water supply in the area is pretty reliable. However, in general, water pressure tends to be low during the night. To be prepared in case of a system failure, stock enough water for at least one day's consumption.

No City Water?

There are many houses in Abuja that are not connected to the city water supply, mostly due to low water pressure. In those cases, tenants drill boreholes, or purchase water from independent suppliers or the Water Board. Prices vary depending upon the quantity of water needed and the distance to be travelled, but it is customary to pay between ₦3,500 and ₦6,000 per lorry. Prices as of 2003 are listed below.

Volume		Charges and Delivery Distance
	5km	10km
2,000 gallons	₦3,500	₦5,000-₦6,000
3,000 gallons	₦4,500	

Some private lorries providing water service can be found in Asokoro, along Murtala Mohammed Expressway, between the Y junction with the road to Nyanyan-Karu-Keffi and the intersection with Yakubu Gowon Crescent. The lorries are parked on undeveloped land in that area.

Electricity Hook-up and Payment

The domestic supply is 220/240 V AC, 50 Hz. Most outlets use 3 pin-flat and/or round plugs (5,13,15 amp) and bayonet or screw-in lamp fittings. Some older properties have two-pin sockets. Many appliances are sold with two-pin plugs attached, and so require adapters.

Contact the local area NEPA (National Electric Power Authority) office if an electrical connection is not already provided. Fees vary depending upon whether the dwelling has one phase, three phases or a commercial hook-up. A certain number of electrical outlets are put on each phase. Small houses usually have one phase; medium and large houses have three phases. Prices in 2003 are noted below.

Categories	Naira per unit kilowatt
Domestic, 1 phase	4
Domestic, 3 phases	6
Commercial	8.5

Bills are delivered to each household every month. However, for some months the meter may not be read. In that case, the amount charged will be based upon the previous months' usage; so, be prepared for a possible increase based upon actual meter readings later.

Bills in Abuja district may be paid at any cash payment office in Abuja. However, it is better to pay the bill in your own area, as the payment record is hand written and it will be easier to follow-up if there are any errors. Cash payment is accepted at each area office. Bring the account statement when making a payment and a receipt will be issued. Be sure to keep the receipt in case there is a dispute over payment later.

Maitama: IBB Way, between Lake Chad Crescent and Danube Street.

Wuse: IBB Way, between Ahmadu Bello Way and Adetokunbo Crescent (north). Opposite British Village.

Garki: Kaura Namoda Street, Opposite Afribank building.

Asokoro: On the South corner of the intersection of Murtala Mohammed Expressway and Yakubu Gowon Crescent.

Disconnection

It is wise to pay NEPA bills within a week after receiving them to avoid disconnection and a consequent reconnection fee.

Supply Reliability

Power outages are common in Abuja. They may last from a few hours to several days during occasional major outages or bill disputes with NEPA. It is, therefore, wise to have a back-up supply via a generator.

Protection of Sensitive Appliances

The power supply deviates considerably from 220V and is often too weak or too powerful to sustain some appliances. In addition, lightening strikes are frequent during the rainy season and can severely damage appliances. It is strongly recommended therefore that residents put stabilisers (voltage regulators) between a wall outlet and any delicate electric appliances such as computers (desk and laptop), televisions/video/DVD recorders, refrigerators, air conditioners, washer/dryers, etc. Stabilisers (voltage regulators) are available at many electric appliance shops and Wuse market, Wuse Shopping Complex, the electronics market near the post office in Zone 3, Grand Supermarket and Park n' Shop to name a few. If you are home during a thunderstorm, unplug the appliances from the wall sockets, unplug modems from telephone jacks and refrain from talking on the telephone to provide the greatest possible protection.

Danger of Fire

In any environment, sockets and plugs should be kept clean and dust-free. Accumulated dust may catch fire, cause a short circuit and a house fire may result. During the dry season, when the wind and the dust from the harmattan is great, special care should be taken. In addition, many imported appliances require the use of an adapter. Be sure to purchase good quality adapters that make a tight seal around the appliance plug and the wall socket to prevent dust from entering and becoming a fire hazard. Air conditioners, in particular, have been known to start fires. They should be checked every three months to prevent fire and health problems.

Generators

Although electricity reliability improves every year, if possible, it is still wise to have a generator. Tenants in houses provide their own generators; landlords of apartment buildings are responsible for providing generators. Different options, from the small generators able to run a few lights and refrigerators to those capable of servicing several houses, can be purchased and installed in Abuja. Be prepared, however, as they are expensive. A drum for fuel storage, a hose/mini-pump for use during refuelling and information on where to purchase fuel will also be needed.

Be sure that the generator connection is properly installed. It must be physically placed after the NEPA line so that payment is not made to NEPA for generator-produced power.

Generator Suppliers

Some generator suppliers used by our readers are listed below.

JMG Ltd.
No. 13, Gana St, Maitama
☎ 09 670-7336; 0802-404-0666; 0803-404-0666; 0804-213-9515
Email: jmg@linkserve.com
Generators, fuel tanks, maintenance (24 hours)

Landmart
NICON Hilton Hotel, 01 Floor
(Aguiyi Ironsi and Shehu Shagari Way)
☎ 09 413-5789
🕒 M-F: 0800-1800
Saturday: 1000-1400
Generators, maintenance

Mikano International, Ltd.
Plot 487 Adetokunbo Ademola Crescent
Wuse II
(Near Chicken House and DHL)

☎   09 523-3997; 523-1994
🕐 M-F: 0800-1900
Saturday: 0800-1400
Generators, maintenance. On call 24 hours.

Fuel Purchases and Delivery

Although Nigeria is a major oil producing country, there are limited refining capacities. Therefore, the majority of its petrol and diesel is imported and there are occasional shortages due to domestic and international conflicts. During those periods, it is not uncommon to wait in line for up to ten hours for petrol.
One station that delivers fuel is listed below.

AP IBB Way Diesel and Petrol Centre
(Corner of Aguiyi Ironsi and IBB Way)
(Opposite British High Commission)
Maitama, Abuja
Mr Segun Olusan (Manager)
☎   09-413-8768; 0802-334-2478

The price per litre will vary based upon the amount needed, whether it is petrol or diesel and whether transportation is required.

Cooking Fuel

Charcoal

Domestic charcoal can be purchased at the local market. Some of the supermarkets also carry imported varieties.

Cooking Gas

Because of frequent power outages and fluctuation in voltage, many households prefer to have gas cooking facilities. Stoves with both gas and electric burners can also be purchased.

There are many suppliers of cooking gas in town, usually quite visible with their gas tanks piled high. Prices vary depending upon the size of the cylinder desired and whether gas is simply being replaced or an entire cylinder is being purchased. The most common cylinder sizes are: 12.5 kg, 25 kg and 50 kg. Prices as at 2003 are shown below.

Content Weight (Size)	Cost of Empty Cylinder	Gas Price	Delivery Charge
12.5kg	₦4,000	₦1,500	₦500
25kg	₦6,000	₦3,000	
50kg	₦12,000	₦6,000	

One home delivery service recommended by our readers is:

Super Gas Home-delivery Service (SHS)

Depot: Rear Gate of Crystal Palace Hotel, 687 Port Harcourt Crescent, Off Ahmadu Bello Way, Off Gimbiya Street, Area 11, Garki Abuja.

Factory: Plot 36, Opposite Bouygues, Idu Industrial Estate, Idu, Abuja.

☎ 09 314-0039; 314-0041; 671-4173; 0802-313-1307, 0803-587-7292

⊕M-Sat.: 0900-1600

Their flyer advertises accurately filled canisters, best prices, constant supply assured even in times of shortage and 24 hour delivery. Prices (Nov 2003): 12.5 kg= ₦1500, 50kg=₦6,000

Television and Satellite TV Hook-up

Nigeria is on the PAL B German television system. Local channels are limited. Most people opt for satellite television, which affords the opportunity to take advantage of international and national television. A multi-system TV compatible video recorder will be necessary if non-PAL videos are to be viewed as well.

The South Africa Digital Satellite (DSTV) provider of M-Net is by far the most popular option for satellite television. There are 44 TV channels, including BBC World, CNN, Sky News, sports channels, children's channels and 26 radio channels. Portuguese, Asian and Arabic channels are available for an additional fee. There are quite a number of businesses selling and installing the decoder and the dish. They are soon to offer interactive TV, hi-speed internet and international call services. Payment for the subscription can be made in monthly instalments. A discount equivalent to one month free is given when payment is made one year in advance (2003 prices = 8,000/month or ₦88,000/year).

If service is scrambled after the bill has already been paid, you can turn your DSTV box to Channel 3, call the office and give them the account number. They should be able to activate your card again. The main office where the monthly show listing and service payments are made is:

DSTV (Satellite TV)
Multichoice Nigeria, Ltd.
Plot 528 Malabo,
Off Aminu Kano Crescent
Wuse 2, Abuja
☎ 09 523-1317; 523-5304; 523-5827
Fax: 09 523-3678

Payments can also be made at Zenith Bank. Some installers recommended by our readers are:

Altech Engineering and Communications Systems
Banex Extension, Aminu Kano Crescent, Wuse II, Abuja
(Next to Park N' Shop Supermarket)
☎ 09 523-8543; 0803-314-0587; 0804-210-1643
🕒 M-F: 0900-1700
Saturday:1000-1400

Digital Telecommunications & Satellite Co, Ltd.
Suite 10, Landmark Plaza
Plot 3124 IBB Way, Maitama, Abuja
P.O. Box 8041, Wuse, Abuja
☎   09 523-8575; 413-8575; 090-800649; 0804-418-0609;
       0804-418-2760; 0803-314-2259
Fax: 09 413-7771

Emeka, Repair Technician
☎   08042101643, 08033140537

Telephone Connection and Telephone Payment (NITEL Land Line)

The state-run Nigerian Telecommunications Ltd. (NITEL), provides telephone service within Abuja, between Nigerian cities and internationally (for an extra fee). It also offers a home internet service and customers can also send telegrams. As mentioned earlier, there are some areas in which it is extremely difficult to obtain a NITEL land line. Therefore, it is wise to rent accommodation with an existing telephone line. If you are unable to do so, applications for telephone lines can be obtained from the exchange offices listed below. A current subscriber will need to support the application and both of you will need to attach passport photos to the forms. A deposit will be required if an IDD (International Direct Dial) line is requested.

Be sure to ask the installer to include telephone and line protection against lightening strikes.

Exchange Offices

Maitama: Madeira Street, Off Aguiyi Ironsi Street, Near MTN, Maitama
☎ 09 413-9555

Wuse: Durban Street, Off Kolda Street, Wuse II.
☎ 09 523-1192; 523-4035

Garki: Orlu Street, Area 3, Garki. In the same building as the Water Board.
☏ 09 234-5670

Asokoro: Yakubu Gowon Crescent, Asokoro.
☏ 09 314-8326

There are different types of fees depending on the service used. Off-peak calls (between 7.00 p.m. and 7.00 a.m. weekdays and all throughout public holidays and weekends) are 50% off peak rates. International calls can be received even if there is no international direct dialling contract.

Bill Payment
1. Collect the bill at the NITEL office in your exchange area. In some cases they deliver the bill.
2. Pay at a designated bank.
3. Make a photocopy of the bank receipt and drop the copy at the NITEL office where the bill was collected.

The payment usually shows up on the bill two months later. To avoid disconnection, submit the copied receipt immediately after payment so that it can be properly credited. Keep all receipts for the duration of your stay in Nigeria.

One company that can help facilitate the installation of telephone lines and internet connections is listed below.

Alpha Data Services
Plot 90 Phase 2 Site 1 Kubwa
☏ 09 670-3231; 0804-410-8660

Precaution Against Crime

Care should be taken while speaking on any telephone. Banking and other personal information should be avoided in discussions and immediately crossed out or destroyed in any fax sent. NITEL customers can also request a security code be placed on their telephones to avoid the use of the line for unauthorised calls by other people in the house or telephone company personnel.

Prepaid Calling Cards

Prepaid international calling cards from several different companies are available in a number of shops including Amigos, Park 'n Shop, etc. Users call their local office/access point and put in the secret code on the card. The card is valid for a certain period of time or until the credit is all used.

Street-side Calling

There are also a number of vendors with mobile and satellite phones from which domestic and international calls can be made.

Mobile Phone Options

Handsets

Many different handsets are available in Abuja. Prices vary depending on the functions provided. Popular types cost between ₦15,000 to ₦40,000.

Options

The options for providers are expanding rapidly. To date, MTN has been the most popular and has the largest capacity for the customers. GLO is a recent entrant on the market. Although it is improving, calls between different providers are difficult to make, as are calls between GSM and landlines. So many Nigerians have several different phones with different service providers. Below is a list of the prefixes for the various mobile service providers and some city codes for Nigeria.

Service Provider	Exchange Prefix
Econet (VMOBILE)	0802
MTN	0803
NITEL (MTEL)	0804
GLO	0805
NITEL Analogue Mobile	090 + 6 digit number*

Some Telephone Codes

City	Telephone Code
Abeokuta	039
Abuja (FCT)	09
Badagry	01
Bauchi	077
Benin City	052
Bida	066
Calabar	087
Ede	035
Enugu	042
Ibadan	02
Ijebu-Ode	037
Jos	073
Kaduna	062
Kano	064
Katsina	065
Lagos	01
Lokoja	058
Maiduguri	076
Makurdi	044
Minna	066
Oshogbo	035
Oyo	038
Owerri	083

*There are still a few analogue phones out there, but they are not used much.

Port Harcourt	084
Sokoto	060
Suleja	09
Warri	053
Yola	075
Zaria	069

Refuse

Households desiring rubbish collection need to apply at the:

FCT Environmental Protection Office
(Corner of Moshood Abiola Road and Ogun Street)
Area 2, Garki, Abuja

The cost for a domestic house with 4-5 bedrooms is approximately ₦18,000/year. Someone from the office will accompany the occupant to the site to verify its size. The charge includes use of two dust bins from their store. However, the customer must arrange transportation of the dust bins from the Environmental Protection's store at the zoo/plant nursery near Aso Rock. The price and dust bins will vary for Embassies and businesses according to the nature and size of the business.

Refuse Collection

The refuse collectors will pick up the dustbins approximately once a week. Sometimes the day of the week differs but they are fairly reliable in terms of frequency. Rubbish bins need to be kept in an easily accessible place. There is no requirement for sorting out different types of rubbish at the moment. Theft of rubbish bins is not a frequent occurrence in the city, so that is not a concern. However, there are a number of persons who may sift through the rubbish in search of useful items, so customers leaving their bins outside their gate may occasionally find them scattered. For this reason, it is extremely important that financial and personal documents are shredded and burned.

Some individuals may wish to arrange for private refuse collection.

Landscaping

Jardin Nigeria Ltd. ♥
Nicon Hilton Hotel
(Aguiyi Ironsi and Shehu Shagari Way)
Office Floor 01
☎   09 413-1500
Fax: 09 413-2638
Email: jardin@jardin.com.ng
🕐 M-F: 0700-1800
Saturday: 0700-1300

Nurseries

There are a number of small plant nurseries on the side of the major roads in the city. For larger selections, try:

Plant Nursery in the National Children's Park and Zoo
(Near Aso Rock, Off Murtala Mohammed Expressway North)
☎   09 314-0475

The office is on the left-hand side of the second roundabout after the gate. Customers are advised to visit the office before 1 p.m.

Plant Nursery at the Nicon Hilton Hotel
(Aguiyi Ironsi and Shehu Shagari Way)
Make a right at the first round about to reach the nursery
☎   09 413-1811-40 (ask for the nursery)
🕐   M-F: 0900-1700
Saturday: 0700-1500
Cut flowers, plants and gardening soil, pots, stands, etc can also be purchased at an office inside the service entrance across from the nursery.

Gardener
Philimon Horticultural Enterprises
For Landscaping and fumigation

Mr Philip Onyewe is an experienced gardener who will regularly oversee the work his gardeners do in your garden and will do short term jobs or arrange longer contracts.
☎ 08055120294

Fumigation (Pest Control)

In some areas of Abuja, termites are a serious problem. Ants, cockroaches, mice and rats can also be a major nuisance for residents. Snakes can also come visiting. Below are some pest control services used by our readers. Possible customers should be aware that the chemicals used by pest control services here are not regulated by the government and may not meet European or U.S. standards for health and safety.

Vet World Ltd
Banex Plaza Extension
Plot 750 Aminu Kano Crescent, Wuse II, Abuja
(next to Park N' Shop Supermarket)
☎ 09 413-8672
◐ M-F: 0900-1600
Saturday: 0900-1600
Sunday: 1430-1700
Email: anodan@hotmail.com
anorued@yahoo.com

Frank Mulega
☎ 0803-332-0677

Appliances (See Stocking-up section for shops and locations)
Appliances can also be purchased from most supermarkets and from the electronics market near the General Hospital in Wuse.
A tumble dryer is recommended (if indoor space to dry clothes is limited) as the rainy season makes drying clothes out of doors difficult

and there is also a significant risk of Tumbu fly eggs being laid on laundry hung outdoors. Tumbu fly lava burrow under the skin and are quite uncomfortable to remove.

Furniture and Furnishings (See Stocking-up for full listings)

There are several shops in town that carry furniture and interior decorations. Most of them deal in imported furniture or furniture made locally with imported materials. In general, the quality is good, but prices are expensive. Some shops specialise in custom-made furniture. Most supermarkets also have furniture floors.

Local Craftsmen

Local furniture craftsmen can be seen selling their products on the roadside. There are a number of workshops along Obafemi Awolowo Way, especially near the former Impresit Life Camp and along the Keffi Road outside of Asokoro. Some specialise in cane furniture. Those used by our readers include:

Jonny Décor Furnishing
Opposite Jabi District -- upstairs, Zhilu Village
☎ 0803-700-4791

Kelly-Bless Furnishing
Opposite former Impresit Life Camp
☎ 0803-349-2375
Skilled craftsman, producing quality work to design specifications in timely fashion and will come to home/office to take orders.

Leo Chiaka and Sons
American International School compound
Lake Chad Crescent, Maitama, Abuja

Rufai
☎ 08034637648

Carpenter
Ibrahim Folorunso
☎ 08055427406
Email: dele4peace2000@yahoo.com

Victor & Emmanuel Ufine Group of Coy
Kado/Life Camp Rd
Behind Agip
Life Camp
Abuja
☎ 08034533462, 08023314565
Cane furniture and interior decorations.

Upholstery
There are a number of places along the side of the road that can re-upholster furniture. One craftsman recommended by our readers is below.

Tom Eton
☎ 0803-451-0818; 0802-300-4716

Interiors (See *Stocking-up* for full listings)

Some of the furniture shops sell carpets, curtains and interior furnishings. Large shopping centres are also likely to have one or two interior shops. There are also numerous shops selling carpets and curtains in Wuse market.

Interior and Exterior Painting

Finitec Finishing Technologies
No 4 Kurra Close, Maitama, Abuja
(Off Lake Chad Crescent)
☎ 09 413-8354;
Fax: 09 413-2357

Post Offices

There are two General Post Offices in town where stamps can be purchased, letters and parcels can be sent, and a P.O. Box can be established. Customs services operate only out of the Garki Post Office.

Garki Post Office
Area 10, Garki, Abuja
Eastern end of Olusegun Obasanjo Way, where it meets with Moshood Abiola Road. This was the first post office to be opened and is the city's main post office.

Wuse Post Office
Along Maputo Street, a few hundred meters off Herbert Macaulay Way, Zone 5, Wuse, Abuja

The master plan calls for a post office for each district and postal agencies for all neighbourhoods. Other post offices are located in Abaji, Kuje and Gwagwalada towns.

Postage

Domestic post is available for letters; aerogramme, post cards and parcels will cover 20 g (₦50) to over 1kg (₦200). International letters can also be posted.

Reliability

Domestic registered mail seems fairly reliable when the receiver has a P.O. Box address. Mail sent to street addresses is not reliable due to the lack of sufficient staff to serve as delivery personnel. International letters also seem to reach their destinations regularly. It is not advisable, however, to send valuables or packages through the mail due to possible theft.

The post office advises that travel times from Abuja are as follows:

To Lagos	within 24 hours
To Asia	by air within 1 week
To Europe	by air within 1 week
To African countries	within 5 days

Personal experience indicates that actual times are about twice those indicated above and can be substantially more around Christmas/Ramadan time.

Security Services

Most residents in Abuja have security personnel at their gates, whether they are guards hired by the residents themselves or provided by a security company. Guard services provide their employees with basic security training and take care of providing relief guards in case of sickness and vacation. In reality, they would probably not be effective against a gang of armed robbers. Guards mostly serve as a deterrent to keep criminals from selecting your home as a target in the first place. Some security companies can provide added protection like mobile patrols and panic buttons. Ask for details on services provided, the length of the shift for the guards and the breakdown of the monthly charge (how much is going to the guards versus overhead for the company, uniform, taxes, etc.). Ask neighbours and friends for references to companies they use. A few companies are listed below.

Bemil Nigeria Ltd.
C/o CBN Executive Qtrs, Karu, Abuja
☎ 0802-308-3295

Prudential Guards Ltd. (Servtrust Ltd.)
Suite 62/63 Corner Shop, Nouakchott Street Zone 1, Wuse, Abuja
☎ 09 670-1896

Gaskiya Security Guards Ltd.
Block 63 Flat 1 Nsadup Close, Area 7, Garki, Abuja
☎   09 234-5212

Profile Security Services
Plot 212E Adetokunbo Ademola Crescent (Behind AP Plaza), Wuse II, Abuja
☎   09 523-5152; 670-7173

EMI Systems Ltd.
Plot 614 Bobo Close, Maitama, Abuja
(Off Gana Street)
☎   09 413-9941; 0803-500-8124
Email: emi@afconx.com
www.emi-systems.com

Personal Effects Insurance

Some residents purchase personal effects insurance to cover their valuables in case of robbery or fire, or more frequently electrical blow-ups.

Industrial and General Insurance Company, Ltd
Abuja Area Office
Plot 1079, Awolowo Way, Area 11, Garki, Abuja
☎   09 234-5542-5

National Insurance Corporation of Nigeria (NICON)
Head Office
Plot 242, Muhammadu Buhari Way, Central Business District, Abuja
☎   09 523-7120-9; 523-8161-70;
Fax: 5237126
Email: infodesk@niconinsurance.com.ng
www.niconinsurance.com.ng

Branch Office
Ground Floor, Nicon Hilton Hotel
(Aguiyi Ironsi and Shehu Shagari Way)
Life insurance and insurance of buildings, house contents and vehicles

Home Repairs (Plumbers and Electricians)

There are a number of building contractors who can help with all sorts of things like major repairs to houses, swimming pools, installing security features, boreholes, etc. One that has been recommended is

Heraklien Nigerian Ltd
Branch Office Abuja
☎ 08033034343 (John.)
If you can do it yourself, there is a tool market off Herbert Macaulay near the Ibro Hotel. Other recommended workmen are below

Abishai Properties, Ltd
Suite C14 Bobsar Complex
Michika Street
(Off Ahmadu Bello Way)
Garki II, Abuja
P.O. Box 10584
Garki, Abuja
☎ 09 314-2649; 0803-322-3559
✉ abishai_ppty@yahoo.com
Repair and maintenance. Ken U. Ndieli, Director of Projects

Austen All Unit Technical
Shop Gwala Auyu Street
Model Market
Garki II, Abuja
☎ 09 234-1213; 0803- 315-6392; 0804-410-3474
Installation & maintenance of refrigeration, air conditioning, office equipment and electrical appliances.

John-Dan-La Refrigeration Works
Block 394 Flat B Kigali Street
Zone I, Wuse
P.O. Box 7569
Wuse, Abuja
☎ 09 523-4772; 0803-316-0742

Refrigerator and air conditioner repairs, electrical installation, gas/electric repairs, sales of spare parts, importer and exporter and general merchants.

Gabriel Gbwong
Block A34 Old Wuse Market
Beside the Police Post, Abuja
Ask for Okey or Gabriel Gbwong
☎ 0804-410-0316
Repairs of electrical appliances, wiring, supplier of all kinds of electrical material, estate surveyor.

Swimming Pool Maintenance

For those lucky enough to have swimming pools, here are maintenance persons recommended by our readers:

Basitex Nigeria Ltd.
Suite C34 Area 7 Shopping Complex
(by UTC)
☎ 09 234-6134

Head Office:
Suite WH 114 Utako Ultra Modern International Market
Abuja
☎ 0803-314-3187

Datress Swimming Pool Experts
Opposite Karmo Police Post, Abuja
☎ 0803-700-6554
Water chemical balance, mechanical and electrical maintenance.

Hiring Domestic Help

Most foreigners employ two or three domestic staff on a full-time basis (five or six days a week). A full-time cook/cleaner, a gardener and 24-hour watchman are the most common domestic staff. Some need a separate cook from the cleaner/maid and a nanny. The quarters provided for the domestic staff— called "boys quarters" — usually has two rooms. The employer decides which staff will occupy those rooms, but it is customarily the cook/cleaner and the nanny (if needed). Some ideas for hiring domestic staff are included below.

Finding Staff
- Check the grapevine. There are always people coming and going — leaving staff behind. Let as many people know as possible that you are looking for someone and they will appear. There is always somebody's "junior brother" or "junior sister" available.
- Put up signs on bulletin boards at schools and work locations to help advertise your need.

Salary
Ask around to friends and colleagues to see what a fair salary is for the services being provided. Transportation is quite expensive in Abuja. So, if the person will need to travel to work, a transport allowance will need to be added to their salary. Be sure to clearly state the basic salary — separate from the transportation — as transportation costs will likely increase more rapidly than the basic salary.

Employer Responsibility
Items that are the responsibility of the employer are noted below. All terms and conditions should be clearly spelled out prior to employment.

- Medical (you may want to make sure they are vaccinated — especially nannies; tests for TB and HIV are not uncommon)
- Transport.
- Uniform (if desired).
- Food*
- Overtime* (Depends upon work hour agreement).
- 17 days leave plus public holidays.

---

*Subject to negotiation.

- 13th month bonus
- Severance in the amount of 1.5 months for each year worked (if the person is not dismissed due to illegal behaviour).

Contract

It is a good idea to draw up a contract with your domestic employees to ensure that the terms and conditions are clearly spelled out. Check with the Human Rights Commission for the latest labour laws.

Hints

- Check references, if at all possible. Resumes or work certificates could be fake.
- Give the person a trial period of a couple of weeks or one month at a lower salary to see if the relationship is going to work out.
- It may not be a good idea to hire a couple. If one of them doesn't work out, two workers are lost.
- Don't give sums of money to domestic employees to pay vendors working at the house in your absence (exterminators, repairmen) as they may be tempted to take a "dash" for themselves and not pay the vendor the full amount.
- Keep a written record of money paid to them (in salary or loans) and have them sign it. That way disagreements over non-payment can be avoided.
- If you do have to dismiss someone (or when you leave finally), document the reasons for unemployment, the severance pay, etc. and have all parties sign it.
- Loans will be requested. It is best not to give loans unless you are willing to "forgive" them. Some employers recommend not loaning more than one to three months salary. Some employers deduct loan payments from the monthly salary (say 1/4 of the salary over a certain time period).

Nannies

The person who will take care of your children has the most important job in the house. It is important to take the time to find the right person for your needs. Ask them about how they discipline children, whether they have first aid experience and their hygiene practices. Review emergency procedures with them in case something happened to the children while you are out of the house. Observe them with the children for a few hours to see how they handle situations [discipline, hygiene (washing hands before meals, changing diapers, etc.). Make sure they are engaging the children in fun and/or educational activities.

Some nannies and other domestic staff seem "shy and reserved" when talking with or in the presence of their employers, this is partly due to culture. They may be different when interacting with the children. So, it is best to also try and observe their activities when they do not know you are looking.

CHAPTER 6

Getting Around

The young goat that rushes wildly to eat leaves will one day swallow prickly caterpillars.

(Nigerian Saying)

Look carefully where you are going or you may end up where you do not want to be.

(Zambian Proverb)

Taxis and Motorcycles

Taxis

Taxis in Abuja are relatively safe and easy to use. There are two types: government sponsored and private. The government-sponsored taxis are green with white stripes. Private taxis can be any type of saloon car. The taxis will honk as they drive by to see if customers want a ride. A wave of the hand will bring them to a stop. There are two possible approaches to payment. A price can be agreed before entering the vehicle or you can just pretend you know what you are doing, and wait to see if the taxi driver complains. Check with friends to ascertain the going rate for a local drop prior to entering so that you know how much you should pay. Prices go up significantly when petrol is in short supply and they are slow to come down thereafter.

As Abuja is a relatively new city, many of the taxi drivers are new as well. They tend to be most familiar with the main locations, so customers may have to assist with directions to less well-known locations.

Motorcycles

Motorcycles, also called "okada", "machine", or "achaba", are plentiful and popular because they are inexpensive. However, given the driving conditions, they are not a safe mode of transportation. The drivers do not have helmets for themselves or their passengers. However, if you get lost driving in your vehicle, you can ask an okada to lead you to your destination.

Importing Vehicles

Duty is imposed on imported vehicles. Vehicles more than five years old are not permitted entry. Newer vehicles may be imported provided they are for the owner's continued use and are not for resale. As Nigerians drive on the right-hand side of the road, it is recommended that the car be a left-hand drive vehicle that has been acclimatised for the tropics with working air conditioning. It is also wise to ensure it is one of the most popular models available in the country for consistency in parts and servicing. Four-wheel drive is recommended if the owner plans to travel out of Abuja on a regular basis. Because of a lack of constant supply of petrol to more remote areas of the country, extra capacity in the petrol tank is also useful.

Documents needed for clearance include: passport (original); certificate of insurance; original purchase invoice with proof of ownership; certificate of road worthiness (for used vehicles);

registration or logbook; make, model and serial number of the vehicle being imported.

Car Hires

There are several options for car hiring services. Customers can negotiate with individual taxi drivers on the street for hourly or daily rates. "Car hires" found at the major hotels are more luxurious ("v boot" Mercedes with air conditioning) and are more expensive. When you first arrive in country, it is a good idea to find a reputable car and driver who can assist in acquainting you with the city. The major car companies are listed below. The rates include the cost of the driver, but remember the driver's overnight costs will also need to be paid as well.

Avis [Rent-a-Car]
Sheraton Hotel, Ground Floor
☎   09 523-0225, Ext 8307
Fax: 09 523-2838

Hertz
Nicon Hilton Hotel
☎   09-4137614

Citi-car Association
Nicon Hilton Hotel
☎   09 413-1811, 413-4720, Ext. 6233

Eco Coty
Peniel Apartments
Plot 137, IBB Way
Wuse II
☎   08033275108

Oasis Car Rental
Sheraton Hotel
☎   09 523-0225, ext 8216

Car Purchases

New cars are expensive because of the import duties on new and luxury items. Nigeria assembles Peugeot 504s. They are considered good cars for the roads as they have high axles. There are also plenty of spare parts and most mechanics know how to fix them. For a new car, they are also relatively inexpensive. Several new car dealerships have opened in Abuja recently.

Ess-Dee Motors (Japanese Sales and Repairs)
Plot 506 Cadastral Zone B4,
Utako-Jabi Expressway,
Jabi, Abuja
☎ 09 523 1711, 5211606

CFAO Motors (Mitsubishi)
Plot 568, Michael Okpara Street
Zone 5, Wuse
☎ 08033432937

Briscoe Motors (Toyota)
105, Olusegun Obasanjo Way
Central Business District,
Abuja
☎ 09 2349224, 801665

ASD Motors Ltd (Peugeot)
Plot 1375, Borno Street, Off Moshood Abiola Way,
Area 10 Garki,
Abuja
☎ 09 2346520, 2346386, 2343480

ATS (for repair of all Japanese cars)
Sokode Crescent
Wuse Zone 5
Abuja
☎ 09 5235001,
08033147999 (Mr Salman)

NMI (for repair of Peugeot)
Plot 2941, Aguiyi Ironsi Way
Maitama
☎   09 4133375, 4133376, 4133377

A number of used cars are imported through the Republic of Benin. Used car markets are located throughout the city and change due to their nature (on squatted land). A major one that has been here for a while is near the electronics market by the General Hospital in Wuse (Behind Tantalizers and Heritage Printers, Off Suleman Abubakar). People also travel to Kaduna or Kano to get a better price on a vehicle.

The purchase and sale of diplomatically imported cars requires the permission of the Ministry of Foreign Affairs. If the buyer does not have diplomatic status, he/she will be required to pay the custom duty. This can take up to a year to get things legally sorted out.

Remember to keep copies of all the car papers and the car insurance papers in the vehicle.

Fuel Servicing

When filling up at the local petrol station, be sure to get out of the vehicle and watch the sale in progress. Attendants have been known to tell customers they have reached the agreed amount when in fact, they have not and then pocket the difference. They have also been known to fail to "zero out" the last purchase before pumping, so the driver pays for the last customer's gas as well. The best time to purchase petrol in Abuja is either early on weekday mornings or on weekends when there are fewer people in town.

Petrol shortages are not uncommon. Some cities suffer chronic shortages, so it is wise for travellers to try and ascertain the availability of fuel at the destination prior to travelling. In an attempt to stop the black market sale of fuel, the government is preventing petrol stations from filling jerry cans. This has made the purchase of extra fuel for emergency purposes more difficult.

Car Servicing and Repair
Reliable car mechanics are difficult to find. Thus, when getting vehicles serviced, it is wise to have someone stay with the vehicle to ensure that the work is done properly. This is also important to make sure that the bill is not inflated by the replacement of additional parts without prior authorisation. You will find mechanics along the road who will change your oil (you may need to bring your own filter and oil), repair and balance tires, etc. There are more expensive but reliable places listed below.

Hidson Engineering Co. Ltd.
(Specialises in Mercedes, but also services other types of vehicles)
915 Alexandria Crescent
(Off Aminu Kano Crescent, near Park 'n Shop)
Wuse II, Abuja
☎ 09 413-4499; 0803-704-4644

Taktouk Nig. Ltd
Michael Taktouk
☎ 08033138217
08044115676

Western Auto Parts and Services Centre Ltd
Plot 178 Ahmadu Bello Way
Aminu Kano Crescent
Wuse II
☎ 2900702, 08037876844
Email: cnwadeyi@gbclimitted.com

ATS
(For repair of all Japanese cars)
Sokode Crescent
Wuse Zone 5
Abuja
☎ 09 5235001,
08033147999 (Mr. Salman)

Chitech Automobile (Mercedes, BMW, Peugeot, Honda, Japanese cars)
Behind Peniel Apartment
Ademola Adetokunbo Crescent
Wuse II Abuja
☎   0803 349 4607
Specialises in Programme Injector System, Automatic Transmission System, air conditioners and carbon cleaning (with machine).

Direction: From IBB Way, turn right on Ademola Adetokunbo Crescent. Continue up to Peniel Apartments, past the paved road on the right (appears to go to a mosque now under construction); take the next turning on the right into a dirty car park. Follow the dirty track around to the right as it turns to the left, then straight to where all the cars are parked. Ask for 'the Master'.

NMI (for repair of Peugeot)
Plot 2941, Aguiyi Ironsi Way
Maitama
☎   09 4133375, 4133376, 4133377

Tyres
There are a number of tyre sales and servicing businesses in an area called Apo Village outside of Abuja. To get there, follow Ahmadu Bello Way past Crystal Palace Hotel. It will end at Apo Village.

Edeemark Group
Apo Office:
Top Hill Station
APO, Abuja
☎   0803-314-3508; 0803-408-0376; 090-84221
Email: edeemark77@yahoo.com
Wheel balancing and alignment done by machines, tire repair.

Infinity Tyres Ltd. ☏
Plot 515B Adetokunbo Ademola Crescent
Near Chicken House
Wuse II, Abuja
☎   09 523-4736; 0803-452-0313
⊕M-F: 0830-1700

Email: infinity@cyberspace.net.ng
Specialise in Pirelli tyres, but also have other brands. Computerised wheel balancing and alignment for all type of tyre.

Head Office
Along Minna Road
Near General Hospital
Box 108, Suleja Abuja
☎   09-500130

Driver's Licence
It is essential that residents in Abuja obtain a Nigerian driver's licence as soon as possible. International drivers' licenses are not recognised. Applicants will need to fill in a form, pay a fee (₦6,500 in 2003), provide passport photos and verification of a valid driver's license from their previous country of residence in order to obtain a Nigerian driver's licence. Once obtained, it should be carried on your person.

VIO (Vehicle Inspection Office)
Off Shehu Musa Yar' Adua Way
Mabuchi
Abuja

Car Insurance
Vehicles require third party insurance coverage. Vehicle registration papers are needed to obtain insurance. Some companies include:

IGI (Industrial and General Insurance Company Limited)
Plot 1079 Awolowo Way
Area 11, Garki
(planning to relocate to IGI House, Off IBB Way, near the intersection with Herbert Macaulay)
☎   09 234-5542-5
Fax: 09 2345544 (first call to confirm fax machine is ready)
⊕ M-F: 0800-1700

Femi Johnson Co.
Nicon Hilton Hotel, 01 Floor
(Aguiyi Ironsi and Shehu Shagari Way)
☎ 09 413-1811 (Extension 6309), 413 1926
Fax: 09 413 1926
☉M-F: 0800-1800

Wideways Insurance Company, Ltd.
24 College Road
Kuje, Abuja.

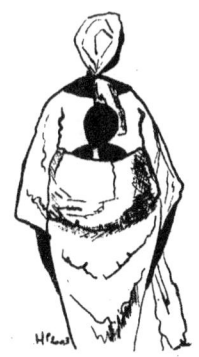

CHAPTER 7

Minding the Children

An elder who is kind to a youth will never starve.
(Nigerian Saying)

Abuja is a comfortable place to raise small children. Between organising your own playgroups, visiting hotel swimming pools, family-friendly eateries and the zoo, there are enough activities to keep children busy in the "old fashioned way", without exposing them to commercial and electronic overload. Secure compounds mean children have the freedom to enjoy the outdoors. Teens will be the ones most likely to miss the more "hip and trendy" things found in larger cities. Below are some ideas, options and opportunities for entertaining and educating small children.

Schools

There are many international schools in Abuja for pre-school, primary and secondary ages but the ones most foreigners consider are listed below. They are all relatively new and are getting fuller every year. Getting children registered and placed on a waiting list (or several) is a good thing to do as early as possible. All of these schools can be contacted by email and most have websites. It is recommended that schools are visited and other parents are spoken to about their experience prior to enrolment. Most people are satisfied with the quality of primary education at these schools. Secondary education is still problematic with fewer options to choose from. Many of the more affluent Nigerians and foreign families send their older children to boarding school. Thus, you may find more teenagers here during the holidays when their schools are on break. Most children have a lively social life and the school community can help broaden your families' network of friends. After school clubs vary depending on the staff and volunteers available for the term and are sometimes open to children from other schools.

Names	
American International School, Abuja	www.aisabuja.com
Phone	+234 9 413 4464, 234 9 413 8063
Fax	+234 9 413 4464
Mobile	0803-3144022
Email	*aisabuja@hotmail.com*
Address	Lake Chad Crescent (Off IBB Way), Maitama, Abuja, Nigeria
Mailing address	8320 Abuja Place, Washington DC 20521-8320, USA
Staff	
Director	Amy Uzoewulu
Assistant Director	Debra Giles
Nationality of teachers	7 Americans, 6 Nigerians, 10 others

Minding the Children 117

Information	
Grade levels – Pre-K to 9	Preschool (age 2-4), Elementary K – 5 (age 5–10), Middle School 6-9 (age 11–14), High School Nebraska Programme 10-12 (age 15–18) – Correspondence Course
School year	August – June;
Hours of day	8.30 a.m. – 12.30 p.m. (preschool), 7.30 a.m. – 1.30 p.m. (Elementary), 7.30 a.m.–2.30 p.m.(Middle School)
Terms and breaks	Term: 3 trimesters; Breaks: Winter (3 weeks), Spring (1 week), Summer (June-August – 2.5 months)
School type	Co-educational, day, private, non-profit
Year founded	1993
Governed by	Appointed and elected Board of Directors
Accredited	Middle States School Association
Regional organisations	AISA, ECIS, NAESP, NASSP
Enrolment	Preschool 50, Elementary 100, Middle School 50, High School 10
Nationality of student body	Over 130 countries represented
Tuition fee currency	US $; can pay in Naira also
Tuition range	$2,337-$9,318
One time fee	Capital levy $3,000
Educational Programme Curriculum	US
Average class size	Elementary 15; middle 10
Language of instruction	English
Language taught	French
Staff specialists	Librarian, computer, art, music, PE/Health, ESL Learning Centre, French

Extracurricular activities	Field trips, Girl Scouts
Sports	Basketball, gymnastics, soccer, swimming,
Clubs	Crafts, French, Tae Kwon Do, drama, soccer, cooking, computer, Indian dance, International Ensemble
Examinations	ITBS and CogAt
PTA and events	Talent show, Yard sale, Bazaar, Art Exhibition, Science. Fair, Carnival, Movie nights, Sports Day
Campus Facilities	
Location	Urban
Campus	Current temporary facility consists of 3 hectares, 3 buildings, 13 classrooms, 1 computer lab with 20 computers and satellite internet access, 1 science lab, covered play area. In the process of developing a new site and facilities in Durumi.

International Community School Abuja	www.ics-abuja.org
Phone	+234 9 523 3520
Fax	+234 9 523 3520
Mobile	0803 349 8741
Email	icsabuja@yahoo.com
Address	Plot 711, Agadez Crescent, Off Aminu Kano Crescent, Wuse II, Abuja
Mailing address	P.M.B. 3972, Abuja
Staff	
Director	Mrs Jan Okpanachi
Finance	Miss Ngozi Okoro

Minding the Children 119

Information Grade levels – Pre-K to 9	Preschool to Grade 9, Age range 3 – 17yrs. (Also has Playgroup for 2 yr. olds & provision for American High School by correspondence with University of Nebraska programme)
School year	Sept to mid-June
Hours of day	Playgroup 9.00 a.m. to 12.00 noon, Preschool (age 3) 7.30 a.m. to 12.00 noon, Prekindergarten (age 4) 7.30 a.m. to 12.00 noon, Kindergarten (age 5) to Grade 5 (age 10) 7.30 a.m. to 1.30 p.m., Grade 6-9 (age 11 to 14) 7.30 a.m to 2.30 p.m (Friday 1.30 p.m.)
Terms and breaks	3 terms of 12 weeks, 3 weeks break in December, 10 days break in the Spring
School type	Co-educational, private, day,
Year founded	1998
Governed by	Board of Directors
Accredited	Accredited by MFCT (Ministry of Federal Capital Territory), also in process of accreditation with CIS (Council of International Schools, formerly ECIS – European Council of International Schools)
Regional organisations	AISA, CIS, PTC
Enrolment	176
Nationality of student body	40% Nigerian, remaining 62% made up of 24 other countries
Tuition fee currency	US $
Tuition range	$1,800 - $5,400
One time fee	None
Educational Programme Curriculum	US; Also prepares students for common entrance exams
Average class size	24
Language of instruction	English
Language taught	French
Staff specialists	Librarian, computer, music, art, PE, language, nurse

Extracurricular activities	Summer Activities, soccer team, basketball & volleyball teams
Special programmes	Parents' Night, Education Fair, Christmas Programme, National Day, Sports Day, International Day, Parents/Teachers Conferences, Music Night, Awards Assembly
Sports	Volleyball, Badminton, Table Tennis, Lawn Tennis, Soccer M, W 3-5, Basketball T, Th 3-5,
Clubs	1:45 p.m.– 3:00 p.m., W & Th: Games, Computer, Science, Art & Crafts, K-1 Fun Club, Music Club, Swimming,
Examinations	Common Entrance (for those students going to Nigerian Secondary schools)
PTA and events	Active PTA, organises events such as Christmas Bazaar, International Food Fair
Campus Facilities Location	Urban
Campus	3 ½ hectares, 1 building, 13 classrooms, computer lab – 10 computers, music room, science lab, 1 playing field with playground area, plus soccer, volleyball, badminton & basketball/tennis courts; library, play area, fully air-conditioned

The Regent School, Abuja	www.regentschoolabuja.com
Phone	+234 9 413-4965/66
Fax	+234 9 413 4965
Mobile	0803 718 4578
Email	See website
Address	Plot 3383, Aminu Kano Crescent, Maitama, Abuja
Mailing address	P.O. Box 502, Abuja, Nigeria

Staff Headteacher	Mr Andrew Moy
Admissions Manager	Mrs Debbie Chukwueke
Nationality of teachers	Host-30, other-10,

Minding the Children

Information	
Grade levels	Early Years (age 2–4), Key Stage 1 (age 5 – 8) Key Stage 2 (age 8 – 11)
School year	
Hours of day	Early Years 8.00 a.m to 1.00 p.m, Primary 8.00 a.m. to 2.00 p.m. Friday closes 1 hour earlier
Terms and breaks	3 Terms with 1 week breaks in Oct and Feb., 3 weeks off for Christmas and Easter holidays
School type	co-educational, primary, day, private
Year founded	2000
Governed by	appointed body
Accredited	Federal Ministry of Education of Nigeria
Regional organisations	AISA, ECIS
Enrolment	Early Years – 120, Key stage 1– 77, Key stage 2 - 98,
Nationality of student body	Host - 80%, 24% other nationalities
Tuition fee currency	US $,
Tuition range	$2520-$5240
One time fee	development levy US$500
Educational Programme	
Curriculum	UK, National
Average class size	20
Language of instruction	English
Languages taught	French
Staff specialists	Computer, music, art
Sports	football
Clubs	Mon and Wed from 2.30 p.m. to 3.30 p.m.– cooking, Tae Kwon Do, football, ballet, computer, art, crafts, dance,
Examinations	SATs, Nigerian Common Entrance Exam
PTA and events	School Fun day (June)
Campus Facilities	
Location	Urban
Campus	1.5 hectares, 1 building, 20 classrooms, 1 computer lab – 25 computers,
	computer in all classrooms, 1 assembly hall, 1 covered play area , 3 playing fields, library with 2,500 volumes, air conditioning in all rooms, studio, art room

German School	
Phone	234 9 521 0942 (Berger Life Camp)
Email	Jbn.dsa@gmx.net
Address	Berger Life Camp, Abuja
Staff	
Head	Mrs Meyer
Nationality of teachers	German
Information	
Grade levels	1 - 10, preschool to secondary
School year	September to June
Hours of day	7.10 a.m. to 12.20 p.m.
Terms and breaks	2 terms, 3 weeks at Christmas, 2 weeks at Easter, half term break in Feb, 8 weeks in summer
School type	Private, co-educational day school
Year founded	1987
Governed by	Board of governors
Accredited	Yes
Enrolment	50
Nationality of student body	25 Host, 20 German, 5 other
Tuition fee currency	US $, Euro, Naira
Educational Programme	
Curriculum	German
Average class size	10
Language of instruction	German
Languages taught	English, French
Staff specialists	Library, computer, music, art, PE,
Sports	Football
Clubs	Various after school clubs
Campus Facilities	
Location	Berger Life Camp, suburban

Ecole Francaise Marcel Pagnol (French school)	
Phone	+234 9 521 2045
Fax	+234 9 521 2045
Email	ecofranab@hotmail.com
Address	BNL (Bouygues Life) Camp, Jabi, Abuja

Staff	
Director	Mr Astier Phone 521 1023
Nationality of teachers	1 Host, 8 French, 8 other
Information	
Grade levels	1 to 6, Age range 3 - 10 years
School year	Sept to June
Hours of day	8.30 a.m. to 11.30 p.m and 1.30 p.m. to 4.30 p.m.
Terms and breaks	3 terms (Toussaint, Noel, Printemps, Paques)
School type	private, day, co-educational
Year founded	1998
Governed by	Ambassade de France
Accredited	Education Nationale Francaise
Tuition fee currency	Naira and Euros
Tuition range	₦135,000 + 1410 Euros
One time fee	₦30000
Educational Programme	
Curriculum	French
Average class size	10
Language of instruction	French
Languages taught	English/Spanish
Extracurricular programmes	Karate, Classic dance, Football
Sports	Piscine, etc
Examinations	BEPC
PTA and events	
Campus Facilities	
Location	Suburb, life camp

Abuja Capital International College	www.acicnigeria.com
Phone	+234 9 670 4466, 4499, 8898
Fax	+23493149492
Mobile	
Email	info@açic.nigeria.com
Address	352/353 Road FHA Estate, Gwarinpa II District, Abuja
Mailing address	P.M.B. 5117
Staff	
Principal	Christine Borowiecki

Assistant Director	Susan Gani
Nationality of teachers	Australian, Nigerian, Philippino
Information	
Grade levels	6-10 Ages 10 to 15
School year	Sept to June
Hours of day	8.00 a.m. - 3.15 p.m.
Terms and breaks	3 terms with half term breaks in Oct and Feb., 3 weeks at Christmas and 2 weeks at Easter
School type	Co-educational, non-denominational, day and boarding, private, secondary
Year founded	2002
Governed by	appointed board of governors
Accredited	Cambridge Certificate
Enrolment	25
Tuition fee currency	US $
Tuition range	$9,500 to $10,500, Boarding $13,000 - $14,000
One time fee	Application fee $100, registration fee $2000
Educational Programme	
Curriculum	British Curriculum
Language of instruction	English
Languages taught	French, Arabic
Staff specialists	Computers, music, art, PE, language, nurse
Extracurricular activities	
Sports	Basketball, volleyball, handball, badminton, table tennis, tennis, soccer, cricket, hockey, gymnastics, track & field, swimming
Campus Facilities	
Location	Suburb
Campus	10,500 m2, air conditioned buildings, 20 classrooms, 4 laboratories, a computer lab, multi-purpose hall with stage, theatre, library, dining room, sports courts, playing field.

Nigerian Turkish International School	www.surat@nigeria.com, www.sercntic.com
Phone	+234 9 413-4731 (Hostel) 413-9285
Fax	+234 9 413 4731
Email	info@suratnigeria.com, info@sercntic.com suratnigeria@hotmail.com
Address	Plot 152, Wuse District Cadastral Zone A7, Ahmadu Bello Way, by Kashim Ibrahim Way,
Mailing address	PMB 4473 Garki, Abuja
Staff	
Managing Director	Mr Hasan Huseyin Aygun
Principal	Mr Tamer Copuroglu
Director of Education	Mr Mevlut Kizilay
Director of Finance	Mr Ferhat Badruk
Nationality of teachers	Nigerian and Turkish
Information	
Grade levels	Junior and Senior School (ages 9 - 16)
School year	September to July, 3 terms
Hours of day	7.45 a.m. - 3.00 p.m. Monday through Friday;
Terms and breaks	mid term Oct, 3 weeks Dec, 4 weeks April
School type	Junior and secondary, co-educational, day and boarding,
Year founded	1998
Governed by	Surat Educational Ltd.
Accredited	MFCT, Federal Ministry of Education
Special Programmes	Science Fairs, Mathematics exam
Enrolment	360
Tuition fee currency	Naira
Tuition range	₦70,000 per term, ₦50,000 boarding per term
One time fee	Non-refundable Caution fee Naira 10,000
Educational Programme	
Curriculum	Nigerian, with a strong focus on the Sciences
Average class size	24
Language of instruction	English
Languages taught	French, Turkish, Arabic, Nigerian
Staff specialists	Nurse, music, art, PE, Computer
Clubs and Societies	Wed 3.00 - 4.00 – Literature, Photography, JET, chess, drama, maths, football, basketball, volleyball, music, astronomy, folklore, computer

Major programmes	Science fair, Mother's Day, Football tournament, Excursion to Turkey, Picnics, Bazaar, end of year programme
Examinations	JSCE (Junior School Certificate Examination), WASSEC (West African Senior School Certificate Examination), accredited centre for the West African Examination Council and National Examination Council, also the venue for Cambridge Exams by British Council
Admission	Entrance exam end of May, followed by interview, application forms available for purchase in Feb.
PTA	Levy ₦1000,
Campus Facilities	
Location	Urban
Campus	60 hectares, 8 buildings, 1 dormitory, 17 classrooms, 1 computer lab - with 15 computers, multi-purpose assembly hall, library, basketball court and football field.

Other schools registered with the "All About Kids Educational Centre" include:

Babyhearts Daycare and After-school Care
Plot 418
Lobito Crescent
Wuse II
☎ 09 4139125, 08044183207, 08023291982
M-F: 0730-1900

Takes children from 3 months of age. You can opt for less than 5 days a week. Has a nurse. Provides after school care and activities for 2-5 year olds. Also has a shop with 'Mothercare' products.

Cedars Park Int'l School
Plot 669
Rhine Street
Maitama.
☎ 09 671-5368
Has holiday clubs and activities during school breaks.

El-Amin Int'l School
Plot 40
Aminu Kano Crescent
Wuse II
☎ 0805-601-2735

Heritage Academy
(Christian Int'l School)
Plot 675
Idris Gidado Road
Wuse District
☎ 0803-313-8155, fax 413-1205

Loyola Jesuit College
Karu-Karshi Road
Gidan Mangoro
☎ 09 523-6240, fax 523-6241

Conducts secondary-entrance exams once a year worldwide for entrance. Enrolment is highly competitive and limited to 100 per year.

Nurul Bayan International School
(Islamic education, boarding facilities)
Off Michael Opara Way, Zone 5, Wuse

A directory listing banks, shops, and activities for kids, as well as 100 Abuja schools is available from:

All About Kids
Suite B2 Wuse II Cornershops Road
Opp. Rockview Hotel, Wuse II, Abuja
☎ 09-4136877, 0803-313-9544
✉ *allaboutkids1@yahoo.com*
Emem Opashi, Co-ordinator

All about Kids also provides educational resource development to schools, playgrounds and parents through educational toys, games and school supplies. They can organise training workshops for schools, day and childcare centres with hands-on, practical workshops for teachers, childcare workers and parents. They also serve as school consultants helping with business plans and advice to schools as well as businesses and others interested in schools or child related activities.

Recreation Options

Playgroups
The best way for young children to interact and for parents to meet other adults and learn new things about Abuja is to join or establish one's own playgroup. Playgroups usually last about two hours. They are held at the home of a different person each week on a volunteer rotational basis. They generally consist of "free play time" for the children and "coffee chat time" for the mothers or fathers that bring them. The community liaison officers at the various Embassies should be aware of any existing playgroups. New ones are easy enough to establish simply by being aware of families as you move about (at the grocery stores, eateries, the zoo, hotels), speaking with them and inviting them to help establish a new one.

After-school Clubs/Lessons
Many of the schools have "after-school clubs" for their students. Some schools allow other students to participate in their clubs even though they do not attend the same school. Some of the clubs routinely offered include: gymnastics, art, swimming, modern dance, ballet, Tae Kwon Do, computer, French, etc. The Nicon Hilton offers tennis and swimming lessons for children. It is possible to arrange group lessons. Other places that offer kids activities are the Dome, Babycare and All about Kids.

Private Lessons

There are also individuals around who can provide private music (mostly piano and guitar) lessons. As they change often, ask around at schools and within Embassy communities for available teachers.

Outings

The National Children's Park and Zoo! ♥ ♥

Along Murtala Mohammed Way
Near "Command Guest House" and the Abuja Nursery
☉ Everyday: 1000 to 1800
☎ 092344853, 08037034162

With the beautiful background of Aso rock, the zoo is the most amazing place for children (and adults) in Abuja. It is well organised and maintained with large open spaces for children and adults alike. The animals are in good condition. Camels, ostriches, impalas, buffaloes, cheetahs, monkeys, horses, tortoises, wildebeests, zebras, giraffes, donkey, horses, goats, gazelles, sheep, water buffalo, rabbits and many types of birds.

As there is little shade, it is better to go first thing in the morning (special arrangements can be made for earlier entry) or in the late afternoon (about 4 p.m.) when it is cooler. There are several large pieces of play equipment and some big rocks to climb. There is also a ping-pong (table tennis) table. There is a "little village" with small houses for the children to play in and around and large open spaces for football. Bring anti-mosquito/fly spray, a hat, a ball, table tennis equipment and a picnic lunch. Snacks and drinks can also be purchased from the lakeside café. They also sell meat pies, hot dog rolls and biscuits. Ice cream and candy are sold from a small kiosk near the monkey area on weekends.

The zoo is a great place for a birthday party or other celebrations. An "event fee" (of ₦10,000 for birthday parties or ₦25,000 for corporate parties) allows guests free entry and reserves a space for setting up your tents, equipment, food and chairs which can be hired from outside vendors. The lake café can also be used for a party, different rules apply to the provision of food and drink, so check with the café manager for details.

For young artists, a painting day can be organised to take full advantage of the beautiful setting. There are three sets of toilets: one close to the lake café; one near the monkey cage; and one near the entrance. Parking is plentiful (but there is no shade). Please do not feed the animals and observe all the rules of the park! The animals receive a special diet and some "people food" may not be good for them. Currently, the gate fee is ₦50 for children and ₦200 for adults. It is usually a very quiet and tranquil place. The only time it gets a little crowded is on Nigerian holidays.

National Children's Park and Zoo

Sheraton Playground and Pool
The playground at the Sheraton is set in sand in a beach-like atmosphere near the pool area. There are several pieces of play equipment and a large area for running around.

Hilton Playground, Pool and Nursery

The playground at the Hilton has several pieces of play equipment on an even larger grassy lawn. There is a bouncy castle on the weekends and a miniature golf course behind the playground area. The nursery on the other side of the complex is also a nice place for a picnic lunch and an hour or so of diversion.

There is a charge for the use of these pools if you are not a member of the hotel's fitness clubs.

HIFA Gardens

Located near Garki Hospital, this nursery and garden area provides a beautiful setting for an outing, picnic or just something to do.

Millennium Park

Inaugurated by Queen Elizabeth in 2004, this new park has a nice walkway with fountains and lights. A good place to walk the dog or come for a picnic. Evenings are especially nice to enjoy the lights. Parking is plentiful and the entrance is off the Three Arm Zone road.

The Abuja Gardens

These gardens are located across from the National Hospital near the Stadium on the road to the airport. They are similar to HIFA Gardens as an outing with or without children. You can go for walks and see the resident crocodile.

Plant Nursery at the Nicon Hilton Hotel

(Aguiyi Ironsi and Shehu Shagari Way)
Make a right at the first roundabout to reach the nursery
☏ 09 413-1811-40 (ask for the nursery)
◉ M-F: 0900-1700
Saturday: 0700-1500

This is a large secluded garden that is suitable for a small party. Reservations for such use are required. Cut flowers, plants and gardening soil, pots, stands, etc can also be purchased at an office inside the service entrance across from the nursery.

Mediterranean Suites Hotel
Plot 1467
Hon. Justice Mamman Nasir Crescent
Asokoro.

☎ 314-8048-9;
Fax: 314-1592
📱 0803-702-3029

There is a nice pool and café to enjoy.

The Dome
Plot 432
Cadastral, Off Constitution
☎ 671 5587, 08042125644

State-of-the-art bowling lanes, cafe, gardens, fitness centre swimming pool and bar.

Games Arcade
For the older children, there is a games arcade above Chum-Chum in the Garki area. There are about 6 machines appropriate for children ages 6 and up.

Savannah Chum-Chum Plaza
Plot 179/7A Ahmadu Bello Way
Garki, A 3 Abuja

Julius Berger Stables
For members, this is a lovely setting near the lake on the road to Kadu. Find someone who has a horse there or buy one. It is not possible to rent horses by the hour. Early morning is the best time to go riding with the children before it gets too hot and before they are too grumpy.

Berger Sailing Club
The Berger Sailing Club at Usman Dam has facilities for their members. Occasionally members outside the Berger Community are allowed to join.

Strabag Rock (Aso Radio Rock)
Let the kids climb Strabag Rock and some of the other hills and domes in the Abuja area. Be careful not to get too close to any military installations. Strabag Rock is 5 minutes from Ministers Hill just off the Abuja-Zuba Road. It has the Aso Radio arriel on top of it. This is difficult to climb with a vehicle so park at the entrance. Sign in at the office and walk to the top for a picnic and a fantastic view of Abuja.

Bwari Pottery Village
Let the kids have a taste of village life by taking them on a visit to the Bwari Pottery Village (see the "Staying Active" section for directions and more information).

Usman Dam (sometimes also called Usuma Dam) ♥
This is a nice place to take a picnic lunch and to go exploring. There is very little shade, so bring beach umbrellas and sun screen! It is also nice to stop at Ushafa Pottery in Ushafa village before the gates to the dam for a quick shopping spree. The area after the gates to the dam is now called Bill Clinton village. Traditional Gwari pots can be found there.

Guara Falls ♥
This is another nice place to take a picnic lunch and to go exploring. Wear good shoes and take bags that are easily carried as the path down to the water can be rather cliff-like. Note: the water can be quite high in the rainy season (see the "Staying Active" section) for directions and more information.

Amusement Parks
There are two amusement parks in Abuja. There are no regulations on the maintenance and safety of the equipment. Some of the rides are rather old and in need of repair. Be warned, there may be no electricity to actually run the rides. Caution should be exercised in the selection of rides for your children.

Abuja Amusement Park
Opposite Park View Hotel
P.O. Box 7629
Abuja
☎   09 523-2203; 523-1157
Email: mjapp@skannet.com

A few rides and bumper cars. No generator so don't venture out if there is no electricity in the area. It is near Sel Sucre so it can be combined with a snack and ice cream.

Monoliza Amusement Park
Go to Shehu Shagari way, take the last right turn before reaching the ring road (R.A.B. Dikko Road), across to Ahmadu Bello. Rides can be seen from the road.

Kid Friendly Places to Eat

There are several kid friendly places to eat. See the "Going Out" section for directions and more information. Our favourites include (in alphabetical order):
A.J.s
Big Bites
Big Daddy
Chase Restaurant (for Sunday brunch for less rowdy kids)
Cherry's (Wuse and Asokoro)
O'Neill's
Roof Top Café (not ideal for children under 5 due to unprotected railing)
Nicon Hotel (swimming pool area; also visit the African Craft village while there)
Sel Sucre
Sheraton Hotel (swimming pool area+buffet in Papillon with a kids menu)
Southern Fried Chicken
Tantalizers

Party and Function Organisers

Just about all of the locations mentioned above would be suitable and available to host a party. Other places that will help you plan and cater a party are:

Conf-Care Services, Ltd ♥
Shop 34 Neighbourhood Centre
Wuse, Zone 3
P.O. Box 2166 Abuja
☎ 09 523-0390; 523-3551
⏲M -F: 0900-1730
Rental and delivery of tents, chairs, tables, red carpets, decorations. Reasonably priced.

Kids Ville
Shop A26 Emab Plaza
Aminu Kano Crescent
Wuse II, Abuja
☎ 09 523-8319; 0803-349-6818
⏲ M -F: 0900-1800
Event planners, kids parties, playgroups, kindergartens, school galas, fairs, promotions, party characters including Barney, Teletubbies and Mr. Chicken. Bouncy castles, giant slides and gladiator ring and equipment. Can also provide popcorn, ice cream, music, face painting and entertainers.

Festive Friends
Suite 20, Abuja Amusement Park
P.O. Box 8504 Wuse 900003, Abuja
☎ 09 523-9833; 0803-329-8729
⏲M -F: 0900-1700
Email: festivefriends2001@yahoo.com
www.festivefriends.com
Event managers, balloon decorations, bouncy castles, party characters, party packs, Santa's grotto, DJ services and canopy, chair and truck rentals are available.

Omega Party Things
'Suite D22 Emab Plaza
(Beside Banex Plaza)
Wuse II, Abuja
☎ 0804-411-3694; 0803-314-5553; 090-808812
Everything needed for a children's party: balloons, accessories and decorations, cartoon characters, clowns, toys, party packs, floral arrangements, candy floss (cotton candy), ice cream, pop-corn, bouncy castle rental, music and MCs.

Mirakon Rentals and Balloon Decor
Suite 15, Area 7A Cornershop
Garki, Abuja
☎ 09 2902435, 09 6717420, 08033216056, 08033172730

Toys and Children Clothes

Supermarkets
The larger supermarkets all have a pretty good choice of children's books, dolls, bicycles and general imported toys. Many of these locations carry clothes and shoes for children as well. (See "Stocking-up" for addresses and contact information)
- Park 'n Shop
- Grand Square
- Amigo's
- 9-11
- Bomas

Wuse, Model and New Markets
Check for toys and bicycles at cheaper prices than at the supermarkets. They also have unusual African instruments that make good presents. Clothes and shoes for children can also be found at the open markets. Take sample clothes and shoes along (or the actual child) as the sizes may be different. (See "Stocking-up" for addresses).

Plazas
There are several plazas that have a number of little shops with interesting items for children. Try Emab on Aminu Kano Crescent and Metro Plaza, Off Herbert Macaulay.

Looking for Something Different for Gifts?
For toys and clothing with an African flavour, try the following shops. (See "Enjoying the Culture" for their locations)

- **Colours of Africa**
  Nice souvenirs for children and teenagers. Selection varies – but sometimes they have shoes, clothes and other children's accessories.

- **Out of Africa, Sheraton Hotel**
  Cards, toys made with batik (Nigerian fabrics), T-shirts (S,M,L) with African pictures and other clothes for children.

- **Signatures Art Gallery**
  Nice lorries, wooden animals (useful for room decorations)

- **Hilton Crafts Village**

- **Abuja Arts and Cultural Centre**

- **Nike Art Gallery**

- **Office Deals Ltd. (at the Protea Hotel)**
  Nice selection of school and art supplies for children.

- **Bazaars**
  Be on the lookout for various bazaars held throughout the year at hotels, schools and life camps. A variety of items are sold at those events suitable as presents for children. For example, the Sisters of Onitsha often sell nice colourful tie-dyed summer dresses for little girls and bathrobes for boys and girls.

Travelling with Children

According to the US State Department, although Nigeria recognises dual nationality, Nigerian-American children (under age 21) may be prevented from leaving Nigeria if the child's father has not authorised departure via a written statement.

CHAPTER 8

Going Out

Ikoko ti yoo jata, idi re a gbona

(Yoruba Proverb)

The pot that wants to eat must have its bottom heated up.

Caveat

Abuja is a growing city with new restaurants, stores and service providers opening weekly. As with any such guide, some entries will be outdated by the time the book goes to print. We apologise for any omissions or errors found within.

Service Symbol Keys
(In Alphabetical Order)

♈	Alcohol Served
👥	Banquet Catering
📱	Cellphone Number
💻	Email Address
⌂	Child Friendly
🕐	Hours of Operation
🏰	Landmarks (nearby)
♪	Music (live)
Ⓟ	Parking (separate lot)
💰	Low Budget
💰 💰	Medium Budget
💰 💰 💰	Top End
☺	We liked it
	No Smoking Section
☎	Telephone Number

Going Out 141

Going-out Notes

Child Friendly

Restaurants receive a child friendly ⋔ sign if:
- customers will receive looks of understanding (as opposed to disapproval) from the management when children do not always behave appropriately;
- there are no dishes to break and/or the dishes will not cost much to replace if broken.

Very few restaurants actually have booster chairs, high chairs or children's menus. If they do, it is noted in the description.

No Smoking?

Likewise, it is rare to find restaurants that have "No Smoking" sections. Some places do have outdoor seating areas and we have tried to be sure to note that in the comments section.

Prices

We did not want to include actual costs in the guide because prices change so rapidly,. Instead, we have developed a relative measure that should survive the test of time. Restaurants included in the guide receive a bargain rating 👛 if you are only paying a little bit more for the food than if you had bought the ingredients in the market and made it yourself. They receive a moderate rating 👛 👛 if you are paying twice as much and a high-end mark 👛 👛 👛 if you are paying three times as much as the ingredients alone would have cost. A plus symbol + after the bags means that the cost is more than three times the cost of the ingredients.

Religious Customs

Some restaurants and stores that do not sell alcohol and pork because of religious prohibitions in the Muslim religion. They are noted within the guide. While some establishments do not sell alcohol, they will allow you to bring it. We have noted those restaurants in the descriptions and mentioned whether they ask for a corking charge.

Credit Card Use
Due to the high rate of credit card fraud in Nigeria, it is best to leave credit cards locked in a safe place and not use them here.

Tipping
Most establishments add 10% gratuity onto the cost of the meal. Tipping is therefore, discretionary. It is not unusual for customers who appreciated the service and/or the ambience to leave an additional 5-10%. At some restaurants the Nigerian workers say that they do not receive the automatic 10% gratuity.

Eateries and Entertainment
For a relatively new city, Abuja has a fair variety of restaurants. Good Italian, Chinese, Indian, Lebanese, continental and African cuisine can be found. There are casual cafes and fast food establishments as well as bakeries with home-made ice cream to be enjoyed as well.

Eateries by Food Type
Hungry for a specific type of food?

Chinese/Oriental	Chase
	Chopsticks
	Grand Mirage Hotel
	Great Wall
	Nicon Hilton Oriental Restaurant
	Talk of the Town
Indian	Sitar
	Talk of the Town
	Wakki's
Italian	Caesar's
	Luigi's
Lebanese	Chase
	City view

Nigerian	Bush Bars (various)
	Mama Cass
	McDowall's
	Shanaco
	Terabah Gardens
Pizza	AJ's
	Amigo's Take-away
	Beiruty
	CIAO
	Hawa's (call and order take-away)
Thai	Thai chi

The eateries below are categorised by type: café, bakery, fast food and restaurant. They are alphabetised within each section. For those that enjoy the "night life," a few bars, casinos, discos and night clubs are included.

Bakeries

Baguette Bakery and Snacks, Ltd
1146B Aminu Kano Crescent
- Banex Plaza, Reliance Bank
  Wuse II
- 8:00 a.m. - 11:00 p.m.
- 413-4507
- 0803-787-7636

Serves pastries, bread, hamburgers, chicken burgers, Philadelphia subs, rice and chicken, and rice and fish plates, milkshakes and Italian ice cream. Birthday and wedding cakes and catering services are available. Seating for 50 persons. No alcohol sold but customers may bring in their own alcohol with no corking charge. Maximum 50-60 persons.

Cherry's Pastry & Bakery
Main Branch:
City Plaza
Plot 2399 Manzini Street
- Chase restaurant near Sheraton Hotel
  Wuse 2, Zone 4
- 8.30 a.m. - 11.00 p.m.
- Main: 523-5777; fax 523-5867
- Asokoro 314-7130;

Fax: 671-1880
0803-705-0578
lebeaini@hotmail.com;
www.cherry-plus.com

Asokoro Branch
Cherry's Plus 2
Asokoro Shopping Mall
T.Y. Danjuma Street
Asokoro

Cherry's at Dunes
Plot 2799 Aguiyi Ironsi Way
Maitama
- 10.00a.m-10.00p.m Mon-Sun
- 4137256

Fax: 413 1910
info@dunescenter.com

Casual café and bakery with indoor seating. On-site bakery for baguettes, bread, pastries, savoury and sweet snacks, coffee (espresso drinks), fresh fruit juice, cakes, chocolate, sandwiches, salads and ice cream. Browse through a nice magazine selection while enjoying food and drink. Seating for 20 persons at each location. take-away items for up to 200 persons. There is also a small gift shop selling chocolate and trinkets at the main branch.

Pinocchio Pastry shop
Plot 81 Aminu Kano Crescent

🏭　　Opposite Park 'n Shop, near Banex Plaza
　　　Wuse II
🕒　　9.00 a.m. - 11.00 p.m. M-Sat
　　　1.00 p.m. - 11.00 p.m. Sun
☎　　413-0200
📱　　0803-590-5410
💰

👥 Casual bakery with indoor seating. Cake, pastries, shawarma, hot dogs, sandwiches, chicken and french fries. Fresh juice, coffee/tea, cappuccino and espresso are sold. Caters children's parties with assorted snacks, cake and ice cream. Seating for 25 persons.

Sel Sucre
CP 27, Nouakchott Street
Zone I
P.O. Box 4261

🏭　　Hali Brothers Filling Station
　　　Wuse
🕒　　9.00 a.m.-10.00 p.m. Monday-Sunday
☎　　523-4130; fax: 523-3777
📱　　0803-787-3696/tel
🚗　　523-4131
💻　　*suzanaj7@hotmail.com*
💰 ☺

👥 ⛳ Casual café and bakery with indoor and outdoor seating. On-site bakery for baguettes, pastries, savoury and sweet snacks, sandwiches, hot and cold drinks (including fresh juices) and ice cream. Cakes can be ordered for special events. Extremely family friendly with smiling and welcoming owners. Seating for 40 persons. Corking charge for alcohol brought in from outside. 🐸 maximum 60 persons.

Both the **Nicon Hilton** and the **Sheraton** also have bakeries with limited seating where fresh pastries can be enjoyed on-site or taken away.

Cafés

Roof Top Café ♥

British Council
Plot 2935 IBB Way

- Maitama Roundabout (intersection of IBB and Shehu Shagari Way) Maitama
- 9.00 a.m.-10.00 p.m. Monday-Saturday, Saturday breakfast 9.00-11.30 a.m.
- 413-1363; 413-7870-7
- 0803-307-3380

Covered open-air casual café serving sandwiches (e.g., baguettes, toasts, burgers), salad, pizza, pasta, and finger food (e.g., suya and chicken wings available in the evenings). Fresh juices, milkshakes, cappuccino/espresso and fun cocktails will quench your thirst. Seating for 54 persons. Corking charge for alcohol brought from outside. maximum 60 persons.

Fast Food and Take-away

AJ's

739 Aminu Kano Crescent

- Park "n" Shop Supermarket Wuse II
- 11.30 a.m. - 10.30 p.m.
- 0804-410-4567; 0803-314-0469

Fast food restaurant serving pizza, sandwiches, falafel, shawarma, burgers, fried rice, chicken, chips, meat pies and ice cream. Covered seating outside available. No alcohol is served or allowed. Seating for 64 persons combined inside and outside. maximum 64.

Amigo's Take-away
Amigo Plaza, Plot 1023
Adetokunbo Ademola Crescent

🏢   Opp. DHL and Chicken House
          Wuse II
🕘   9.00 a.m.-10.00 p.m.
📱   523-4067, ext. 16

💰

🍴 Fast food take away serving pizza, shawarma, burgers, meat pies, and egg rolls. Quick pizza (15 minutes).

Big Bites
Big Bites Nigeria Ltd Plaza
411 Plaza
Adetokunbo Ademola Crescent

🏢   411 Plaza
          Wuse II
🕘   24 hours a day/7 days week
☎   413-1987 0803-317-5154
🚗   0803-349-7066
💻   eroms29@hotmail.com

💰 Ⓟ

🍴 Casual fast food restaurant with indoor seating upstairs and downstairs. Serves African and continental fast food (e.g., chicken and rice plates, hamburgers, sandwiches) and pastries. Seating for 100 persons. 🍽 maximum 50 down/50 up, outdoor catering services also available.

Big Bites
7A Yakubu Gowon Crescent

       Ecowas Secretariat Road
          Asokoro

148 Around and About Abuja

🕐 24 hours a day, 7 days a week
☎ 314-8728
📱 0803-727-8021
🚗 0803-349-7066
💻 eroms29@hotmail.com
💰

👪 Casual fast food restaurant with indoor and outdoor seating. Serves African and continental fast food and pastries (e.g., chicken and rice plates, hamburgers, sandwiches). Seating for 200 persons.
👥 maximum 50 indoors/150 outdoors.

Big Daddy
Shop No.4
Addis Ababa Crescent
🏨   Sheraton Hotel
        Wuse II, Zone 4
🕐 8.00 a.m. - 12 midnight
☎ 523-7133
📱 0802-311-9845 📱 0803-704-0231
💰

👪 Indoor casual fast food. Serves Continental, Mediterranean, African and International fast food such as shawarma, humus, salads, seafood, soups, gari, plantain, and jollof rice. No corking charge for alcohol brought from outside. Seating for 100 persons.
👥 maximum 1000 for catered events

Mr Bigg's

Location 1:	Location 2:
Lagos Street	A.Y.A. Abuja
Garki Village	Asokoro

Location 3:	Location 4:
Zone IV	Aminu Kano Crescent
Corner Shop	Wuse II

Location 5:
Kwowa
- 🕐 7.00 a.m. - 10.00 p.m.
- ☎ Head Office 671-3308
- 📱 0802-311-9845 📱 0803-704-0231
- 💰 Ⓟ (at most locations)

 Casual fast food. Serves Continental, African and International fast food such as hamburgers, hot dogs, meat, chicken, jollof rice, fried rice, and ice cream. Some locations also have a few games for children.

Chop-Chop Take-away/Eat-in Food
Shop 21
Ladi Kwali Street
- 🏨 Sheraton Hotel and Towers
  Wuse, Zone 4
- 🕐 8.00 a.m. - 11.00 p.m.

💰

 Serves African fast food including chicken soup, meat balls, beef burgers, chicken and rice, and Continental food. Seating for 33 persons.

Colby's Pizza
- 📱 0803-315-5091

💰

Homemade pizza delivered to your door.

Hawa's Gourmet Pizza Take-away
#7 Ontario Crescent
Off Mississippi Street
Maitama
- 🕐 8.00 a.m. - 10.00 p.m.
- ☎ 413-2137

📱   0803-590-1679

🛍 🛍 ☺

Large deep dish American style pizza. Orders need to be made 3 hours in advance. This is not a restaurant, but a call-order service.

O'Neal's Food Pastry and Snacks
Plot 116 Adetokunbo Ademola Crescent
🏢   Peniel Apartments
        Wuse II
🕐   8.00 a.m. - 12 midnight everyday
☎   670-8554
📱   0803-306-2150; 0803-306-3153
🛍

👨‍👩‍👧 Y Fast food eat-in or take-away serving pizza, shawarma, burgers, meat pies, and egg rolls. Quick pizza (15 minutes). Small playground for kids out front. Large lawn for parties. No corking charge for alcohol brought in from outside. Smoking and non-smoking sections.

Rasi Cafeteria
Plot 10B Mohammed Idrees Way
Ahmadu Bello Way
🏢   Beside Chum-Chum
        Garki
🕐   7.30 a.m.-12 midnight daily
☎   671-5905

🛍

👨‍👩‍👧 Cafeteria style service. Continental and African food including, chicken, salads, rice, suya, etc. Seating capacity 36. 🍴 Indoor and outdoor catering.

Savannah Chum chum

Location 1:
Plot 179/7A Ahmadu Bello Way
Garki, Zone 3

Location 2:
Massana Street
Opposite Agip Petrol Station
By old Hall Brothers, Zone I
Off Obasanjo Way
Wuse

🕐   24 hours, Everyday
☎   234-9737
💰   Ⓟ

👥 Serves fast food, African and Nigerian dishes. Clean bright setting. Extremely child friendly with booster seats and different types of arcade games for children. Seating for 80 persons. 👥 maximum 100 persons.

Southern Fried Chicken

Plot 1268 Arthur Unegbe Street
(Off Ahmadu Bello) Area 11

🏢   Near NuJ/NNPC Housing Estate Garki
🕐   9.00 a.m. - 10.00 p.m. everyday
☎   314-9470-1
💻   *www.southern-fried-chicken.com*
💰   Ⓟ

👥 Serves "Kentucky Fried Chicken" style chicken, hamburgers, chicken strips and nuggets, coleslaw, french fries, pizza, kids meals and ice cream. Clean bright setting. Extremely child friendly. Seating for 50 persons. 👥 maximum 80-100 persons.

Tantalizers

Location 1:
Rochas Plaza
Conakry Street
Off Sultan Abubakar
🏛 Near Ministry of Foreign Affairs/General Hospital
Wuse, Zone 3

Location 2:
Aminu Kano Road
Wuse 2
☎ 09 671 9341

Location 3:
Udjah Street Garki 2
☎ 09 671 9048

Location 4:
Borno Street
Area 10, in Villa Hotel
☎ 09 671 9050

🕐   7.30 a.m.-10.00 p.m.
☎   671-9049
📱   0803-373-4855
💰   ⓟ

👥 Casual fast food chain. Serves Continental, African and International fast food such as hamburgers, sandwiches, hot dogs, french fries, beef roll, chicken pie, scotch egg, spring rolls, jollof rice, fried rice and doughnuts. Friendly atmosphere. Seating for 150 persons

Restaurants

Al-Basha Restaurant

643 Sassandra Street
Off Usuma Street, off Gana Street
Maitama
🕐   12.00 noon - 12 midnight
☎   413 8038, 4138039
📱   0803-3940142
💰 💰

👥 Serves Lebanese and continental food. Alcohol available. Seating for 110 persons, plus garden with room for 100.

SPECTRUM BOOKS LIMITED

Visit us at our Abuja Office

**UNIC Insurance Building
Plot 1046, Ahmadu Bello Way,
Garki II, Abuja FCT.
Tel: 08023246754,**

Spectrum titles can be purchased on line at
www.spectrumbooksonline.com

...placing worthy books in worthy hands since 1978

Bolingo Restaurant
at the Bolingo Hotel
Independence Avenue
- Opposite "Ship House"
  Garki, Area 10
- 7.00 a.m. – 10:30 a.m. Breakfast,
  12.30 pm – 4.00 p.m. Lunch,
  and 7.00 p.m. – 10.30 p.m. Dinner.
- 234 4701
- gmphabuja@yahoo.com

💰💰💰 ☺ ⓟ ⊛

Situated in the Bolingo Hotel, the Bolingo Restaurant serves International and Nigerian dishes à la carte. There are meal menus available according to the time of day and snacks are available any time between 7.00 a.m. – 10.30 p.m. Seats a total of 80-100 persons but can also cater outside functions. Other facilities at the Protea Hotel include a cocktail bar (live music Monday – Saturday evenings) and three conference rooms that can be catered separately for up to 800 guests. maximum 800 persons. There is a "no smoking" section in the restaurant.

Caesar
Mississippi Crescent
- beside Chopsticks
  Maitama
- 6.00 p.m. – 11.00 p.m. (closed Sunday)
- 413 1451-3

💰💰💰 ☺ ⓟ

Serves Italian cuisine. Take out menu. Located next door to Chopsticks. Telephone orders are welcome.

Chase Restaurant & Seafood bar
City Plaza
Manzini Street
- Sheraton Hotel

Wuse II, Zone 4
🕐 12 noon - 12 midnight
☎ 523-8220; fax 523-3001
📱 0803-705-0578
💻 lebeaini@hotmail.com

💰💰💰☺℗

🍸 Serves Lebanese, Continental and Chinese dishes. Sunday buffet brunch is not to be missed. It features a wide variety of Lebanese and Continental dishes. Spectacular views of the city from the rooftop outdoor seating area. Guests may also dine indoors. Seats a total of 165 persons. 👥 maximum 200 persons.

Chopsticks
Mississippi Crescent

🏢 This is a landmark on its own. Drive till you see the white wall with Chinese letters on it.
Maitama

🕐 12.30 p.m. – 4.00 p.m. &
6.30 p.m. – 11.00 p.m.

☎ 413 1451-2

💰💰💰☺℗

🍽 Serves Chinese cuisine. Located next door to Caesar. Has take-away menu. Seats a total of about 75 persons. 👥 maximum 200 persons.

CIAO
Monsterrado Street Shop 20
Wuse Zone 4, near NEPA office
Near NEPA Office

☎ (09) 2904854
📱 08035923719
🍸 Serves Italian.

City View Restaurant and Imperial Bakery
IBB way, Wuse 4

🏢   On IBB way, turn right at the signs for Chase instead of left.
Open for lunch from 11.30a.m

☎   670-4224 or 0803/314-1350

Crystal Palace Hotel Royal Restaurant
Plot 687 Port Harcourt Crescent
Off Gimbya Street

🏢   Itself a landmark
Area 11, Garki

🕐   24 hours

☎   314-0033, 36, 38; fax 314-0034

💻   crystalpalacehotel@yahoo.com

💰 💰

🍴 🍷 Buffet lunch and dinner includes Nigerian, continental and Mediterranean dishes. Seating for 40 persons in the restaurant. 🪑 maximum 50 persons — but also has a meeting hall that can be used for banquets that seats about 150 people.

Galaxy
Corner Shop
Ladi Kwali Street

🏢   Farmer's Supermarket
Wuse II, Zone 4

🕐   8.00 a.m. - 12.00 midnight

☎   523-9282

📱   0803-700-3019

💻   GalaxyRestaurant@hotmail.com

💰 💰

🍴 🍷 Casual restaurant serving Oriental and Continental dishes. Seating for 80 persons.

Grand Mirage Hotel
Ming's Restaurant
Plot 691 Port Harcourt Crescent
Garki 11

- 🏨 Crystal Palace Hotel Garki
- 🕘 11.00 a.m. to 11.00 p.m.
- ☎ 314-2912
- 💰💰 ⓟ

🍴 Serves Chinese and Indian food. Seats 40 persons. 👥 maximum 50 persons.

The Great Wall
Landmark Plaza
Plot 3124, IBB Way

- 🏨 Federal Housing Authority Flats Maitama
- 🕘 11.00 a.m.-11.00 p.m.
- ☎ 413-2372; 413-2895
- 📱 0803-590-5739
- 💰💰 ⓟ

🍴 Authentic Chinese food in large open setting. Customers may bring their own alcohol. Seating for 300 persons. 👥 maximum 500 persons

Mama Cass Restaurant Ltd
Location 1
336 Aminu Kano Crescent
Wuse II

Location 2
Corner Shop
Ladoke Akintola Boulevard
Garki

Location 3
Federal Housing Authority

Off Limpopo
Maitama
🕐 7.00 a.m. - 12 midnight daily
☎ 523-8549; fax 01 493-4601
📱 0803-700-0397
💰

👫 🍸 Indoor casual restaurant. Serves a variety of Nigerian and other African dishes such as seafood, soups, gari, plantain, and jollof rice. Seating for 90 persons (Garki). Nice place for the kids. Comfortable and clean. 💬 Garki board room seats 20; children's party room seats 50.

McDowals Restaurant and Take-away

Location 1:
Suite No. 6
Addis Ababa Crescent
Wuse, Zone 4
🏢 Chase Restaurant
🕐 8:00 a.m. - 12:00 midnight
☎ 523-3177, 523-6791
📱 0803-787-7535

Location 2:
11 Federal Housing Estate
Off Limpopo, off Yedseram, off IBB,
Maitama
🏢 Behind Maitama Stores
🕐 8.00 a.m. - 12.00 midnight
☎ 413-0391; fax 413-4382
💰 💰 ☺

👫 Casual restaurant serving Continental and African cuisine. No alcohol served or allowed. Good mixed clientele. Some outdoor seating available. 💬 maximum 62 persons

Mediterranean Suites
100 Degrees Bar and Restaurant (Also known as the Sky Lounge Bar)
Plot 1467 Hon Justice Mamman Nasir Crescent
Gombe State Governor's Lodge

Asokoro

24 hours

314-8048-9; fax 314-1592

0803-702-3020

Seats 80 people. Bar on one side with tables and chairs. The other side is a nicely decorated restaurant. This whole hotel is one of the undiscovered jewels of Abuja. There is a small zoo at the hotel for the children to enjoy. maximum 120 persons.

Oriental Restaurant Nicon Hilton
Aguiyi Ironsi and Shehu Shagari Way
Floor 01

7.00 p.m.-10.30 p.m.

413-1811, Ext. 6351; fax 413-2418

Hilton_Abuja@hyperia.com

Buffet meal featuring Chinese and Asian food. Thai food featured on Saturday evenings. Customers may choose from pre-made dishes or create their own at the "Mongolian BBQ" grills. Dine in a tastefully decorated setting. Select from indoor or outdoor seating. Undeniably the best restaurant at the Hilton and the highest rated restaurant in our survey. Seating for 180 persons. Banquet manager ext. 6419

Fulani Pool Bar and Restaurant Nicon Hilton
Aguiyi Ironsi and Shehu Shagari Way
Pool Area

12.00 noon - 9.30 p.m.

☎ 413-1811, ext. 6250; fax 413-2418
💻 Hilton_Abuja@hyperia.com

💰 💰 💰 ➕ Ⓟ

🏛 ⛾ Outdoor covered poolside setting. Lunch time offerings include pizza, salads, hamburgers and pastries. Grill Bonanza on Wednesday evenings, Tandoori Grill Monday, Tuesday, Thursday, and Friday evenings. Buffet lunch and BBQ on Saturday and Sunday. 👥 maximum 72 persons, banquet manager ext. 6419.

Zuma Grill Nicon Hilton

Aguiyi Ironsi and Shehu Shagari Way
Lobby Floor

🕐   7.00 p.m.-10:30 p.m.
☎   413-1811, fax 413-2418
💻   Hilton_Abuja@hyperia.com

💰 💰 💰 ➕ Ⓟ

⛾ Cooking demonstration every Wednesday and Thursday. Mediterranean food. Italian food on Wednesdays. Large wine selection. Live music. 👥 banquet manager ext. 6419.

Shanaco Resort and Garden

Ahmadu Bellow Way
(Between Benue Plaza and NIIT)

🏛   Bridge by Benue Plaza
           Wuse 2
🕐   12.00 p.m. - 12 midnight
☎   0802-319-7987

💰 Ⓟ

🏛. Advertises itself as "the African Choice." Serves Nigerian dishes (pounded yam, roasted fish, cow legs, soups, egusi, okra, bush meat, fresh and dried fish, roasted chicken, pepper soup, cow tail, etc.) To get there customers need to drive down a rough road. Thatch covered area seats about 50 people. A separate thatched area is rented for parties and ceremonies. Nice open atmosphere.

Boat House Abuja Sheraton Hotel and Towers
Ladi Kwali Street
Wuse 2, Zone 4
- 🕐   10.30 a.m. - 11.00 p.m.
- ☎   523-0225; Ext. 8365/8116
- Fax: 523-1570/1

💰 💰 💰   Ⓟ

👪 🍸 Outdoor thatch-covered poolside setting. Relaxed family friendly setting. Serves a la carte Continental and African dishes with a touch of Caribbean spices. Kids menu available. Seating for 40 persons. 👶 maximum 45 persons.

Papillon Restaurant
Abuja Sheraton Hotel and Towers
Ladi Kwali Street
Wuse 2, Zone 4
- 🕐   6.30 a.m. - 10.30 p.m.
- ☎   523-0225; ext. 8196/8308
- Fax: 523-1570/1

💰 💰 💰 Ⓟ

👪 🍸 Serves buffet Continental, Nigerian and International dishes for breakfast, lunch and dinner. Tandoori oven for good Indian cuisine. Kids menu (ask for it). Two high chairs available (the chairs can also be moved to Luigi's or the Boat House on request). Seating for 125 persons. 👶 maximum 125 persons.

Luigi's Italian Restaurant
Abuja Sheraton Hotel and Towers
Ladi Kwali Street
Wuse 2, Zone 4
- 🕐   6.30 a.m. - 10.30 p.m.
- ☎   523-0225; ext. 8192
- Fax: 523-1570/1

💰 💰 💰 Ⓟ

THAI CHI

World Class Dining

Extensive & Authentic Thai menu
Full cocktail bar & Quality wine list
Covered roof terrace & Modern interior design
Functions & Takeaways

Reservations: 09 523 6798
Office: 09 670 6470

The Penthouse, Safire Plaza,
Adetokumbo Ademola Crescent,
Nitel Junction, Wuse 2, Abuja

☥ Serves Italian and Continental cuisine. Known for Steak Night on Thursday evenings when imported beef is cooked to order. Wednesday is Italian buffet night with imported Italian anti-pasta and "cook to order" fresh pasta. Seating for 70 persons.
🕸 maximum 70 persons.

Sitar
Plot 664
Usuma Street, Off Gana Street
🏢   UNICEF, Zenith Bank
      Maitama
🕒   12 noon-3.30 p.m.; 6.30-10.30 p.m.
☎   413-9833/4; fax 413-9834
📱   0803-787-6345
💻   *ipnm@hotmail.com; itk@linkserve.com;sitar@linkserv.com*
💰 💰 💰 Ⓟ (some)☺

☥ Serves good authentic Indian food. Stylish décor and quiet ambience. Seating for 100 persons. 🕸 maximum 100 persons.

Sky Chef
25 Addis Ababa Crescent
🏢   Sheraton
      Wuse
🕒   24 hours
📱   0804-214-7968

💰

☥ Serves Nigerian dishes. Good for a taste of the local dishes. Seating for 70 persons. 🕸 maximum 50-60 persons.

Thai Chi
Safire Plaza, Plot 1066
Adetokunbo Ademola Crescent
Wuse II (in the Equity Bank building),
☎ 09/670-6470.
Landmark: Amigo supermarket

Talk of the Town Restaurant
Plot 635 Usuma Street
Opp. Nicon Hilton

    911 complex
    Wuse II

    12.00 p.m. - 11.00 p.m.

    413-6465; 413-8441

🍶 🍶 🍶 Ⓟ

Serves Chinese and Indian cuisine. Tastefully decorated interior. Seating for 100 persons. maximum 50-100 persons.

Wakkis ♥
Shop No. 56
Off Ladi Kwali Street

    Opposite Abuja Sheraton and Towers
    Wuse II, Zone 4

    12 noon - 11.30 p.m., 7 days a week

    523-5436; fax 314-4740

    0803-454-2929

    521-0018

    titus_beena@yahoo.com

🍶 🍶 ☺

Comfortable, cute and casual setting to eat authentic Indian cuisine. Customers sit at "picnic style" tables and benches and can watch as their food is cooked on the Tandoori grill. Take-away. Delivery available. Seating for 40 persons. maximum 15 persons in-house. Outdoor catering services available.

Fish Bars

There are a number of good fish bars (also referred to as "Bukaterias") in Abuja serving inexpensive fish, chips, rice and other Nigerian dishes. Most, however, just have fish and chips and most serve beer and minerals only. As many are informal establishments on squatted land, what may be there today, may not be there tomorrow.

Good current locations include under the bridge, off Ahmadu Bello Way, between Aminu Kano Crescent and Adetokunbo Ademola Crescent; and on Shehu Shagari Road. They are sometimes brightly lit with "fairy" or "Christmas" lights.

Bars

> If the fly sitting on top of a palm-wine calabash says it is drunk, what will the fly inside the calabash say.
> **(Nigerian Saying)**

Caveat
Please remember to drink responsibly and to have an expert, sober driver take the wheel. A recent study on HIV/AIDS infection rates in Nigeria indicates that the adult prevalence has risen to 7% of the general population and is a serious concern. As in all places these days, care should be exercised in intimate relationships. See the Staying Healthy section for more information on HIV/AIDs in Nigeria.

Blake Resort Hotel
Plot 50 Ahmadu Bello Way
Cadastral Central Zone, Garki
📱 08044102676
Live band most nights, cover charge ₦200

Crystal Mini Bar
Crystal Palace Hotel
Plot 687 Port Harcourt Crescent
Off Gimbya Street

🏙	Itself a landmark
	Area 11, Garki
🕐	24 hours
☎	314-0033, 36, 38; ext. 334 or 339
Fax:	314-0034
💻	*crystalpalacehotel@yahoo.com*

💲 💲 ⓟ

🍸 Serves drinks only. Seats 7 people.

Fairwinds
MPlot 660, Usuman Street,
Off Gana street, opposite Nicon Hilton Hotel
Maitama
- 🕐 24 hour service
- ☎ 314-1311-2; fax 314-1310

💰 💰 Ⓟ

Everyday nightclubbing and dancing establishment with bar and restaurant, snooker, billiards, darts, karaoke.

Grand Mirage Hotel
Moonlight Bar
Plot 691 Port Harcourt Crescent
Garki II
- 🏨 Crystal Palace Hotel
  Garki
- 🕐 24 hour service
- ☎ 314-1311-2; fax 314-1310

💰 💰 Ⓟ

🍸 🎵 🍽 Outside seating area for drinks and live music nightly. Grilled fish and chicken and chips or order off the Ming(Chinese and Indian) menu. African and Continental cuisine is also served. 👥 maximum 500 persons.

Grand Mirage Hotel
Monaco Bar
Plot 691 Port Harcourt Crescent
Garki 11
- 🏨 Crystal Palace Hotel
  Garki
- 🕐 24 hour service
- ☎ 314-1311-2; fax 314-1310

💰 💰 ☺ Ⓟ

🍸 🎵 🍽 Small bar, seats about 20 people. Serves African and Continental, food. Ask for all three menus available. 👥 maximum 100 persons.

Hilltop Bush Bar
Garki II,
Off Murtala Mohammed Expressway
🏘 Near Benue Links Bus stop, before Apo roundabout

Nice sunsets and city views. Live Tiv music and dancing later in the evening. (This is similar to "lap dancing" and the place is probably not best for families after dark).

Lakeside Bush Bar
Berger Camp

This is a Lakeside Bush Bar near the Berger Life Camp from which dramatic sunsets and lake views can be seen.

Leisure Castle
Gana Street
Maitama

🍸 🍽 Live music nightly after 10.00 p.m. Really gets going after 1.00 a.m. Good jazz. Serves fish.

Capital Nicon Hilton
Aguiyi Ironsi and Shehu Shagari Way
Lobby Area
🕐   Wed. 3:00 p.m. -1:00 a.m.;
           Sat-Sun. 12:00 noon - 1:00 a.m.
☎   413-1811, ext. 6234 fax 413-2418
💻   Hilton_Abuja@hyperia.com

💰 💰 💰 Ⓟ

🍸 🍽 Live music. Snacks available: suya, sandwiches, fish fingers, prawns, spring rolls, etc.

Piano Bar Nicon Hilton
Aguiyi Ironsi and Shehu Shagari Way
Lobby Area
🕐 M-F   7.00 a.m. - 12 midnight;

Sat.　　3.00 p.m.- 12 midnight;
　　　　Sun Closed
☎　　　413-1811, Ext. 6221 fax 413-2418
🖥　　　Hilton_Abuja@hyperia.com
Ⓟ

🍸 🍽 Quiet place during the day time. Live music, nightly. Piano bar setting with nooks and crannies for private discussions. Snacks available: suya, sandwiches, fish fingers, prawns, spring rolls, etc.

Mediterranean Suites
Swimming Pool Bar
Plot 1467
Hon Justice Mamman Nasir Crescent
🏙　　　Gombe State Governor's Lodge

　　　　Asokoro
🕐　　　24 hours
☎　　　314-8048-9; fax 314-1592
📱　　　0803-702-3020

💰 💰 💰 Ⓟ

👥 🎵 🍽 🍸 Seats 80 people. Clean and tastefully decorated. Finger food. BBQ area. Thursday, Friday and Saturday there is live African and Jazz music. 👥 maximum 100 persons.

Mediterranean Suites
Okavango Bush Bar
Plot 1467 Hon Justice Mamman Nasir Crescent
🏙　　　Gombe State Governor's Lodge

　　　　Asokoro
🕐　　　24 hours
☎　　　314-8048-9; fax 314-1592
📱　　　0803-702-3020

💰 💰 💰 Ⓟ

♪ 🍽 🍸 Seats 27 people. Appetisers and pizza available. Traditional African Bush Bar with style décor. 👥 maximum 33 persons.

Raviolis
Kwame Nkrumah Crescent
Asokoro
Food, music and karaoke

Elephant Bar
Abuja Sheraton Hotel and Towers
Ladi Kwali Street
Wuse 2, Zone 4
🕐 6.00 p.m. - 1.00 a.m.
☎ 523-0225; ext. 8178
Fax: 523-1570/1
Ⓟ

Discos /Night Clubs
Several of the Bush Bars in Garki also have live music. The foreign crowd usually frequents the Nicon and the Sheraton night clubs. A few foreigners also frequent Point and Mirage. Care should be taken when travelling late at night. It is best to travel in groups and to make sure that someone in the group knows the area well.

Hotel Broadway
Garki
Live African Jazz weekends with Baba 2010

Crystal Club
Crystal Palace Hotel
Plot 687 Port Harcourt Crescent
Off Gimbya Street
🏛 Itself a landmark
    Area 11, Garki
🕐 24 hours

☎ 314-0033, 36, 38; ext. 336 fax 314-0034
🖥 crystalpalacehotel@yahoo.com.

💰 💰 Ⓟ
🍸 🍽 Serves snacks and drinks. Buffet available at hotel. Seats 36 people. 👥 maximum 36 persons.

D'Matrix
Amazon Street

Grand Mirage Night Club
Centenario Club
Plot 691 Port Harcourt
Garki II
🏨 Crystal Palace Hotel
Garki
🕐 10.00 p.m.- 5.00 a.m.
☎ 314-1311-2; fax 314-1310
💰 💰 Ⓟ
🍸 🎵 🍽 DJ Music, drinks, finger food. VIP section upstairs.
👥 maximum 500 persons.

Nicon Hilton Safari Club
Aguiyi Ironsi and Shehu Shagari Way
Lobby Area
🕐 11:00 p.m. - 5:00 a.m.
☎ 413-1811; fax 413-2418
🖥 Hilton_Abuja@hyperia.com
Ⓟ
🍸 For up-market clubbers. Men must wear collars. DJ music.

Point Lounge
2022 Aminu Kano Crescent
🏨 Bridge between Regent School and Emab Shopping Plaza

Wuse Ii
🕐 24 hours
📱 0805-517-7645

🍶 🍶

🍸 🎵 🍽 Serves Continental, Chinese food and Indian food. Seating for 150 persons. Up-market clientele. 💺 maximum 200 persons.

White House
Plot 820 Uyo Crescent, behind IGI
Area 11
Garki, Abuja

Sheraton
Dazzles
Abuja Sheraton Hotel and Towers
Ladi Kwali Street
Wuse 2, Zone 4
🕐 11.00 p.m. - dawn
☎ 523-0225; Ext. 8361-8363
Fax: 523-1570/1
Ⓟ
🍸 Dancing, DJ, bar (no food).

Sky Chef
25 Addis Ababa Crescent
Upstairs from the restaurant
🏬 Sheraton

Wuse
🕐 10.00 p.m. to 4.00 a.m.
📱 0804-214-7968

Casinos

Nicon Hilton Casino
Aguiyi Ironsi and Shehu Shagari Way
- 🕐   4.00 p.m. to 4.00 a.m.
- ☎   413-1811, Ext. 6132; 6134;
- Fax: 413-2418
- 💻   *Hilton_Abuja@hyperia.com*
- Ⓟ

Summerland
Casino
Plot 1374
Borno Street
Area 10
☎ 8.00 p.m to 3.00 a.m. Sun-Fri.

CHAPTER 9

Stocking-up

If a chicken does not dig, it does not feed
(Cameroonian Proverb)

No one bargains for yams that are still in the soil.
(Nigerian Proverb)

Shopping is something many of us enjoy and some hate. Shopping in Abuja could make you switch sides. If you have the time and are a bit adventurous, it can give you the chance to experience 'real' Africa, with all the sights, sounds, textures and smells that go along with it. You will see people 'making market' everywhere. A stoplight is an opportunity to sell and buy those vital necessities - phone cards, toilet paper, rat killer, watches, food, towels, shoes, newspapers, etc.

You will usually need to bargain, but some things do have set prices. It never hurts to ask for a reduction, just as the vendor may feel it never hurts to double the price and see if they get lucky. There are a growing number of supermarkets if you have more money than time, but you will pay for the convenience of these 'one stop shops'.

Appliances and Electronics

Appliances and electronic equipment can be purchased from most supermarkets. The Grand Square, Park and Shop, Amigos and 9-11 have a reasonable selection. The local electronics market could offer some savings if you want to work a bit harder. This is in the **Neighbourhood Shopping Centre**, Zone 3 Wuse between Conakry Close and Maputo Street off Herbert Macaulay Way. Turn right again past the Methodist Church, police station, fire service into the shopping centre between the two roads. There, opposite Wuse General Hospital, are many little shops selling TVs, videos, refrigerators, washer/dryers, etc. This would be a good place to enquire for electronic repairs as well.

Electronics
Kristonie Daniels, Ltd.
Shop No. 1, Block 11
Wuse Market

Binatone
Block 12, Lafia Close, Off Ilorin Street, Area 8, Garki
☎01/234-0811

FarEast Mercantile Company
M.G. Plaza (Ground Floor)
Plot 1921 Dalaba Street
Wuse Zone 5, Abuja
☎5232855

A tumble dryer is recommended (if indoor space to dry clothes is limited) as the rainy season makes drying clothes out of doors difficult and there is also a significant risk of Tumbu fly eggs being laid on laundry hung outdoors. Tumbu fly lava can burrow under the skin and are quite uncomfortable to remove.

Art and Crafts
AB Artworld
EMAB Shopping Plaza, Shop E9
Plot 51 Aminu Kano Crescent,
Wuse II
(before Park 'n Shop)
☎ 0802-300-0104
Art and architectural materials, frames and surveying equipment.

(See "Enjoying the Culture" section for more information on local arts and crafts)

Butchers

Chicken House
Near Amigo, at the IBB Way and Ademola Adetokunbo Crescent junction.

Felak Meat 🌸
13, Ahmadu Bello Way
Jos, Plateau State
☎   073-248364, 08034508567
Email: felakent@cetracom.net

Zartech
Cold store/retail shop
Plot 792 Ademola Adetokunbo Crescent
(Rockview Hotel Junction, opposite Big Bite Fast Food)
Wuse II, Abuja
☎   09 413-0022; 09 413-0023; 0803-312-0184
🕐 M-F: 0800 - 1700

Sat: 0800-1600
Service: Since 1984

Products: for fresh and frozen chicken - whole, breasts, nuggets, wings, laps, gizzards, burgers; turkey, minced meat, beef fillet, sausages, sea food - prawn, calamari, sole, shrimp, lobster, crab; croaker and salmon, eggs.

The main supermarkets also have good meat counters.

Amigo
Grand Square ♥
Park n' Shop

Drinks

Fizzy drinks like Coke and Fanta are known as 'minerals'. These can be purchased anywhere you see full crates along the road. If you don't have a crate of 'empties' you will need to pay a deposit on the crate and bottles. You will then exchange yours for a new crate when you refill. The going rate in December 2003 was ₦650 for a refill. Some stops people have recommended are:

- Corner Shops across from the Rockview Hotel
- Near Grand Square on the road to Lemingsway
- Limpopo Street, Maitama near Maitama stores; sells ice as well.
- Corner of Yedseram and Limpopo
- Beer at Langfield Foods and Beverages Ltd, Sani Abacha Way, behind Wuse Old Market
  ☎ 5239805, 3142929, 314 2928

Florists

Flower-Plus

11B Gana Street, Maitama
(Same building as Agatha's Interiors – Furniture Shop)
☎ 0805-610-9880
🕐 M-F: 0800-1800
Sat: 0800-1600
Cut flowers, dry flowers, flower arrangements for social events.

Petals & More
Crystal Palace Hotel, Port Harcourt Crescent, Area 11, Garki, Abuja
☎ 09.314-0038-40; 0803-787-4444
🕘 M-Sat: 0930-1830
Specialists in weddings, banquets, conferences.

Petals 'N' Sepals
Inside Park 'N' Shop
Aminu Kano Crescent, Wuse II, Abuja
☎ 09 413-5892
🕘 M-Sat: 0900-2100
Sunday: 1100-2100

Cut flowers are also available at Park 'n Shop and Grand Square Supermarkets.

Fish-Fresh and Frozen Sea/Ocean Food

Raph-Fish Enterprises
7B, Marine Road
Live Pool Jetty, Underbridge Apapa
☎ 0803-723-4835

Suppliers of all kinds of fish including lobsters, prawns, shrimp, and octopus. Fish is delivered to homes in Abuja upon request.

The Fish Man
📱 08056012473

Flies in from Lagos every 3 weeks or so with fresh fish on ice. Call to arrange delivery.

Grand Square also has a refrigerator van deliver fresh sea food and fish every Friday morning in the parking lot from 10.00 a.m. to 12.00 a.m.

Furniture and Furnishings

There are several shops in town that carry furniture and interior decorations. Most of them deal in imported furniture or furniture made locally with imported materials. In general, the quality is good, but prices are expensive. Some shops will custom-make furniture. Supermarkets (9-11, Park 'n Shop and Grand Square) also have furniture floors.

Agatha's Interior
11b, Gana St. Maitama, Abuja
☎ 0804-212-6851; 0802-326-0754
🕐 M-F: 0830-1830
Saturday: 0900-1600
Home and office furniture

Ausken Royal Furniture
Plot 678 Aminu Kano Crescent, Wuse II, Abuja
☎ 09 523-4035; 523-4056; 0803-453-4145
🕐 M-Sat: 0800-1830
Leather furniture

BeeVee Interiors
Park 'n Shop Complex
Aminu Kano Crescent, Wuse II, Abuja
☎ 09 413-9786; 413-9461, 0803-311-5162
🕐 M-F: 0900-1900
Saturday: 1000-1800
Furniture, interiors

Cherry Wood
6 Gana Street, Maitama, Abuja
☎ 09 413-4197
🕐 M-Sat: 0800-1700
Imported leather furniture

Stocking-up 177

Choice
Plot 536 Adetokunbo Ademola Crescent, Wuse II
☎ 09 523-8774; fax 523-8781
🕐 M-F: 0830-1800
Saturday: 0900-1600
Leather furniture, marble, granite, décor, carpet, curtains, many items imported from Italy

Grand Products Co. Ltd.
(a.k.a., The French Supermarket)
Plot 270 Muhammadu Buhari Way, Central District, Abuja
Ground Floor and 1st Floor (South wing of the building)
☎ 09 523-0064; 234-5030; 234-6612
🕐 M-Sat: 0900-2100
Ligne Roset furniture

Heroes
Plot 13 Adetokunbo Ademola Crescent, Wuse II, Abuja
☎ 0803-311-5194
Leather furniture

Kaduna Furniture and Carpets Co, Ltd ♥
15 Inuwa Abdulkadir Road, Kaduna South
P.M.B. 2224, Kaduna
☎ 062-213243; 062-233043
Furniture (excellent quality locally constructed) and carpets

Kautal Hairu Company
Park 'n Shop Complex
Aminu Kano Crescent, Wuse II, Abuja
☎ 09 413-9323; 413-9324
🕐 M-Sat: 0900-1700
Doors, bathroom units, floor materials, furniture

Linea Italia
12A Gana Street, Maitama, Abuja
☎ 09 413-6489

🕘 M-F: 0900-1900
Saturday: 0900-1800
Furniture, kitchen units, etc. imported from Italy

Nuconcept Ltd.
No.1 Barawa St, Maitama, Abuja
☎ 09 413-3697; fax 413-3723
🕘 M-F: 0800-1730
Saturday: 0800-1600
Commercial and residential interiors

Park N' Shop
Aminu Kano Crescent, Wuse II, Abuja
2nd and 3rd Floors
☎ 09 413-5892
🕘 M-Sat: 0900-2100
Sunday: 1100-2100

Silhouette
Millennium Verdict Plaza
Plot 1159 Adetokunbo Ademola Crescent, Wuse II, Abuja
☎ 09 523-2537; 0803-311-3831
🕘 M-F: 0900-18.00
Saturday: 0900-1400
Locally made, good quality, custom orders

SILMA Global Furniture
JITAU Plaza
Plot 1173 Adetokunbo Ademola Crescent, Wuse II, Abuja
☎ 09 523-9705; 523-0081; 0803-705-3488
🕘 M-F: 0800-1800
Saturday:1000-1500
Leather furniture

Universal Furniture Ltd.
Plot 1247 Aminu Kano Crescent, Wuse II, Abuja
☎ 09 523-0197; 0803-402-1468; fax 523-0198

⏰ M-Sat: 0800-1800
Locally made, good quality

VINA International Ltd.
4 Adetokunbo Ademola Crescent, Wuse II, Abuja
☎   09 523-5196; fax 523-4143
⏰ M-F: 0800-1800
Saturday: 0900-1300
Locally made, good quality, characteristic light wood

Green Grocers

Shagalinku Farmers Market
Zone 4 Corner Shop
Constantine Street, between Ladi Kwali and Addis Ababa Street, (Near Chase Restaurant, down the street from the Sheraton)
☎   09 423-6025
⏰ M-S: 0800 - 2200
Service: 1 year
Alcohol: No
Products: food items, cosmetics, fresh produce, seeds, housewares.

Amigo Fruit and Vegetable Stand
1023 Adetokunbo Ademola Crescent
Wuse II, Abuja
To the left of the entrance of Amigo shop
⏰ M-Sat: 0900-2300
⏰ Sun: 1000-2100

Legends Fruit and Vegetable Stand 🍃
Outside Legends supermarket
27 Port Harcourt Crescent,
Off Gimbiya Street
Across from Crystal Palace Hotel
Ahmadu Bello Way, Area 11,
Garki, Abuja
⏰ M-Sat: 0900-1800

Other places to find fresh fruit and vegetables are in the local Wuse and New Markets each of which has a section for these goods. Local vendors along roads such as IBB Way sell local produce at reasonable prices, but you cannot guarantee they will be selling what you need.

Many people make use of delivery services from Jos. This is a main vegetable growing area of the country and is about a four-hour drive away. There are several producers who will deliver fresh produce once or twice a week (usually on a Tuesday and/or Friday). They can be contacted by email or phone to place orders. Orders should be placed several days before delivery. The cost will be slightly more for medium to very high quality goods.

Plateau Fruits and Vegetables
☎ 0803-720-1436
Email: garuti@afrione.com

Zamani Farms Limited ♥
Farm: Kuru Jenta, Jos, Plateau State.
Office: BP 1486 Metropolitan Avenue, Tudun Wada, Jos.
☎ 073-464091, 08034504225
Email: norma-jos@hetnet.nl, norma@AfriOne.com

Rosda Ventures
5, Rangama Close
Sabon Bariki Bukuru,
P.O. Box 6967
Jos, Plateau State
☎ 073-280592; 0803-498-2254
Email: rosda201@yahoo.com

There is also a butcher service operating out of Jos that provides home delivery.

Felak Meat ♥
13, Ahmadu Bello Way
Jos, Plateau State
☎   073-248364, 08034508567
Email: felakent@cetracom.net

Interiors and Household Accessories
Some of the furniture shops sell carpets, curtains and interior furnishings. Large shopping centres are also likely to have one or two interior shops. There are also numerous shops selling carpets and curtains in Wuse Market.

Belle Maison
Sheriff Plaza (B10-12)
Plot 739 Kade Street
(Off Aminu Kano Crescent, next to Park 'n Shop)
Wuse II, Abuja
☎ 09 670-1014
Bedroom, bathroom and kitchen accessories

Nike Interiors
Suite #A15 Kenaz Plaza
Plot 2413 Kashim Ibrahim Road
(Near Wuse Market)
Wuse II, Abuja
☎   09 523-4488; 0802-320-4376
Email: nike_akanbi@yahoo.com
Interior décor, blind accessories, wrought iron and marble

OTI Carpets and Furnishing Co. Ltd.
1001 Adetokunbo Ademola Crescent, Wuse II, Abuja
◷M-F: 0830-1830
Saturday: 0830-1430
Carpets, frames, doors, etc.

Prestige
NICON Hilton Hotel
(Aguiyi Ironsi and Shehu Shagari Way)
☎   09 413-1811
🕘M-F: 0900-1800
Tableware, towels

Tiffany Boutique
Shop 60 Area 11,
Corner Shop,
Wuse II, Abuja
☎   09 314-8221-2; 314-8219,
🕘M-Sat: 0900-1930
Sells plates, pots, stainless products, kitchen utensils, ceramic wares and marble ceramic tiles imported from Italy.

Cookmall
Suite B2, B3 Mc Lewis Shopping Plaza
Adetokunbo Ademola Crescent
Wuse II, Abuja

Exclusive Kitchen and dining wares, expensive but high quality utensils, glasses and ceramic wares.

U.O.O. Nigeria Ltd
Shop C8 Kenaz Plaza
Plot 2413 Kashim Ibrahim Road
(Near Wuse Market)
Wuse II, Abuja
☎ 09 523-6034; 0803-310-0398
Curtains, vertical blinds and interior decoration

Local Nigerian Markets
For those wishing to pay less than premium prices the local markets are the places to go. There are two large African markets in Abuja which offer a wide variety of goods at prices that will have to be

negotiated, so it is a good idea to have priced items elsewhere before buying. Bargaining in the market is a game – everyone knows where it will end up, but you have to go through the motions anyway. The usual tact is to offer a third of the original asking price and settle for half of the original price. Vendors will usually greet you and encourage you to look at their goods in a way that may appear aggressive at first. Returning greetings is an important part of being polite in this culture and a good chance to practice a bit of the local language while you walk on by. If you hire a "barrow boy" to carry your shopping (for ₦50) he can help you find what you are looking for and will keep the other barrow boys from bothering you. It also leaves your hands free and he will be able to help you find your way out again.

It is a good idea to avoid the markets if unrest is predicted. Also, the authorities occasionally crack down on the illegal stalls in and around the market area by breaking them up and burning them. If it sounds like trouble is starting - get out.

The Old **Wuse Market** is quite easy to find but parking is rather difficult. It is not recommended to drive your vehicle inside the market, although there is a parking area inside. There will be many cars parked between the market and the expressway but be warned against theft and occasional clearing of the area by the police as it is not a legal parking area. There is a new Langfield supermarket with parking just at the bottom of the market. Behind this yellow supermarket is a wholesale beer supplier which has very competitive prices. Wuse Market is a good place to find cloth, tailors, electrical goods, household items, carpets, books, office supplies and fresh fruit, vegetables, rice, etc.

The **New Market** is much bigger and located off Constitution Avenue, a one way road system, and Olusegun Obasanjo Way. There has been some talk of this market being "relocated" so ask around about it. In general, the variety of goods there is better and the prices are lower. Parking is also difficult, so going by taxi or with a driver is a good idea. Some readers have also said that parking is easier if the market is accessed from the road in from the airport. The market has fresh meat, fish, musical instruments, crafts, fruit and vegetables, grains, etc.

Many areas of town have their own smaller markets that can be interesting to wander through. Some of the following, as mentioned elsewhere in the book are **Garki Model Market** and the **Market by Berger Life Camp**. For information on markets in outlying villages, see "Enjoying the Culture" section.

Supermarkets

Almost anything (or a reasonable substitute) can be found in Abuja these days. The 'easiest' places are the big, air-conditioned, supermarkets. These usually stock fresh and frozen goods, canned foods, dairy products, as well as household items ranging from furniture to electrical appliances. Several also have bakeries and butchers. It is always a good idea to check the expiry date before purchasing items.

Some local brands to look out for are **Farm Fresh**(milk, butter, yoghurt, cheese), **Maizube Farms** (milk, yoghurt) **Zumani Farms** (vegetables), **Fan Milk** (ice cream), **Supreme** (ice cream).

The main supermarkets as of December 2003 are:

Amigo
1023 Adetokunbo Ademola Crescent
Wuse II, Abuja
☎   09 523-8624; 09 523-4067
M-Sat: 0900-2200
Sun: 0930-2000
Established: 1997
Alcohol: No

One main floor with sections above and below, plus additional businesses on the ground and second floor, air conditioned with some parking outside.

Products include weekly deliveries of fresh and imported fruits and vegetables, butchery has fresh lamb, beef and chicken (no pork), dairy products, bakery on site, toys, cosmetics, household goods, electronics, stationary, seasonal items, food products, juices, confectionery, jewellery, mobile phones. Also there: Amigo Suya

Snack, Amigo Saloon, Gift shop, Fresh fruit and vegetable stand and second hand books outside.

Grand Square ❤
Plot 270 Muhammadu Buhari Way
Central District, Abuja
☎ 09 234-5030; 234-6612, 523-0064;
⏰M-Sat: 0900 - 2100
Established: 2003
Alcohol: Yes

New, on several floors, air conditioned with plenty of secure parking.

Products: Supermarket (groceries, toiletries, fresh and frozen food, butchery, eggs, bakery, pastry, home made ice cream, drinks and wines), electronics, household appliances, suitcases, toys, CD/DVD shop, music items, hi-fi, lights, furniture, BBQs, flowers and cafeteria on site.

Park 'n Shop Supermarket and Departmental Store
740 Aminu Kano Crescent
Wuse II, Abuja
(Next to Banex Plaza)
☎ 09 413-5892; 09 413-5893-95
⏰M-Sat: 0900 - 2100
Sun: 1100 - 2100
Alcohol: Yes

Four floors, air conditioned with plenty of secure parking.

Products: Groceries - fresh vegetables and fruits, cheese products, butter, milk, ice cream; butchery - beef, pork, lamb; bakery, pet food, toiletries, household items, luggage, beverages, various wines, whiskey, cigars, cigarettes; electronics - televisions, DVD/CVD, music systems, household and kitchen appliances, cameras, phones and faxes, air conditioners, fridge/ freezers, washer/ dryers, cookers, fire proof safes, lawnmowers; clothes and shoes, home and office furniture, lights.

9-11 Superstores
Maitama, Plot No 635
Usuma Street, Abuja
☎ 09 413-0441
⏰M-Sat.　0900 -2300
Alcohol:　Yes
Established:1998

One large floor, air conditioned with some secure parking.
Products: General items, food stuffs, alcohol, canned and dry goods, electronics, household items, furniture, magazines, greeting cards, cosmetics, soft ice cream, popcorn and snacks.

Some other stores include:

Legends of Abuja
27 Port Harcourt Crescent, Off Gimbiya Street
Across from Crystal Palace Hotel
Ahmadu Bello Way, Area 11,
Garki, Abuja
☎ 09 314-8809
Fax:　09 314-8808
⏰M-Sat.　0900 -2300

Air conditioned with secure parking.
Products: Imported dry and canned goods, butter, cheese, some frozen foods (local chicken, fish, prawns, African fabrics, cleaning products, dishes, water, stationery, luggage, toys, electrical items, canned soft drinks, some fruit and vegetables, furniture, second hand books, maps, magazines.

Also: good fresh fruit and vegetable stand outside.

Metro Plaza
Plot 991/992
Fourth Cadastral
Central Area, opposite War College of Nigeria

⊕ M-Sat: 0900 -2100
Sun: 1200 - 2100

This is a multi-storey shop with 2 big shops on the ground floor and many small shops and businesses on the floors above.

Products: canned and dry food goods, toys, electronics, drinks, clothes.

Also in the lobby you can buy soft serve ice cream and popcorn.

Metro Plaza

Sahad Stores (can be congested on weekends)
Plot 272,
Bengazi Street, near Chase restaurant
Wuse, Zone 4
Abuja
☎ 09 5231954
⊕ M-Sat: 0800 - 2300
Sun: 1000 - 2300
Alcohol: No
Products: Canned and dried foods, sweets, household and cleaning products, cloth, magazines.

Lemingsway Stores Ltd.
Supermarket and Bakery
Plot 323 Leventis Close, Central Area District, Abuja
(Opposite Wuse New Market/NNPC Mega Station)
- ☎ 09 314-8034; 0803-587-1317
- ⏲ M-F: 0900 - 1900
- Sat: 0900 - 1800
- Established: 1998
- Alcohol: No

Products: Furniture, electronics, fresh foods (fish, meat, cheese, butter, bacon, prawns, etc), canned foods, perfumes, cosmetics, books, cards, cooking utensils, clothes, pillows, household/kitchen wares, toys, stationery, wall units, games, equipment, fresh bread and other confectioneries (from own bakery), lighting accessories, rugs, etc

Bomas Supermarket
Iluobe Filling Station
Plot 598 Aminu Kano Crescent
Wuse II, Abuja
- ☎ 09 523-7415
- ⏲ M-Sat: 0800 - 2200
- Sun: 1700 - 2200

Products: many Wuse Market goods, food products, household items, clothing, current magazines, Nigerian movies.

There are many smaller supermarkets in each area of the city and in addition to being close to home, roadside fruit and vegetable shops offer good value. Eggs, vegetables, fruit, palm oil, yam, etc. can be purchased on the road. Maitama has two good small shops for fresh milk, flour, sugar, rice, bread, house cleaning supplies and some household goods. They are listed below.

Maitama Stores
LS(B) Street, Block 4 FHA
Maitama, Abuja
- ☎ 09 413-742
- ⏲ 0800 - 2200

Majindadi Store
FHA Quarters
Corner Shop No. 4
Limpopo St.
(Off Yedseram, parallel to IBB way, behind the Great Wall of China)
Maitama, Abuja
☏ 09 413-0294; 09 413-4429

Toys, clothes and shoes
Supermarkets
The larger supermarkets all have a pretty good choice of children's books, dolls, bicycles and general imported toys. Many of these locations carry clothes and shoes for children as well.
- Park 'n Shop
- Grand Square
- Amigo
- 9-11
- Bomas

Wuse, Model and New Markets
Check here for toys and bicycles at cheaper prices than at the supermarkets. They also have unusual African instruments that make good presents. Clothes and shoes for children can also be found at the open markets. Take sample clothes and shoes along (or the actual child) as the sizes may be different.

Plazas
There are several plazas that have a number of little shops with interesting items for children.

Emab Plaza
Plot 751 Aminu Kano Crescent, Wuse II, Abuja
Close to Park 'n Shop
(Lots of parking available)

- **Art World**
  Shop E9
  Art supplies for little artists.

- **Omega**
  Suite D22
  ☎ 09 671244, 080844113694, 08056157617,
  ⊕ M -Sat: 0900-1800

Well stocked with toys for presents, balloons, etc. Also does party packages with many dressed up characters and clowns, rents bouncy castles and popcorn machines, cups, food warmers, chairs, canopies, etc.

- **Pyramids**
  Shop 1190 located on the last floor of the middle block sells kitchen items, toys, cards, shoes and dresses for kids and adults

- **Zero to Ten**
  Shop 24
  ☎ 08055423880
  ⊕ M -Sat: 0900-1900
  Clothes for children age 0 to 10; shoes, bags some toys.

Metro Plaza

The shops on the first floor have a variety of toys and gifts

The Babyheart Shop
Plot 418
Lobito Crescent,
Off Adetokunbo Ademola Street
Wuse II
☎   09 4139125, 08044183207, 08023291982
⊕ M-Sat: 0900-1900
Mothercare authorised distributor in Abuja.

Children's Affairs
1079 Kolda Link
Off Adetokunbo Ademola Crescent
Near Nitel Junction
Wuse II, Abuja
☎   09 523-0759
🕘M-F: 0900-2000
A three-storey building with everything for children ages new-born to 12 years old. Toys, cards, party accessories, sweets, movies and much more.

Children's World Investment Ltd.
Prime Plaza
Plot 1012
Ademola Adetokunbo Crescent
Opposite Rockview Hotel
Wuse, II, Abuja
☎   09 413-5830
Fax: 09 413-5932
🕘 M -F: 0900-1700
Opened in March 2003. It stocks toys, cards, shoes, dresses, trousers, furniture and accessories for children ages new-born to 14 years old.

Cute 'n Chic
Shop 1:
Abuja Shopping Mall
Shop B14
Near Ministry of Foreign Affairs
Wuse Zone 3, Abuja

Shop 2:
F15 Metro Plaza
Plot 991-992, 4th Avenue
Off Herbert Macaulay Way, Opposite War College
Central Area, Abuja
🕘 M -F:0900-1700
Children's toys, gift items, baby accessories, clothes and shoes.

Trendy Kids
Poly Plaza, Suite B1 Plot 1073
Adetokunbo Ademola Crescent
Beside AP Plaza Wuse II
Abuja
Toys, clothes, party bag stuffers

Kiddies Corner Toy Shop
At the Hilton Pharmacy, on the ground floor across from the bakery.

Nadina Babies
Shop F23 Metro Plaza
Plot 991-992, 4th Avenue
Off Herbert Macaulay Way, Opposite War College
☎ 0803-452-1534
Mostly clothes for newborns to 14-years old

Mitaire S. Oraegbu
Shop A72
Area7 Shopping Complex
Behind UTC
Garki, Abuja
☎ 09 234-4559
Hand-made clothes made with African cloth for children and adults.

In addition, there are several markets in villages outside Abuja that take place on certain days of the week. See "Enjoying the Culture" for more details.

CHAPTER 10

Getting Rest

A day of peace in times of stress is like a thousand days in paradise.
(Nigerian Proverb)

Hotels and Service Apartments.

There is no doubt about it, hotels that are safe, clean and easily accessible in Abuja are expensive. We have only included a detailed description of those hotels at which we would feel comfortable inviting our parents to stay. This is not the **Lonely Planet,** and younger, more patient souls could give you a plethora of other options. We have included a list of hotels and contact numbers for hotels that we did not personally visit but that are listed with the Federal Ministry of Culture and Tourism. Again, new hotels are being built continually and others are closing their doors, so we apologise for any errors or omissions.

Getting Rest Symbol Keys

- 🕴 Meeting Rooms
- 📱 Cellphone Number
- 💻 Email Address
- 🏔 Landmarks (nearby)
- 🎵 Music (live)
- 🍸 Gym
- 🛁 Swimming Pool
- 🖧 Business Centre
- ✂ Beauty Salon
- 🔒 Security Guards
- 🍽 Restaurant
- ✈ Airline Reservations
- 🚗 Car Hire
- Ⓟ Parking (separate lot)
- 💰 Low Budget
- 💰💰 Medium Budget
- 💰💰💰 High Budget
- ☎ Telephone Number
- 🚑 Emergency (after hours number)

Getting Rest Notes

Prices
Room prices will usually add 5% VAT and 10% service charge on top. With the exception of the Amana Suites, none of these hotels are low budget (for a standard room). The remainder have been divided into medium and high budgets with some rating 👜 👜 👜 + for a standard room. Because of problems with guests leaving without paying their bills, most of the smaller hotels expect payment in advance. Guests are cautioned to ensure that their bill does not exceed their deposited amount or they will be literally locked-out of their rooms until payment is made.

Stable Current
All of the hotels included have backup generators in case of power outages.

Telephone
They also all have telephones in the rooms and the capability of making international calls either via direct dial or via the operator. The rates, however, are usually quite high. Please remember that all calls can be monitored and so gauge topics of conversation accordingly.

Taxis and Car Hires
Unless otherwise stated, it is relatively easy to find taxis from these hotels. The term "car hire" can be used to describe two things in Nigeria: one is the international standard meaning - to rent or hire a self-drive vehicle for a day or more. The other is getting a high standard car (e.g. Mercedes with air condition) with a driver to take the guest to a desired location. These "car hire" drivers are found at the larger hotels and they charge more than "street" taxi drivers. The symbol for car hire 🚗 refers to the availability of vehicles for hire or rent.

Hotels

Agura Hotel
#10 Moshood Abiola Road
Area 10, Garki, Abuja

🏢	International Conference Centre
☎	234-2500; 234-1757-9; 234-1753;
📱	0802-332-3472; 0803-723-3063; 0803-408-8419
🚗	234-2000
💻	agurahotels@yahoo.com
🍸 ⚓ 🖧 ✈ 🚘 ✂	casino
🦟	tennis (1), squash (1), massage, laundry/dry cleaning
🍽	(3) ♪ (2)

Ⓟ 🍾 🍾 🍾

Room types: Standard, Business Suite, Deluxe Suite
Naira rates for residents and non-residents

There are 169 rooms with guest capacity of 180 each. In operation since 1987. All rooms include air conditioning, satellite TV, a refrigerator and cups/glasses. Deluxe rooms also include coffee pots. Bookings can be made via phone, fax or email but a letter is preferred. There are two lifts.

   There are meeting rooms available to hold from 40 to 600 people. On site are also boutiques, perfumery, bureau de change, video centre and car wash.
   There is plenty of secured parking. Drivers receive security entrance tickets that must be returned upon leaving the hotel.
   The hotel is one of the landmarks in the busy Garki area. One of the first hotels in the city, it is located near the International Conference Centre. There is a garden with large trees in front of the hotel for relaxing.
   10-20% or more discount can be negotiated for long-stay guests.

Amana Suites

Sokode Crescent
Off Michael Okpara Street
Wuse Zone 5, Abuja
P.O. Box 7317, Wuse, Abuja

  🏭   Nigeria Engineering Works
  ☎   523-0888; 523-0883; 523-7641;
           523-8664; 523-7270; 523-8671

🍸 🖧 🚗 📢

laundry/dry cleaning

🍽 Ⓟ 🗝 💰

Room types: Exclusive, Executive, Deluxe, Royal Delux, Presidential Suites.
Rates for residents in Naira and non-residents in US Dollars.

There are 60 rooms. In operation since 1999. All rooms include air conditioning, satellite TV, a refrigerator and coffee pot with cups/glasses. Deluxe and Royal rooms also include a CD player. Presidential and Deluxe suites include a microwave oven, a VCD player and an electric cooker. Bookings can be made via phone or fax.

    Bungalow type rooms with green space between the bungalows. Kitchen is available for an additional fee. There is a meeting room capable of holding 100 people.

    There is secure parking for the guests and their visitors. The entry and exit of vehicles is checked by security guards. The hotel is situated in the downtown area of Wuse off of major streets. Taxis are not located on site, guests would need to walk a little way to find a taxi or ask the guards to call one for them.

    15% discount for long-stay guests. 20% discount for Saturdays and Sundays.

Chelsea Hotel
Plot 389 Muhammadu Buhari Way
Cadastral Zone AO
Central Area, Abuja
P.O. Box 487
Garki, Abuja

- Grand Square Supermarket
- 234- 9080-98; fax 234-9074; 234-9077
- chelseahotel@linkserve.com;

  chelseahotel@rosecom.net

tennis (2), laundry/dry cleaning

(1), ♪ (1 bar)

Ⓟ

Room types: Superior, Deluxe, Executive, Business Suite
   Rates for residents in Naira and non-residents in US Dollars.
75 rooms; guest capacity 150. In operation since 2000. All rooms include air conditioning, satellite TV, a refrigerator, cups/glasses and computer internet hook-ups. Executive rooms and business suites also include coffee pots. Very good internet connections. Doors are operated with key cards. Non-smoking rooms are available. Bookings can be made via phone, fax or email. There is one lift.
   There are two meeting rooms available. One large conference room holds 350. Another small room holds 70.
   There is also plenty of secured parking. Security guards check entry and exit of visitors.
   This mid-sized hotel has a friendly atmosphere. The swimming pool is small but well maintained. The hotel faces a major street and is visible from a distance. It is close to Nicon Plaza and the NNPC Corporate Headquarters and a three minute drive to the Federal Secretariat. A free shuttle bus to the airport operates daily. 10% discount can be negotiated for long-stay guests. Weekends rates available for Friday, Saturday and Sunday night stays.

Crystal Palace Hotel
687 Port Harcourt Crescent
Off Ahmadu Bello Way,
Off Gimbiya Street
Garki, Abuja

🏢   International Merchant Bank
☎   314-0033; 314-0040; fax 314-0034
💻   *crystalpalacehotel@yahoo.com*

🍸 🚇 ✈ 🚗 ✂

🗣   massage, laundry/dry cleaning

🍽 (1)

♬ (1 bar, 1 night Club)

Business Centre

Ⓟ 💧 💧 💧

Room types: Crystal Corporate Suite, Special Executive Suite, Royal Jumbo Suite, Ambassadorial Suite, Suite Majestic, Presidential Suite and Presidential Apartment
    Naira rates for residents and non-residents
    There are 41 guest rooms. In operation since 2000. All rooms include air conditioning, satellite TV, a refrigerator, coffee pots, and cups/glasses.
    Bookings can be made via phone, fax or email.
    A small hotel with a friendly atmosphere. One of the most popular beauty salons in Abuja is located at the hotel. There is also a large supermarket across the street. The hotel is one of the landmarks in the Garki area. As it is not facing a major street, it is rather peaceful. There is no garden/green space and the parking area is not large. Security guards are posted at the gate. By Abuja standards, it is an embodiment of good value for money.
    30% discount for long-stay and weekend guests.

Nicon Hilton Hotel ♥

Aguiyi Ironsi and Shehu Shagari Way

🏨	Itself a landmark
☎	413-1811-40; 0803-901-3000
Fax:	413-2417-8
💻	hilton_abuja@hilton.com

🍸 ⚓ 🚂 ✈ 🚗 ✂ ⚿ casino ♟ tennis (3), squash (3), massage, laundry/dry cleaning

🍽 (4) Oriental, Zuma, Fulani Pool and Bukka, Piano Lounge

♪ (3 bars; 1 Night Club)

Ⓟ 🛏 🛏 🛏 🛏 ✚

Naira rates for residents, US Dollar or Credit card for non-residents

Standard Rooms: Twin, King, King Deluxe, King Alcove, Royal, Executive Suite, Royal Suite, Ambassador Suite and Presidential Suite

Executive Floor Rooms: Twin, King, Deluxe, Alcove, Executive Royal room, Executive Royal Suite, Penthouse Suite, Ambassador Suite and Presidential Suite

There are 670 rooms; guest capacity 1500. The largest, best quality and most expensive hotel in Abuja. The hotel is spread across three towers and is a major landmark in the city. There is a wide variety of rooms from which to choose. All rooms include air conditioning, satellite TV, refrigerator and coffee pot (w/cups, glasses). Some of the nicer rooms include kitchens, video, DVD players, internet access and balconies. The hotel is undergoing major refurbishment. Doors are operated with key cards. Non-smoking rooms are available. There are 9 lifts. Bookings can be made via phone, fax or email.

The grounds are well landscaped and maintained. There are several shops and services on the ground and 01 floor levels, including DHL, pharmacy/boutique, airline companies, travel agents, dentist, perfumery, book and stationer, jeweller, barber and clothiers to name a few. The sports facilities and the gym are well equipped and maintained. Residents in the community can join the "Hiltonia Club" and have access to the facilities.

There is a large children's playground and a mini-golf course. On weekends there is a bouncy castle in the playground and a large floating toy in the pool. Bring a ball and clubs for the mini-golf or ask at the fitness centre. Non-guests and non-members of the club pay a fee for entry to the pool. The handicraft village below the mini-golf course has a large selection of Nigerian arts and crafts at reasonable prices (by Abuja standards).

There are 22 meeting rooms ranging in capacity from 30 to 1200 persons. Outside catering services are also available. There is plenty of parking and security guards are placed at the gate and throughout the hotel on a 24-hour basis. Drivers receive security entrance tickets that must be returned upon leaving the hotel. Large events held at the hotel can sometimes cause congestion. Clean and well managed, the hotel has high standards and is frequented by foreigners and Nigerians alike. Discounts can be negotiated for long-stay guests.

Services on the executive floors include private check-in and check-out; complimentary cocktails on arrival, complimentary Executive Breakfast, complimentary afternoon tea, complimentary pre-dinner canapés, exclusive cocktail bar, use of personal computer, use of fax and photocopier and a wide selection of local and international newspapers and magazines.

Bolingo Hotel Abuja

Independence Avenue
Area 10, Garki, Abuja
P.O. Box 4654, Garki, Abuja

- 🏰   The National Stadium, Ship House, site for new US Embassy and British High Commission
- ☎   234-4701-9; fax 234-4710
- 💻   www.bolingo@bolingo hotel and towers plc.com

Y ⚬ ⚬ ✈ 🚗 ⚭ casino
● tennis (2), massage, laundry/dry cleaning

🍽 (1) 🍸 gym, swimming pool

🎵 (2 bars; 1 night club)

Ⓟ 💰💰💰💰

Room types: Standard, Executive Studio, Executive Suite, Diplomatic Suite, Presidential Suite
Naira rates for residents, US Dollar rates for non-residents

There are 350 rooms; guest capacity 700. It was newly renovated in 2003. All rooms include air conditioning, satellite TV, a refrigerator and cups/glasses. All but the Standard rooms also include computer internet hook-ups. Doors are operated with key cards. Bookings can be made via phone, fax or email. There are five lifts.

Guests are met by a dramatic water fountain and an attractively arranged reception area. There is plenty of secured parking. Drivers receive security entrance tickets that must be returned upon leaving the hotel.

There are several sports facilities, a shopping mall area with several stores, medical facilities and a spacious, well-landscaped garden. There is a nice office supply store and business centre with satellite internet service in the shopping mall.

The hotel is easily visible from a distance and is fast becoming a landmark. It is located on the main airport road near the central business district where several embassies are being built.

Long-stay residents, groups and corporate entities can negotiate a discount.

Rockview Hotel

Plot 789 Adetokunbo Ademola Crescent
Wuse II, Abuja
☎ 413- 6722-38; fax 413-6768; 413-6720
💻 info@rockviewhoteltd.com
🍸 🚬 🖧 ✈ 🚗 ✂ 💈 tennis (1), massage, laundry/dry cleaning

🍽 (2) Bistro Restaurant; Pool Restaurant and Bar

♪ (1 bar) Spring Bar

Business Centre

Ⓟ 🍾 🍾 🍾

Room types: Standard, Superior, Executive, Ambassador Suite
Naira rates for residents, US Dollar rates for non-residents.

    There are 106 rooms. Opened in 1996. All rooms include air conditioning, satellite TV, a refrigerator, cups/glasses. Bookings can be made via phone or fax. There are two lifts. It is extremely important to prepay for rooms here as reservations are not held for unpaid rooms.

    There is plenty of secured parking. Drivers receive security entrance tickets that must be returned upon leaving the hotel. There are three meeting rooms: one large enough for 400 (cocktail style), one for 80; and one for 25 persons. There is also a mini-mart and pastry shop on the hotel grounds. Live music is provided on the weekends. Residents can also join the fitness centre and have access to the pool and tennis courts.

    Discounts can be negotiated for long-stay residents, groups and corporate entities.

Rockview Hotel Extension
Plot 789 Adetokunbo Ademola Crescent
Wuse II, Abuja
☎   413-0168-75, 413 0041-93
Fax: 413-0176-77
💻   *info@rockviewhotelltd.com*

Opened a new extension with 211 rooms in 2004. Uses same amenities as the Rockview Hotel above.

(Abuja) Sheraton and Towers
Ladi Kwali Way
P.O. Box 14?

Around and About Abuja

	Itself a landmark, near Mosque Wuse, Abuja.
☎	523-0225-244; 523-8101-131
Fax:	523-1570-1
📱	0802-500-4000-3
💻	*reservationsabuja@sheraton.com*

🍸 ⚡ 🚻 ✈ 🚗 ✂ casino

👤 tennis (4), squash (2), massage, laundry/dry cleaning

🍽 (3) The Papillon, The Boathouse, Luigi's Italian, Obudu Grill

♪ Elephant Bar, Dazzles Night Club

Ⓟ 🛏 🛏 🛏 🛏

Room types: Standard, Classic, Junior Suite, Diplomatic Suite, Ambassador Suite, Presidential Suite

Naira rates for residents and non-residents

There are 575 rooms; guest capacity 950. One of the largest hotels in Abuja. The hotel is spread across three towers and is a major landmark in the city. The 7th, 8th and 9th floors of the towers have been renovated and now include private lounge check-in, complimentary breakfast and refreshments. 235 executive rooms have also been refurbished to a high standard. All rooms include air conditioning, satellite TV, refrigerator, coffee pot (w/cups, glasses) and a balcony. All suites and executive rooms include internet access. There are 5 lifts. Bookings can be made via phone or fax.

There is a children's park/beach area near the pool. Residents can join the club and have access to the pool, gym and sports facilities. Non-guests can also pay a fee to use the pool for the day. Several stores and services are located on the ground floor including boutiques, arts and crafts, video rental, doctor's offices and pharmacies. The KLM airline also has its office here. There is plenty of parking and security guards are placed at the gate and throughout the hotel on a 24 hour basis. Drivers receive security entrance tickets that must be returned upon leaving the hotel. Large events held at the hotel can sometimes cause congestion.

The hotel is located close to the central Mosque and in a preferred restaurant area and meeting place for Nigerian and foreigners alike. The view from the upper floors is magnificent.

An automatic $1 donation to UNICEF is added to guests' bills. It can be omitted upon request.

Discounts can be negotiated for long-stay guests.

Le Meridien Hotel
Tafawa Balewa way
Area 11, Garki
Abuja

🏢	Conference centre
☎	09-2342082, 2342818
Fax:	2341897
💻	*www.lemeridien.com*

🍸 ⚓ 🚲 ✈ 🚗 🎤

tennis (3), squash, sauna, laundry/dry cleaning
🍽 Pool restaurant, Asian, Chinese
♪ Night Club

Casino is planned

Ⓟ 🍾 🍾 🍾 🍾

Room types: Standard, Classic, Junior Suite, Diplomatic Suite, Ambassador Suite, Presidential Suite.
There are 577 rooms, with 220 ready in 2004. All rooms include air conditioning, satellite TV, and internet access.
Discounts can be negotiated for long-stay guests.

Other hotels listed with the Federal Ministry of Culture and Tourism as "Silver Standard" (defined as almost as good as the top hotels, but for less money) include:

Ibro Hotel
Michael Okpara Street,
P.O. Box 2122
Zone 5, Wuse

☎ 09 523-3200-9, 233-2009
Fax: 09 523-1263

Savannah Restaurants and Suites
Area 3 Garki
☎ 09 234-1090

"Bronze Standard" hotels are those with less than 30 rooms. They are reasonably furnished with air-conditioned rooms, telephone, local and satellite TV and a restaurant. As standards vary, the Ministry advises a personal inspection of the rooms and facilities before checking in. They are listed in alphabetical order below.

Abuja Lovebet Hotel
Plot 579 Panama Street
(Off IBB Way)
Maitama, Abuja
☎ 09 523-2102

Admiralty Suites
Plot 656 (No. 10)
Asokoro District
P.O. Box 5064, Abuja

Admiralty Suites (Wuse)
Block 155 Bissau Street
Wuse, Abuja

Airwaves Hotel
Plot 513
Wuse II, Abuja
☎ 09 523-2215

Akalaka Guest House
Plot 7 Yaounde Street
Wuse, Abuja
☎ 09 234-1297

Arcade Club Suites
Plot 68,
1st Ave by Shehu Shagari Way,
Zone AO, Central Business Area, Abuja
☎ 09 5240570-4
Fax: 09 5240575

Arewa Suites
3rd Avenue
(Off Herbert Macaulay Way)
Central Area, Abuja

Aso Guest Inn
No. 5 CBN Road
Garki II, Abuja

Banex Plaza Hotel
Plot 750 Aminu Kano Crescent
Wuse II, Abuja
☎ 09 – 413 6420-25
Fax: 09 413 6423

Capital Restaurant and Guest House
Area 10 Garki
P.O. Box 4654, Abuja

Chida Guest Inn
Plot 302 Cadastral Zone A4
Area 11 Junction
(Off Shehu Shagari Way)
P.O. Box 3461, Abuja
☎ 09 234-4714, 234-7195; 234-7332
Fax: 234-7332

Citi Cena Guest House
Plot 47 Imo Crescent
Section 1, Area 1, Garki
P.O. Box 4246, Abuja
☎ 09 234-4437; 234-5053; 234-5054

Dayspring Hotel
Plot 2382 Tuba Street
Wuse, Abuja
☎ 09 523-8714; 523-8816
Fax: 523-8817

Duhu Guest Inn
Plot 2119 Ladi Kwali Way
Wuse, Abuja
☎ 09 523-3898-9

Eddybina Hotel Ltd.
Plot 350 Cadastral Zone A8
(Behind the Ministry of Solid Mineral Development)
Wuse II, Abuja
☎ 09 523-9400

Eddy-Vic Motels Ltd.
Plot 466 Ahmadu Bello Way
(Behind Central Bank main office)
P.O. Box 308, Garki II, Abuja
☎ 09 234-5576

Elyte Guest Inn
Plot 440 Zungeru Close
(Off Jos Street)
Area 3, Garki, Abuja
☎ 09 234-0404
Fax: 234-5062; 234-0406

Empress Hotel
Near CBN Staff Quarters, Wuse II
P.O. Box 5416, Garki, Abuja
☎ 09 523-3673

Imperial Suites
Plot 226 Zone II, Wuse
P.O. Box 5113, Garki, Abuja
☎ 09 234-4264

Jalli Guest Inn
Plot 561 Owo Close
Area 10, Garki, Abuja
☎ 09 234-3950; 234-2748
Fax: 09 234-3956

Kantoma Resort
Block 2A Mambolo Street
Zone 2, Wuse, Abuja
☎ 09 523 4667-8

Kore Hotels
Plot 121 Benue Crescent
Area 1, Section 1
P.O. Box 570, Abuja
☎ 09 234-4076-77

Leisure Castle
4 Gana Street
Cadastral Zone A5, Abuja
☎ 09 523-6320-2
Fax: 09 523-6320

Maitama Guest House
Yedseram Street, Block 25
(Off IBB Way)
Maitama, Abuja
P.O. Box 6852, Wuse, Abuja
☎ 09 523-0219; 523-7514
Fax: 09 523-7518

Muna Guest Inn
Plot 816 Uyi Close
(Off Obafemi Awolowo Street)
Area 11, Garki, Abuja

National Centre for Women Development Guest House
Better Life Street
Central Area, Abuja
☎ 09 234-0961-7; 234-0607

New Rendezvous Hotel, Ltd.
Block 3, Plot 188 Makemi Street
Wuse Zone 6, Abuja
☎ 09 523-1195

Niger Link Hotel
Plot 243 Malanje Street
Zone 4, Wuse, Abuja
☎ 09 523-5291; 523-5293,
Fax: 09 523-5292

Omega Hotel
Plot 1981 Lome Street
Zone 7, Wuse, Abuja
☎ 09 523-6770-2

Optima Hotel
Plot 2005 Owo Close
Area 10, Behind Post Office
Garki, Abuja
☎ 09 234-6848-9

Oriental Hotel and Plaza, Ltd.
Plot 772 Sudan Street
P.O. Box 7130 Wuse, Abuja
☎ 09 523-6908-9

Otiti-M-Plaza
Zone A7, OAU Quarters
(Opposite CBN Quarters)
Wuse II, Abuja
P.O. Box 3344, Garki, Abuja
☎ 09 523-6044; 523-3666
Fax: 09 523-3666

Pechez Inter Hotel Ltd.
Plot 926 Aminu Kano Crescent
Cadastral Zone A7
(Near Banex Plaza)
Wuse II, Abuja

Prime Resorts Hotel
Plot 679 Ogbomosho Street
Area 8, Garki, Abuja
P.O. Box 3543, Garki, Abuja
☎ 09 234357, 236027
Fax: 09 234-3665

Retsham Lodge
Plot 808 Oyo Crescent
Area 11, Garki, Abuja
P.O. Box 2325, Garki, Abuja
☎ 09 234-0806

Rosebud Hotel
Port Harcourt Crescent
Off Ahmadu Bello Way
Garki

Rocuno Hotel Ltd.
Plot 1392 Abidjan Street
(Off Herbert Macaulay Way)
Zone 3, Wuse, Abuja
☎ 09 523-4570-1

Rodze Hotel
Wuse Zone 5, Abuja

Royalton Hotel
Plot 1970 Gongola Street
Area 2, Section 1, Garki, Abuja
☎ 09 234-4915-7
Fax: 09 234-4913

Salem Guest Inn and Restaurant
Plot 845 Yedseram Street
P.O. Box 3835
Maitama, Abuja
☎ 09 523-5999; 523-6666

Villa Hotel
Borno Street
Area 10 Garki
☎ (09) 2342228/9
Fax (09) 2347650/2
Landmark: Tantalizer
Email: *thevillahotel@hotmail.com; ifad20@hotmail.com.*

Service Apartments

Marble Court Luxury Service Apartments
Kumba Close, Off Buchanan Crescent
Off Aminu Kano Crescent
Wuse II, Abuja
🏢 Park and Shop
☎ 413-9077; fax 413-9722
📱 0803-786-7867; 0804-411-0710
💻 *marblecourt@yahoo.com*
⌨Ⓟ ♨ ♨ ♨ ♨ ✚

Six fully serviced and furnished flats. In operation since 1987. All rooms include air conditioning, satellite TV (with dedicated decoder), video CD player, closed circuit TV camera, refrigerator, full kitchen with cooker, microwave oven, plates, glasses, cutlery and coffee pot. Each flat has a cook and a steward included in the price. Bookings can be made via phone.

The doors to the rooms are bullet proof and the lock is a special cylinder lock that does not unlock from the outside once locked from the inside. The closed circuit TV system adds additional security for viewing and screening visitors. There is just enough secured parking for the residents (approximately 10 spaces). Guests need to walk a bit to get a taxi.

Located in a residential area in Wuse, the apartments are close to Park 'n' Shop. It is a three storey-building and does not have a lift or garden area.

Discounts can be negotiated for long-stay guests.

Dunes Apartments

2799 Aguiyi Ironsi Way
Maitama

☎   413-1911; 413-4052; 413-4053
Fax: 413-1910
💻   apartments@dunescenter.com.
         laundry/dry cleaning

🚗 Ⓟ 🛏 🛏 🛏 🛏 ✚

Room types: studio, two-bed, three-bedroom

Fully serviced and furnished flats. Opened in 2004. All rooms include air conditioning, satellite TV, refrigerator, microwave oven, kitchen, plates, glasses, cutlery and electric kettle. No washing machines or dryers but a laundry service is available. Limited room service is available. There is a Cherry's Plus snack shop below. A supermarket and various shops are planned. The apartments are tastefully decorated and well-maintained.

Peniel Apartments

Plot 137 IBB Way
Off Adetokunbo Ademola
Wuse II, Abuja

☎ 413-0058; 413-1066; 413-0501
Fax: 413-0062
📱 0802-322-8795
💻 penielapartments@hotmail.com

🍸 ⛓ 🖥 🚗
🍷 laundry/dry cleaning
Ⓟ 🛍🛍🛍🛍 +

Room types: One-bed, two-bed, special apartment

There are 70 fully serviced and furnished flats. In operation since September 1999. All rooms include air conditioning, satellite TV, VCR, full-sized refrigerator, full kitchen with cooker, microwave oven, plates, glasses, cutlery, electric kettle, iron and ironing board and safe deposit box. No washing machines or dryers but a laundry service is available. Separate phone connection to Nitel can be requested and paid for. While there is no restaurant, room service is available with a full menu of breakfast, lunch, snack and dinner items from which to choose. Bookings can be made via phone, fax or email. However, reservations made in person are preferred.

Located in a quiet residential area in Wuse, the apartments are tastefully decorated and well maintained. A swimming pool is currently being built. The buildings are four stories high. There is no lift. The parking lot is large. Each block of apartments has a receptionist at the entrance for security. The staff is efficient, helpful and friendly.

Discounts will be provided to long-term guests on the basis of full advance payment prior to commencement of stay and are customarily 7% for stays from 1-6 months and 14% for stays from 7-12 months. Foreign guests are expected to pay in foreign currencies unless they hold a resident permit.

Protea Hotel Apo Apartments 💕
2 Ahmadu Bello Way,
Apo, Abuja
☎ 09-231-1237-1
💻 www.proteahotels.com

CHAPTER 11

Getting Down to Business

A girl who goes to the stream early in the morning fetches clean water.

(Nigerian Proverb)

Public Holidays

Month	Date	Description
January	1	New Year's Day
2 months & 10 days after Ramadan	Announced when the moon is sighted	Id-el-Kabir
March/April	(Varies)	Good Friday Easter Monday
May	1	May Day
	May/June (Varies)	Id-el-Maulud (Birth of the Prophet)
	29	Nigerian Democracy Day
October	1	Nigerian National Day (Independence Day)
Every 11 months		Id-el Fitri (End of Ramadan – fasting)
December	25	Christmas Day
	26	Boxing Day

Business Hours

In general, business hours are Monday to Friday from 8.30 a.m. to 5.00 p.m. Government offices are open weekdays from 7.30 a.m. to 3.30 p.m. Banking hours are Monday to Thursday from 8.00 a.m. to 3.00 p.m. and Friday until 1.00 p.m. Due to the Muslim holy day on Fridays many offices and businesses reduce staff or close early on Friday afternoons.

Central Bank

Business and Investment Information

Abuja Chamber of Commerce, Industry and Agriculture
Block 12
Zone 3, Wuse
P.O. Box 86 Garki, Abuja
☎   09 523-0453
🕘 M-F: 0900–1700

The Chamber is a non-governmental organisation that disseminates information about industry, commerce, agriculture, mines, legislation, etc. affecting businesses in Nigeria. The Chamber organises an annual Trade Fair in October.

Abuja Investment and Property Development Company (AIPDC)

Plot 770 Central Business District
(Opposite the National Mosque)
P.O. Box 3302
☎: 09 523-352-284
Fax: 09 523-352-92
🕘 M-F: 0900–1700

Established by the FCDA and the Ministry of the Federal Capital Territory (MFCT) to stimulate and promote industrial, commercial and property development in FCT. It provides information to potential investors and is also itself an investor in wholly owned and joint venture projects.

Banks and Banking

There is a plethora of banks in Nigeria. Check with friends and colleagues for recommendations. There is a tendency for some smaller banks to become "distressed" and close their doors. Reputable banks will require the following documentation to establish an account:

1. 2 passport photos
2. Form of identification (e.g., national I.D. card, passport)
3. Alien card or resident permit
4. Official letter from the employer introducing the client
5. Reference from an existing account holder introducing the client
6. Tenancy agreement or utility bill establishing proof of residency.

Many banks now offer debit schemes where you can deposit a sum of money and use a "Value Card" to pay for goods.

Money Changing

The spread between the official and the black market rates has been closing. However, it is still a widespread practice to change money on the parallel market. Money changers can be found near the Sheraton Hotel on Ladi Kwali Way. Customers can drive up and conduct business from the vehicle. There are also a number of Bureaux de Change in that area that provide comparable rates. As mentioned in the "Hints to Foreigners" section, the best rate is provided for $100 bills (only the new ones with the big heads are accepted). The denomination of the notes for the Pound and the Euro do not matter and are also commonly exchanged. Over 2002-2004, the exchange rate varied from $1 = ₦125-₦157; £1 = ₦158 – 260, and E1= ₦125 – 175.

Farsman Bureau de Change
Corner Shop No 15
Addis Ababa Crescent, Off Ladi Kwali Street
☎ 09 523-3882
For Travellers Cheques

Dala Bureau de change Nig. Ltd ♥
35A, Corner Shop
Zone 4, Wuse
☎ 09 523-7037

Internet Cafes (See "Staying in Touch" section)

Courier Services

As mentioned in the "Getting Settled" section, the regular postal service is not the fastest or most reliable way to send mail. There are several courier services available in Abuja that provide faster service.

DHL
Main Office
Adetokunbo Ademola Crescent
(Near Durbar Street, across from Amigo)

☎ 09 523-8712
🕘M-F: 0800–1800
Saturday: 0900–1700

Second Location:
Nicon Hilton Hotel
(Aguiyi Ironsi and Shehu Shagari Way)
Lower Lobby Area
☎ 09 413-1339
🕘 M-F: 0800-1700
Sat: 0900-1500

UPS
Main Office
Plot 781
Awolowo Street
Area 11, Garki
☎ 09 234-7979
Fax: 09 234-7583
🕘M-F: 0800-1800
Sat: 0900-1400

Second Location
Ibro Hotel
Michael Okpara Street,
P.O. Box 2122
Zone 5, Wuse
☎ 09 523-3872
🕘M-F: 0800-1800

Office Supplies

Fil Fembs Investments Ltd.
Emab Plaza
751 Aminu Kano Crescent
Wuse II, Abuja
☎ 09 671-1051; 0802-309-7445
🕘 M-S: 0800-1800

Stationery, computer accessories, drawing materials, general supplies.

Officedeals Ltd.
Showroom —Bolingo Hotel
Bolingo Centre
Area 10
Garki, Abuja
☎ 09 671-1790-2

Large stationery shop with good selection of imported and locally produced material. Customised printing, large selection of back-to-school items, special orders for items not in stock. Free delivery in Abuja for corporate customers.

Computer/Office Equipment Repairs/IT Consulting

Centre Point Network
Prime Plaza
Plot 1012 Adetokunbo Ademola Crescent
Wuse II, Abuja
☎ 09 670-3542; 524-2346; 0803-453-7489; 0803-330-0955;
Fax: 670-3542
Email: cpn@rosecom.net

Quick and reasonable computer repair and servicing. Computer supplies, educational CDs for children, welcoming staff.

Infoware Nigeria
Kola Falayajo
No. 30, 54 Road,
Gwarinpa Estate Phase II.
☎ 0803-787-5852; 0804-611-8782
Email: infowareng@yahoo.com

Information systems analysis and development, database systems design and development, and hardware systems support.

Smartmicros
Emmanuel Nwokolo
Suite B29 Emab Plaza

751 Aminu Kano Crescent
Wuse II, Abuja
☎ 09-523-8771; 0803-786-6927; 0803-317-4710
Email: emma@smartmicros.com;smartobi@yahoo.com; emma@worldgategroup.com; www.smartmicros.com
Provides computer technical support, sales, maintenance, networking and structured cabling, software development and internet solutions.

TLG Engineering Ltd
Plot 1111
(Off Aminu Kano Crescent, Off Dar-es-Salaam Street
Beside Redeemed Church, Wuse II, Abuja
☎ 09 670-1638
Network solutions, computer systems, communications, UPS and other power systems.

Graphic Design and Website Development Companies

CNE Graphics Studio ♥
A Division of CNE Engineering Company, Ltd.
Suite 8 People's Shopping Centre
Plot 1263 Jere Street
Garki II, Abuja
☎ 09 290-0405; 0803-317-3299
Email: info@cnenigeria.com;www.cnenigeria.com
Specialises in website development. Tailor-made site configuration, email domains, music and video streaming, order forms and guest books.

MDZ Multimedia Nig. Ltd. ♥
Plot 21 Shehu Shagari Way
(near Berger Dam)
Maitama
☎ 0803-787-4835
Email: mdzmultimedia@aol.com
Full package graphic consultants and project managers from

concept, graphic design, and editing to printing. Brochures, reports, newsletters, magazines, and general publishing needs. They produced the *Abuja City Guide* fold-out map.

Printing Companies

The printing technology in Abuja is not as good as it is in Lagos or some other countries. The availability of quality paper is also limited. Often, companies will purchase paper from abroad and supply it to the printer. Also, be sure to give the company an earlier deadline than when the document is actually needed. It is also essential to proofread it several times before going to press to ensure that the final product is accurate.

Heritage Press Ltd.
636A Sultan Abubakar Way
Wuse A2, Abuja
☎ 09 523-3927, 523-5701
Fax: 09 523-3926

Roman Print Services Ltd.
☎ 09 670-1799
Did an excellent job printing "Nigeria Awaits: The 8th All Africa Games Abuja 2003" brochure.

Corporate Image Promotion Materials

Beekas Investments Ltd.
Plot 463 Lobito Crescent
Wuse II, Abuja
☎ 09 413-8725
Fax: 09 413-6537
Email: beekasinvest@hotmail.com
Business and promotional gift items. Modern factory can place logos on almost any type of item.

Photocopies/Photocopiers

There are a number of small shops providing photocopies. The best quality and most reasonably priced we have found is:

Afro-Folly Systems Nig. Ltd. ♥
(Sharp Dealership)
Abuja Office:
Suite 10 Cornershop Layout
Opposite Rockview Hotel, off Adetokunbo Ademola Crescent
Wuse II, Zone A8, Abuja
☎ 09 413-6105; 0803-319-2043; fax 523-6106
◐ M-F: 0900-1800
Email: afrofolly@yahoo.com
Photocopies (black and white and colour), lamination, office equipment, sales, service and repairs.

Furniture Rentals

Conf-Care Services Ltd. ♥
Shop 34 Neighbourhood Centre
Wuse, Zone 3
P.O. Box 2166 Abuja
☎ 09 523-0390; 523-3551
Rental and delivery of tents, chairs, tables, red carpets, decorations. Reasonably priced.

Sound/Lights

DOXA Digital
Dayo Benjamin-Laniyi, MD
Suite B3 Opposite C.A.C. Main Gate
By NNPC Housing Estate
Area 11, Garki, Abuja
☎ 09 314-0225; 234-3808; 0802-308-0341; 0803-315-4763
💻 doxadigital@yahoo.com; www.doxadigitalnigeria.com
Provides sound and light equipment for events

Film Developing

There are several shops that develop film to varying degrees of quality. The ones recommended by our readers include:

Climax Photos International
Bobo Street
Off Gana Street, after the Japanese Embassy, behind a satellite dish
Maitama, Abuja
Passports, video coverage of birthday parties and outside services.

Visual Concepts Photo and Video
Plot 15, Limpopo Street, (Opposite NDIC quarters)
Off Yedseram, off IBB way
Maitama, Abuja
☎ 09 413-5803; 090-801-415
🕘 M-F: 0800-1900
Does passports (American size as well) for ₦350, while customers wait for ₦800 when there is film in stock. Next day pickup for developing rolls of film. Portraits can also be done there.

CHAPTER 12

Staying in Touch

It is the wind that tells the trees the kind of dance to dance
(Nigerian Proverb)

Staying in touch with friends and families and up-to-date on current events is not as hard as it used to be and is improving all the time. Internet connections from home to secure sites are as safe here as anywhere in the world (see the "Staying Safe" section). Local and international newspapers, magazines and radio; as well as local and satellite television help keep residents informed on local and international events.

Internet hook-ups

There are several Internet Service Providers (ISPs) available in Abuja. More are being added monthly. Note that in addition to the monthly fee paid to the ISPs, there is also a ₦5 per minute charge from NITEL for the use of the phone line. Also, although the internet connection to secure sites is safe, care should still be maintained in sending personal information via email because the ISP will have access to the email (unless it is encrypted). Therefore, it is not recommended that personal information such as social security or credit card numbers be sent via email. The connection speed is somewhat slow and service sometimes goes out temporarily. The more reputable ISPs in operation as of December 2003 are listed below.

Rosecom.net
Plot 138B Adetokunbo Ademola Crescent
Wuse II, Abuja
☎ 09 413-1844, 413-1845
🖥 *info@rosecom.net*
www.rosecom.net

PremierNet
569 Durban Street
Off Adetokunbo Ademola Crescent
Wuse II, Abuja
☎ 09 523-1903,
Fax: 09 523-1901
🖥 *info@premiernetng.net*
www.premiernetng.net

Linkserve
569 Durban Street
Off Adetokunbo Ademola Crescent
Wuse II, Abuja
☎ 09 523-1821; 523-1826
Fax: 09 423-1826
🖥 *abv@linkserve.net*

Nitel

Possibly the best value in terms of publicly available internet connection is NITEL's (Nigerian Telecommunications Ltd.) no-frills dial-up service that operates at around 41Kbps if accessed through a main telephone exchange in Abuja. The service slows down during work days and is occasionally unavailable.

An annual subscription cost ₦39,900 of December 2003 and free application forms are available at the following location:

Internet Department
NITEL
Plot 1083, Emeka Anyaoku Street
Garki, Area 11
Abuja
☎ 09 234-8702

To process an application for a single user dial-up internet access facility, NITEL requires the following documents/items:

- A Completed "Single User Dial-Up Application Form".
- Personal identification, such as an international passport or an organisation's ID card.
- An "Application Letter" addressed to the Senior Manager (Marketing), Internet Services, Area 11, Abuja, requesting internet access and signed by the applicant.
- Two endorsed passport-sized photographs.
- (If relevant) An authority letter from the applicant to endorse a third party agent acting on their behalf. The agent should also be in possession of adequate personal identification.
- Receipt for payment of ₦39,900 into NITEL Internet Account at the Prudent Bank. Once payment is made, it is not refundable.
- A customer-designated "User Name" and "Password"

Startech Connections Ltd

Startech is a new entrant to Abuja-based internet service providers. Startech provides a range of telecommunications services and its home-oriented dial-up internet service is piggy-backed on its own telephone network. For home use, the IDD-capable telephone network and internet access are provided together and can also support fax communications. Annual, unlimited internet connectivity costs ₦48,000; connection to the phone network is just under ₦22,000; and an initial deposit of at least ₦5,000 is required. The start-up package is therefore expensive, but at ₦1.5/minute it promises the cheapest dial-up service currently available in Abuja. Although phone calls cost around 20-30% above NITEL's local tariffs, you may want to chose this option if internet browsing makes up the biggest portion of your home phone bill.

Startech Connections Ltd
Rivers State House
Opposite Ministry of Finance
☎ (09)222 1083

Satellite Internet
Now available through Multichoice Mnet connected with the DSTV satellite service. You need a DStv W4 Satellite Dish, a modem, an M-Web Satellite Card, and M-Web PC software. All of this is available from

Multichoice, Nigeria
Plot 528 Malabo, Off Aminu Kano Crescent
Wuse II, Abuja
☎   08033119743 (Tunde) .
💻   www.mwebnigeria.com

Television
Nigerian television is accountable to the Federal Government (Nigerian Television Authority) or in the case of state channels - to the states themselves. Income from advertising is provided to them as revenue. The NTA produces and broadcasts news bulletins, round-table talkshows and serials. It also broadcasts foreign programmes. The news bulletins are shown at 1900hours, 2100

hours, 2300 hours. Satellite systems are popular here. A dish and decoder are required. There are several levels of service available. See the "Getting Settled" section for more information.

Radio
Some of the radio stations are broadcast from Abuja while others come from Lagos. The stations operational as of December 2003 included:

92.3	FM Asoradio - government
92.9	Kapital - news, radio Nigeria
93.7	Rhythm FM
96.7	Cool FM
100.5	Raypower
106.5	Raypower - *rebroadcasts BBC news at the top of the hour at 0600 and 0700
	0830 - 0900 Network Africa
	1100 BBC news
	1300 News hour
	18:05 Focus on Africa
	23:00 - 00:00 - The World Today

Newspapers

International newspapers are sometimes available in the big hotels and supermarkets (Grand Square has a good selection). A few vendors are downloading, printing and supplying electronic copies of newspapers. For more information contact:
www.NewspaperDirect.com; info@NewspaperDirect.com or

Connect 2 Africa
☎ 08037277908
🖥 eanih@connect2africa.com

---

*Rebroadcasts of live foreign programmes, including the BBC, are banned at printing.

Around and About Abuja

Nigerian English-language newspapers include: *The Guardian, This Day, Daily Times, Daily Sun, New Nigerian, Nigerian Tribune, Post Express* and *Vanguard*. The newspapers are usually not available first thing in the morning as majority of them are produced in Lagos.

Post office (refer to the "Getting Settled" section)

Websites

More information can be obtained from the following sites:
http://www.abujacity.com
http://www.afrione.com
http://www.allafrica.com/Nigeria
http://www.cnenigeria.com
http://www.discovernigeria.com
http://www.e-nigeria.com
http://www.everything-nigeria.com
http://www.FOSNigeria.com - Federal government site
http://Allafrica.com/Nigeria -newspaper stories
http://www.motherlandnigeria.com
http://www.nigeria.com
http://Nigerianet.com

Libraries

There is a National Library being built at the moment but as of December 2004 it was not yet functioning. The International schools have their own school libraries. There are also a number of bookstores such as Bookmine and Integrity that run book clubs. Members can join and pay a rental fee for the books they are reading in the book club.

The British Council
Plot 2935 IBB Way
Maitama, Abuja
☺ Mon: 1200 - 2000
Tue. Thur. Fri.   1000 - 2000

Wed: 1100 - 2000
Sat: 1000 - 1630
☎ 09 413-7870-9; 413-4559-64;
Fax: 413-7883; 413-0902
💻 *abuja.info@ng.britishcouncil.org*

The Abuja office of the British Council opened in 2001 and is located at the Maitama roundabout (intersection of IBB and Shehu Shagari Ways). Membership is based upon the recommendation of an existing member. There is a fee of ₦10,000 for an annual membership. Members are entitled to attend cultural events, borrow books and periodicals. A fee is charged for the late return of materials. Free 1-hour per day internet access is also available. British Council also facilitates information exchange regarding scholarships and admission to British Universities. It also occasionally hosts Book Fairs.

Bookstores and Stationers

The larger hotels (NICON, Sheraton) have small stores that sell books, magazines, periodicals and cards. Also, the larger supermarkets (Park 'n Shop, Amigo, Bomas, Grand Square, Legends) sell new and second hand books and magazines. There is a small second hand bookshop outside Amigo next to the produce stand. The selection is limited so bring or buy at the airport. You can also order by internet or make friends with avid readers out here. Informal international book clubs are often running, ask around.

The weekly local magazines available on the streets are *Tell* and *Newswatch*.

Abuja Book Exhibition
Merit House
Aguiyi Ironsi Road, between Shehu Shagari and IBB ways,
Maitama, Abuja
This the venue of an annual, week-long, book fair which brings educational and school children age reading books up from Chelis Bookazine Limited, in Lagos.
💻 *chilis@cyberspace.net.ng*

Bookmine
Suite 04 Yasuha Plaza
Adetokunbo Ademola Crescent
(Behind AP Plaza)
Wuse II, Abuja
☎ 0804-412-9008, 0804-211-6528
✉ bookminenigeria@hotmail.com

Bookseller
City Plaza (Ground Floor)
Ahmadu Bello Way
Area 11, Garki II
Abuja

CSS Limited Bookshops
Bamenda Road
(Behind Abuja Shopping Mall – Beside All Saints School)
Wuse Zone 3, Abuja
☎ 09 523-3551
✉ cssbookshops@skannet.com.ng

Integrity Books Ltd.
C14 Emab Plaza
(Near Banex Plaza)
Wuse II, Abuja
☎ 09 424-0325; 0804-410-5882; 0803-453-6099

Reedbooks
Suite C11 Poly Plaza
Wuse II, Abuja
☎ 0804-411-2982

Spectrum Books Ltd (Publishing House)
UNIC Building
Plot 1046, Ahmadu Bello Way,
Garki II,
Abuja

☏ 09 413-9051; 0802-324-6754
✉ admin1@spectrumbooksonline.com

Officedeals Ltd
Protea Hotel
Bolingo Centre
Area 10, Garki
☏ 09 671 1790, 671 1791, 671 1792

Pen and Pages
Metro Plaza Suite F5
First Floor
Central Business District
☏ 08033201197
✉ www.penandpages.com

Cyber Cafes

Akrifa Cyber Cafe
Plot 1145 Aminu Kano Crescent
Reliance Bank Building
(Near EMAB Plaza)
Wuse II, Abuja
☏ 09 413-3645; 0803-332-7876
🕐 24 hours a day 7 days a week
✉ www.akrifa.com

VSAT connection; ₦100 per hour, international calls ₦35 per minute, international connection from residence/office ₦40 per minute, scanning, webcam, CD/DVD writer, international faxes, membership available

Highwaves Communications Ltd.
Suite 111-112 1st Floor Millennium Verdict Plaza
Plot 1059, Adetokunbo Ademola Crescent
Wuse II, Abuja

📠 09 523-4615
🕘 M-S: 0800-2000

This is a full service business centre (email, internet browsing, photocopying, faxing, printing, laminating, document binding, graphic/letterhead design etc.). It has eight computers available in a relatively spacious layout, charging ₦10 per minute (or ₦500 per hour) for internet access and ₦100 per page for received email as of December 2003.

Startech Connections
Plot 83 Ralph Shodeinde Street
Rivers State Office Complex
(Opposite Federal Ministry of Finance)
Abuja
📠 09 524-0677; 0803-408-0383
💻 *www.startechconnections.com*
VSAT connection

Westwood Business Services Ltd
Millennium Verdict Plaza
Plot 1059 Adetokunbo Ademola Crescent
Wuse 2, Abuja
📠 09 523-2370
🕘 M-S: 0800-2130
📧 *westgeneral@hotmail.com*

This is a full service business centre (email, internet browsing, colour and B&W photocopying and printing, faxing, laminating, document binding, graphic/letterhead design etc.). It has three computers available at purpose-built workstations in a close but business-like environment and internet access was a standard ₦10 per minute as of December 2003.

9-11
🖳   09 413-8441
🕒M-S: 0900-2300
Sun: 1100-2300

NetXpress
Usuma Street
Just after Zenith bank, big blue sign, building set back from road
Internet provider and cyber café
🕒24 hours a day

Big Bites in Wuse II and Asokoro also have cyber cafes and business centres.

CHAPTER 13

Staying Healthy

He who volunteers his head for the breaking of a coconut should not expect to eat from it.
(Nigerian Proverb)

Rigakafi ya fi mägàni
(Hausa Proverb)
Prevention is better than cure.

Just like any other city in the world, there are certain basic risks taken in visiting or living in Abuja. However, by staying informed and by taking necessary precautions with your health and safety, potential problems can be avoided and remedies can be quickly found. This section attempts to inform and offer possible solutions to health concerns.

Prevention

With common sense, the maintenance of up-to-date immunisations, sound hygiene and sanitary conditions, it is not difficult to stay healthy in Nigeria. This section provides suggestions on how to prevent illness. The Volunteer Service Organisation (VSO) Nigeria Health Handbook served as an important reference for the information found here. That resource also refers to a book called *Travellers Health* by Dr Richard Dawood (3rd edition).

Some key steps that can be taken to prevent illness include:

- Avoid getting run down:
  - get plenty of sleep;
  - eat a balanced diet;
  - exercise regularly;
  - live a balanced life by setting aside time for fun and personal activities;
  - recognise when something is not right and seek treatment; and
  - recover fully from illness before resuming normal activities.

- Take multivitamins and minerals. Minerals may actually be more important as fresh fruit often fills vitamin requirements.
- Keep immunisations up-to-date.
- Take anti-malarial medication (Larium, Doxycycline, or Paludrin and Chloroquine).
- Ensure good personal and food hygiene. This includes washing hands frequently, especially after handling money.
- Protect yourself against the sun by using sunscreen and hats and by avoiding long exposure to the sun (even during the harmattan). This is especially true for children. Sunglasses are also recommended.
- Wash vegetables and fruit that are not peeled with clean water and Milton™ or Permanganate™, following the product instructions.
- Use a condom **every time** for sexual intercourse.
- Boil and filter water used for drinking, brushing teeth and

cleaning vegetables and fruit.
- Drink a lot of water: two to three litres per day, up to 5 litres on hot days and when exercising.
- Keep skin as clean and dry as possible to avoid skin problems and infections (e.g., use powder, wear cotton, shower daily). Avoid nylon and synthetic fibres that stick to the skin in high heat.
- To avoid contracting bilharzia (a disease spread by freshwater snails) do not bathe, swim or walk in stagnant or slow moving water. Treated swimming pools are not contaminated.
- Avoid mosquito bites. Sleep under treated mosquito nets, use mosquito repellent and cover arms and legs (especially if out at dusk).
- A tumble dryer is recommended (if there is not space to dry clothes inside) as the rainy season makes drying clothes out of doors difficult and there is also a significant risk of Tumbu fly eggs being laid on laundry hung outdoors. Tumbu fly larva burrow under the skin and are uncomfortable to remove. Therefore, clothes dried in the open air (including underwear) should be carefully ironed in order to kill any possible parasites/ eggs that might lodge themselves under the skin.

Purifying Water

Contaminated drinking water can cause cholera, diarrhoea, dysentery, giardiasis, Hepatitis A, typhoid and worms. Therefore, it is essential that the water used for drinking, making ice, cleaning teeth and washing fruits and vegetables is clean. Although the Water Board says that the water in Abuja is potable, so many things can happen to it between its source to the tap (contaminated pipes, dirty storage tanks, etc.), that it is best to treat it before using. Boil water for 20 minutes to destroy all viruses, bacteria and cysts. After boiling, use a water filter to clarify and remove larger particles. Filtering alone is not sufficient to make water drinkable. Be sure to check the water filter regularly, clean the candles weekly and replace them regularly. Remember to store filtered and boiled water in clean bottles with lids.

Water Irofocatopm tablets (Puritabs or Aquatabs), when used

according to the manufacturers directions, make water safe for drinking. The taste of the water will not be pleasing but it will be potable and can be used for emergencies when travelling.

Alum is a chemical that settles out inorganic matter from dirty water and makes dirty water look clean. It is sold in the markets and is useful for cleaning water that will be used for washing clothes, etc. but does not make the water potable. The long-term effects of drinking water to which alum has been added are not clear, so it is best not to add it to the water you plan to drink either before or after boiling it.

Purchasing bottled water in the stores is another option. Most of the locally produced bottled water has been through a process of disinfection called "reverse osmosis."

Food Hygiene

The general rule of thumb is:

"Boil it, peel it, wash it or forget it"

Fruit such as bananas, oranges and mangoes with thick skin provide natural protection against bacteria and parasites for the "meat" inside. Therefore they do not need to be washed in a disinfectant solution prior to eating. Make sure, however, that your knife and hands are clean and dry when peeling and eating to avoid contamination.

Other fruits and vegetables need to be cleaned in a disinfectant/sterilising solution. Products specifically made for this purpose can be bought in the grocery stores, e.g., Milton™. If you use chlorine bleach you should use 15 ml of bleach to 4 pints disinfected water. The food should be left in the solution for 30 minutes. Although rinsing after soaking is not necessary, if you still choose to rinse make sure you do not use tap water. Rinsing should be done with disinfected, sterile water. Once cleaned with this method, fruits and vegetables can be eaten raw. Alternately, vegetables can be boiled and then eaten.

Kitchen Hints

Hygiene in the kitchen is extremely important. Everyone who uses the kitchen should be well trained on kitchen hygiene.

- Clean the countertops, ceramic tile and the floor daily with a disinfectant solution, such as Dettol soap or a solution made with bleach.
- Anyone working in the kitchen (including yourself) should wash their hands thoroughly with a disinfectant soap and use a brush to clean under their nails.
- Clean the refrigerator often (white vinegar is good for this).
- Use plastic containers with tops for keeping food in your refrigerator.
- If you have an air-conditioner inside the room be sure to have the filter cleaned every month (it is good to do this throughout the rest of your house every three months).

Immunisations

As mentioned in the "Hints to Foreigners", persons living in Nigeria should have the following immunisations: Hepatitis A, Hepatitis B, Meningitis A and C, Polio, Rabies, Tetanus, Typhoid and Diptheria, Yellow Fever and BCG (against TB).

Be sure to keep your immunisations up-to-date during your stay. Current booster requirements are noted below, but be sure to check with whatever health professional you choose to make sure the prevailing wisdom has not changed.

The table given here is a guideline for most common booster vaccines. Please check with your doctor as some brands may not follow the norm.

Vaccine	Booster Dose
Hepatitis A	Every 10 years
Hepatitis B*	Every 5 years
Meningitis	Every 3 years
Polio	Every 10 years
Rabies*	Every 2 years

* Be sure to follow closely the initial recommended course of treatment as in some cases second and third doses are needed for initial immunity. The Cholera vaccine is no longer recommended.

Tetanus	Every 10 years
Typhoid	Every 3 years
Yellow Fever	Every 10 years

Evacuation Insurance

If possible and feasible, it is wise to purchase evacuation insurance that will cover an emergency medical situation that cannot be properly treated in the country. The most popular companies used for this service are SOS International and BUPA.

International SOS Assistance (UK) Ltd.
6th Floor, Landmark House
Hammersmith Bridge Road
London, UK W6 9DP
Admin phone:+44 (0)20 8762 8000
Alarm phone: +44 (0)20 8762 8008
www.internationalsos.com

BUPA International Russell Mews
Brighton,
UK
BN1 2NR
☎   +44 (0)1273 323563
Fax: +44(0)1273 820517

Expat Health Centre
+1 800 234 1862, +1 703 299 6001
info@worldtravelcentre.com

When You Are Ill

You should seek medical advice immediately if:

- You have a high fever [38.5 °C (101.3 °F) or more]
- The illness is not getting better after four days or it seems to

get better but then returns a few days later
- The treatment tried has not made the symptoms get better or they are getting worse while on the treatment
- You have diarrhoea for more than 24 hours or the diarrhoea has blood in it
- If a cough lasts for more than a week and does not improve
- You have severe abdominal pain
- You are unsure or are worried as to what is happening to you.

These are general guidelines. But the more specific prevention, symptoms and treatment of some of the most prominent illnesses in Nigeria are outlined below.

Health Hazards

The most common ailments affecting foreigners and local nationals are malaria and typhoid fever. Malaria is one of the main causes of death in Nigeria and so should be taken seriously. Other health hazards include: diarrhoea; sexually transmitted diseases; skin problems; upper respiratory infections; and worms. Below (in alphabetical order), several of the most serious illnesses and conditions are discussed in terms of prevention, symptoms and treatment.

Bilharzia (Schistosomiasis)

This disease is spread by freshwater snails that live in muddy, stagnant or slow moving water.

Prevention: Avoid swimming, walking or wading in slow moving or stagnant water (streams, lakes, rivers).

Symptoms: Blood in the urine or stools.

Seek Medical Advise Quickly, If:
You have these symptoms and have had skin contact with questionable water.

Cholera

Cholera often comes in epidemics, but there can also be regional outbreaks. It is often contracted through drinking or ingesting contaminated water.

Prevention: Good hygiene and sanitation.

Symptoms: Severe diarrhoea with stools that look like "rice-water," vomiting and severe dehydration.

Treatment: Oral re-hydration fluids. Loss of body fluids can be very rapid. Cholera can be fatal within 9 hours.

Seek Medical Advise Quickly If:
You think you have this condition. Get to the hospital urgently for antibiotic treatment and intravenous fluids (drips). Be sure to take someone with you who can help attend to you and verify the cleanliness of the needles used for the IV (Intravenous fluid drip).

Dehydration

The lack of fluids in the body. This condition can be life-threatening.

Prevention: Drink plenty of fluids (adults usually need a minimum of 2-3 litres per day; 3-5 litres are needed on extremely hot days or after lots of exercise or to replace fluids lost due to fever or diarrhoea.)

Avoid drinking alcohol as it stimulates urination and worsens dehydration.

Avoid walking in the hot sun.

Symptoms: Low output of dark yellow urine. Dehydration can also be accompanied by headache, dizziness, lethargy, cramps, dry mouth and weakness.

In serious cases there will be no urine output, inelastic skin and vomiting/nausea.

	Women may have burning, painful urination. They may suspect a urine infection (cystitis) but the symptoms are actually due to the concentrated urine, which irritates the bladder.
Treatment:	Drink three-five litres of fluids daily, preferably Oral Re-hydration Solution (ORS). ORS is a mixture of water, salt and sugar. You can use ORS sachets or make your own solution (see below).
	Also eat/drink home fluids such as: soups, rice water and fruit juices. Lemon/lime mineral (Sprite, 7-up, etc.) is also a good alternative when travelling especially if a little salt is added.

Seek Medical Advise Quickly If:
    The condition does not improve after taking ORS.

Diarrhoea

Most long-term visitors will get this at some point. Caused by ingested bacteria, it usually lasts between one and three days and does not require antibiotics or anti-diarrhoea medicine such as Imodium. Anti-diarrhoea medicine can actually prolong the diarrhoea because the bacteria is not allowed to pass through the system.

Prevention:	Can be avoided by good nutrition, sanitation and hygiene, including the proper preparation, cooking and storage of food and water.
Symptoms:	Frequent loose or watery stools, abdominal distension and pain, loss of appetite, nausea or vomiting.
Treatment:	Drink a glass of ORS (Oral Re-hydration Solution — see below) every time a watery stool is passed or vomiting occurs. Eat bland foods the first couple of days (e.g., rice, bananas, bread, boiled or scrambled eggs).

Seek Medical Advice If:
The diarrhoea lasts more than three days; it is recurring frequently or it is accompanied by a fever that has lasted more than two days; there is blood or mucus in the stool; you are unable to keep enough fluids in your body to prevent dehydration; or you have relatively mild diarrhoea that becomes chronic or keeps relapsing.

Oral Re-hydration Solution (ORS)
Prepare according to the directions on the sachet or make it yourself following the directions for a Sugar-Salt Solution (SSS) below.

Sugar-Salt Solution (SSS)
For 1 glass (250 ml):
Mix 2 level teaspoons of SUGAR
Pinch of SALT in
1 glass of clean WATER

For 1 litre:
Mix 8 level teaspoons of SUGAR with 1 level teaspoon of SALT in 1 litre (3 mineral bottles) of clean WATER.

Ensure that the SSS is not stored longer than 24 hours. Keep it covered and in a cool place. Recipes for SSS differ. The most important thing is that the solution should **not taste saltier than tears.**

Dysentery

Prevention: As for diarrhoea.
Symptoms: There are two types of dysentery:
Amoebic dysentery causes diarrhoea with mucus and blood. There are abdominal cramps, nausea and sometimes vomiting. It may not be severe but can relapse and become chronic.
Bacterial dysentery causes diarrhoea with blood and can be accompanied by fever.

Treatment: Drink a glass of ORS every time a watery stool is passed or vomiting occurs. Eat bland foods the first couple of days (e.g., rice, bananas, bread, boiled or scrambled eggs).

Seek Medical Advice If:
You have the symptoms noted above. The doctor will conduct a stool test and prescribe antibiotic treatment. A test is necessary since amoebic dysentery and bacterial dysentery require different drugs.

Fever

Normal body temperature is between 36.5-37.5 °C (37°C is 98.6°F). A fever is an abnormal elevation in body temperature. A high fever (39-42°C or 102-108°F) is a dangerous situation and needs medical attention. Likewise, a temperature of 35°C (95° F) is too low and should also be evaluated. A fever can be the result of a virus (e.g., influenza), bacteria (dysentery), fungi, protozoa (giardiasis), dehydration, disease (typhoid fever, hepatitis A, malaria) or illness (pneumonia). The most important of these for seeking immediate medical treatment is malaria.

Prevention: Can be avoided by up-to-date immunisations, malaria prevention, good nutrition, sanitation and hygiene.

Symptoms: Feeling warm to the touch, weakness, shivers.

Treatment: Determine the cause of the fever and have it properly treated. Cool the body with cool water, a wet cloth or a fan (even if you already feel cool). Take aspirin or paracetamol (1 or 2 tablets every 4 to 6 hours) to lower the fever. (Do not take aspirin if you are asthmatic or get indigestion.) Drink plenty of fluids (especially if the cause of the fever is dehydration).

Seek Medical Advice If:
>See a doctor immediately if you suspect malaria. If you do not suspect malaria, but the fever does not clear up in 48 hours also seek medical advice.

Giardiasis
Contaminated food and water can cause this faecal-oral illness. This protozoa infection of the intestines is common amongst travellers, due to inadequate hygiene and sanitation.

Prevention: See diarrhoea.

Symptoms: Yellow, bad smelling and frothy (bubbly) diarrhoea. No mucus or blood. Chronic or intermittent diarrhoea. Swollen belly with gas, mild intestinal cramps and flatulence. Severe cases can result in weight loss, weakness, anaemia and food allergies.

Treatment: Good nutrition: giardia infections sometimes clear up by themselves.

Seek Medical Advice If:
>The condition does not improve or becomes worse. A stool examination confirms existence of the protozoa and appropriate treatment will be prescribed.

Hepatitis
Hepatitis is an infection or inflammation of the liver that usually results in the yellowing of the skin and eyes (jaundice). There are many causes of hepatitis including excessive alcohol intake, bacteria, parasites, viruses (Hepatitis A), sexual intercourse with a contaminated person or contact with contaminated blood (Hepatitis B). The Hepatitis A virus is usually spread via food or water that has been contaminated with infected faeces.

Prevention: Immunisations, good sanitation and hygiene, boiling and filtering drinking water, responsible alcohol intake, safe sexual practises (e.g., using a condom

every time) and avoiding blood transfusion and contaminated needles/razors.

Symptoms: Low-grade fever, loss of appetite, weakness, nausea, vomiting and jaundice.

Seek Medical Advice If: You have the symptoms noted above. The doctor will confirm the diagnosis but there is no drug treatment for hepatitis.

Treatment: Antibiotics are not effective against viruses and they can potentially harm the liver in its already weakened state. Drink plenty of fluids and eat a healthy, low fat diet. Rest as much as possible; recovery can take a long time. Avoid alcohol for at least six months after fully recovering.

Malaria

As mentioned earlier, malaria is one of the main causes of death in Nigeria. It is caused by a parasite called Plasmodium and is spread through the bite of an infected female *Anopheles* mosquito. Here we are exposed to mainly two different species of this parasite. The most dangerous and most common in Nigeria is *Plasmodium falciparum*. It causes malignant malaria. If left untreated plasmodium falciparum infection can progress to cerebral malaria and attack the brain and cause severe headache, convulsions, confusion, reduced level of consciousness and death. *Plasmodium vivax* causes benign malaria which, while extremely unpleasant, is not fatal.

Prevention: Anti-malaria medication is such a controversial and important topic that we hesitate to provide advice here. Each person needs to fully research the options and recommendations and come to his/her own conclusions. The in-house doctors servicing the foreign missions here strongly recommend the use of anti-malaria pills. The perfect drug for malaria prophylactic has not yet been found and there are several different options. Consult medical resources such as your local doctors, books, literature and the web prior to deciding which is best for you. They each have different advantages, disadvantages and side effects. The options most commonly recommended are: mefloquine (Lariam), doxycycline, proguanil (Paludrine) plus chloroquine (Nivaquine), or chloroquine alone.

Physical Precautions. Mosquitoes, in general, usually bite at dusk and dawn. Mosquito bites can cause diseases, including: Malaria, Dengue Fever and Yellow Fever. Physical forms of protection against mosquito bites are extremely important.

Cover-up as much as possible. Wear long sleeved shirts and long trousers or dresses. Light coloured clothing is preferred as mosquitoes are attracted to dark clothing. Mosquitoes are also attracted by dirt and sweat so maintaining good personal hygiene is essential.

Use mosquito repellents, especially when outside. The chemical diethyltoluamide or "DEET" is the most common and effective active ingredient (usually in concentrations of 30%) found in mosquito repellents. Be sure to read the directions for proper usage. There are also alternatives for those sensitive to DEET, such as Mosiguard Naturel, a eucalyptus-based product and essential lemon grass oil. Ankle bracelets and wrist-bands impregnated with DEET are also sold at travel shops/clinics overseas. For extra protection, it is also possible to soak cotton clothing in DEET. Knock-down sprays and mosquito coils can also be helpful.

Use a bed net. Remember to take a net with you

when you travel. You can also impregnate the net with Permethrin, which kills mosquitoes that come into contact with the net. Nets should be re-impregnated after washing and/or every six months. Be sure that the net is properly tucked in and that any tears are mended quickly.

Screen doors and windows with fine mesh netting. The netting can also be impregnated with insecticide.

Symptoms: — Fever (can be intermittent or continuous)
— Sweating
— Rigour (shivering)
— Headaches
These may also be accompanied by:
— Diarrhoea
— Abdominal pain
— Jaundice

Seek Medical Advice If:
Because of the severity of malaria, you have any of the symptoms above. Seek medical advice from a reputable lab immediately. Malaria is diagnosed by a finger prick test. A drop of blood is examined under a microscope and the parasites are seen in the red blood cells. There are simple tests available where blood from a finger prick is put on a strip and line indicators show in minutes if malaria is present.

Even though a blood slide test may be negative, an individual could still have malaria and treatment may be recommended if symptoms persist.

Treatment: As with the malaria prophylactics, there are different advantages, disadvantages, allergies and side effects to the drugs used for the treatment of malaria. Be sure to question the prescribing doctor fully about them prior to taking treatment.

Meningococcal Meningitis

This is a serious bacterial infection that causes swelling of the outer part of the brain and the spinal cord. It is passed through the inhalation of bacteria when an infected person sneezes or coughs. It usually occurs in epidemics in crowded areas and is more common in the North of Nigeria during the dry season.

Prevention: Immunisation and ensuring adequate ventilation in crowded areas.

Symptoms: Severe headache and stiff neck. Sensitivity to light, fever, rashes, vomiting.

Seek Medical Advice If:
You have the symptoms noted above.

Treatment: Antibiotic injection will be needed immediately.

Rabies

This is a fatal disease that must be taken seriously. It is spread through the saliva of an infected mammal when it bites, scratches or licks on a wound. Once such contact has been made, it is essential for the infected person to seek treatment immediately. Once the symptoms appear on the person, the disease is fatal.

Prevention: Dogs are the most common transmitters of the disease to humans. Stay clear of stray dogs. Ensure that your own animal is immunised every year. Make sure your own immunisation is up to date — it will give you more time (one-two days) to get treatment.

Symptoms: Pain and tingling in the area of the bite, difficulty in breathing and swallowing, headache, fever, paralysis. At that point the patient usually falls into a coma and dies.

Seek Medical Advice If:
You have been bitten, scratched or your wound was licked by a mammal you do not know. Even if a dog has "just" licked a small wound on you (e.g., cut or scratch), do not wait for the symptoms to appear!

Treatment: Wash the wound thoroughly with plenty of soap and running water for 5-10 minutes. Apply an antiseptic agent (e.g., iodine) and leave the wound open. Seek medical attention immediately. You will need two booster shots if you are fully vaccinated. If you are not, you may need rabies antiserum, six injections, an anti-tetanus booster and possibly antibiotics.

Keep the animal under observation for 10 days. If it starts behaving strangely (restless, sad or aggressive) or dislikes water, the animal needs to be destroyed immediately.

Sexually Transmitted Diseases, including AIDS

Sexually Transmitted Diseases (STDs) include a wide range of infections such as herpes, Pelvic Inflammatory Disease (PID), gonorrhoea, Hepatitis B, syphilis and chancroids and HIV/AIDS. Anyone who has unprotected sexual intercourse is at risk.

HIV-AIDS in Nigeria

AIDS is a fatal disease for which there is no cure. It is a worldwide problem and is presently growing in Nigeria. Some cultural beliefs and practices (men having several wives, the belief that sperm makes women healthy, and using a condom means you don't trust someone) make it difficult to stop the spread of the disease.

The first AIDS case was reported in Nigeria in 1986 and the epidemic has rapidly grown since then. The adult HIV prevalence has increased from 1.8% in 1991 through 4.5% in 1996 to 5.8% in

2001. Estimates using the 2001 HIV/Syphilis sero-prevalence sentinel survey among women attending ante-natal clinics indicates that more than 3.5 million Nigerians aged 15-49 years may be infected with the virus. The epidemic in Nigeria has extended beyond the commonly classified high-risk groups and is now common in the general population.

A new survey is due out in February 2004 and is expected to show that the prevalence has risen to about 7% of the adult population. In Nigeria, transmission is mainly through unprotected heterosexual sex and some through transfusion of infected blood. The rates of infection vary significantly between states and between population groups. Sex workers, truck drivers and the armed forces are all considered to be at highest risk level of contracting HIV. Also at-risk, however, are married women who are unable to demand that their husbands use condoms. Young people, unaware of the risks of unprotected sex are adding to the statistics at an alarming rate.

There is considerable stigma which people living with HIV-AIDS (PLWHAs) face in their day-to-day lives, making citizens reluctant to seek help and to find out their sero-status. Negative messages about condom use and claims of miracle cures from some religious organisations add to the difficulty of getting practical prevention messages across to the people who need the information.

The National Action Committee on AIDS (NACA) is the multi-sectoral body under the President's office that is leading the campaign against HIV-AIDS.

You won't notice HIV-AIDS. People living with HIV can look and feel healthy for years and most do not know they have it. This is why it spreads so silently and dangerously.

You won't contract HIV unless you have unprotected sex with an infected person, receive unscreened infected blood, share a dirty needle, razor or other items that contain infected body fluids. Even these will not automatically infect you, but might. If you employ a person with HIV, there is no risk to you or your family and it is good to keep PLWHAs employed as they need more income to pay for good food and treatment. As an employer, you should not demand an HIV test from your employees, but you can tell them about HIV-

AIDS and offer to cover the cost of any counselling, tests and treatment of opportunistic infections if requested.

If a person tests positive, they need plenty of moral support. They should be allowed to continue with their job as long as they can do it. If they are becoming weak and very ill and are unable to take the anti retroviral treatment, then you should consider ways in which you can support this person to lead a comfortable life.

Be aware that once Anti retroviral drugs are started they **must be** continued for life.

Prevention: Celibacy. Minimise the number of sexual partners, practise "safe sex" by ALWAYS using a condom EVERY TIME you have sex whether it is with an "occasional" or "permanent" partner. Avoid oil-based lubricants that can weaken the condom or cause it to slip off, avoid blood transfusions, broken skin infections, skin piercing and the sharing of needles and razors. Make sure that any injection you receive is given from an auto-destruct syringe.

Symptoms: *For HIV/AIDs:*
There are no initial symptoms. If you have engaged in any risky behaviour, chances are high for infection. Testing and counselling are recommended.
For STDs:
Sometimes there are no symptoms. Penile discharge in males or vaginal discharge in females sometimes accompanied by itching. These symptoms may appear for a short time only to come back more seriously after a period of time if not treated.

Seek Medical Advice If:
For HIV/AIDS, if you have been sexually assaulted or exposed to a needle stick injury. Ask for Post Exposure Prophylaxis (PEP) if you are worried that you might have been exposed to HIV. This is the antiretroviral treatment given for a short period

and can only be given up to 72 hours after exposure. Standards of testing, confidentiality and counselling may vary, so be sure to use a trusted resource. Testing, counselling and treatment are available at various medical facilities, such as:

National Hospital
Plot 132 Central District
P.O. Box 425
Garki, Abuja
☎ 09 234-2686-9, 2341328, 234 7241, 234 2686-9

Center for the Right to Health
Plot 718, Minna Street
Off Muhammadu Buhari Way,
Area 8, Garki, Abuja
☎ 09 234 6657
☎ 0823199192
Email: crhaids@yahoo.com

National Network of People Living with HIV/AIDS
Block 2, Lafia Close
Area 8, Garki
☎ 08033061278, 6710755, 413 5944
Dr Pat Matemilola.

Society for Positive Action Against AIDS
Suite 12, DMK House Plot 735
Kadoe Street, Off Aminu Kano Crescent
Wuse II
☎ 4132462, 8500989, 08037004937
Email: femi tomi@yahoo.com.

Organisation of Positive Productivity
Durumi Phase II
Garki, Abuja
☎ 08034533760, 08035871859
Email: oppnigeria!@yahoo.com

Catholic Action Committee on AIDS
Block 8, Flat 2
Catholic Secretariat
Area 2, Garki

Women Matters Initiatives
c/o State House Clinic
Abuja

> For STDs, seek medical attention immediately if you have symptoms to prevent serious complications such as sterility in women and urethral stricture in men.

Tuberculosis

Tuberculosis (TB) is infectious and can be passed from the infected person to others from droplets in the air. It is common to request a test for TB before employing a new person.

Symptoms: Cough, night sweats, loss of weight.

Seek Medical Advice If:
   You have the symptoms noted above.

Typhoid

Typhoid or typhoid fever is a bacterial infection that is fairly common in Nigeria. Contaminated food and water can cause typhoid and it often comes in epidemics. It is over-diagnosed in foreigners who have been vaccinated and, therefore, test positive for the Widal-test which measures anti-bodies in the blood.

Prevention: Immunisations, good sanitation and hygiene.

Symptoms: Flu and cold symptoms: headache, sore throat, dry cough. A fever that increases every day while the pulse gets slower (about 80 beats/min). Hot and dry skin. Sometimes there might be abdominal discomfort accompanied by bloody diarrhoea or constipation and vomiting. If it progresses there will be a high fever, a rash on the body, trembling, delirium, weakness, weight-loss and dehydration.

Seek Medical Advice If:
You have the symptoms noted above. As mentioned, the Widal test is misleading for everyone who has been vaccinated against typhoid because they have the typhoid bacillus antibodies present in their blood. The only way to diagnose the disease in vaccinated patients is to make a culture (i.e. to grow bacteria) of blood, stool and urine.

Treatment: Seek medical advice for appropriate drug treatment. Cool the body and take paracetamol to lower the fever, drink plenty of fluids, get good nutrition and rest, and practice good hygiene to prevent spreading the disease to others.

Worms

Worms are parasites that enter the body by drinking water or eating food that is contaminated by faeces, through dirty hands or flies. Hookworms enter the body via the feet. Tapeworms develop when eating infected meat (especially pork) that is not thoroughly cooked. Guineaworms are contracted from dirty drinking water.

Prevention: Always drink clean water. Use good hygiene by thoroughly washing your hands and covering food and drink to protect them from flies. Wear shoes when walking outside (hookworm). Some residents de-worm themselves every six months or so with levamisole (Ketrax) available from the pharmacist.

Symptoms: The main symptom is weakness. There can also be abdominal discomfort and diarrhoea (whipworm). One symptom for roundworm is also a cough. Threadworms cause itching at the anus.

Seek Medical Advice If:
You have the symptoms noted above. A stool sample will be taken to confirm the diagnosis.

Treatment: Medical tests are necessary to determine which drugs will best treat the different types of worms. Good nutrition, especially food rich in iron will also help to rebuild strength.

Seeking Medical Advice

Doctors in Nigeria are not used to being questioned about the diagnosis they are making or their prescribed course of treatment. They may, in fact, become offended when you do so. Yet you have the right to understand clearly what is going on with your body Below are some suggestions as to how to handle that situation.

- Tell the doctor you would like this information for your health record and as a reference for other health providers. Ask him to write down the diagnosis, the tests that were completed. the names of the drugs prescribed and their dosage. Ask him to specifically identify those that need to be taken as a complete dosage.
- As you may want to check with other medical sources before starting the course of treatment (e.g., *Travellers Health*, other doctors), tell the doctor that you do not need to purchase them from the in-house pharmacy, that you want to check and see what you might have at home first. This will give you time to double check the recommendations without offending the doctor.
- If you are prescribed an injection, ask the doctor for an alternative medicine in tablet form.

Drugs

Over-prescribing and Full Course
Most diseases can be treated with one or two drugs, but often you

are likely to be prescribed several more. This is partly due to the culture, which believes that the more drugs taken, the better. There is no benefit in taking more drugs than needed and the risks of damaging side-effects is increased. If you believe you have been over-prescribed for an illness, get a second opinion or check *Travellers Health* or other medical resources. Likewise, there is a tendency to prescribe drugs for a full course when they may not be needed. Be sure to ask your doctor which drugs need to be taken as a course (usually antibiotics, anaemia medication, anti-inflammatory drugs, etc.) and which ones can be taken only when necessary.

Injections

In Nigeria, it is believed that injections are much stronger and work much faster than tablets. Therefore, it is the preferred route of drug administration. However, consider the opposing view that injections can be more dangerous for several reasons. They can produce infections and abscesses, serious allergic reactions and the side-effects are likely to be more serious when given by injection. In addition, there is the slight chance of HIV infection, if needles are re-used. Therefore, it is best to take the medicine in tablet form as long as you are able to keep the tablets down.

Fake Drugs

Estimates of the amount of fake drugs on the market in Nigeria vary between 40-90%. It is difficult to spot fake drugs because they often claim to have been made in the U.S or the U.K. Buy drugs in individual blister packs with an outer cardboard container. Look for good quality packaging and the brand names of well known companies like Glaxo-Smith-Kline, May & Baker, Bayer, Pfizer, etc. If you buy drugs locally, make sure they are stamped "approved by NAFDAC" on the print of the packaging. Do not purchase the type of drugs counted out from a bulk container. Ask the pharmacist for the "sachet kind" not the "counting ones".

Maternity Facilities

Most foreigners return to their home countries to give birth. Antenatal care including preparation and relaxation sessions and post-natal care can be available in Nigeria for non-complicated births.

Hospitals and Medical Clinics: In Case of Emergency

The Nigerian Department of Health and Social Services runs Health Centres in three districts, clinics for neighbourhoods and dispensaries for rural areas. While many of the doctors may be well trained, the facilities often lack equipment and medicines. It is advisable to have medical evacuation insurance. In case of "life/death" emergency situations, foreigners can get in contact with their Embassies as some of them have their own medical clinics, which are normally strictly for use by employees but may be used to assist citizens of their countries in critical situations.

The following types of medical facilities are found in Nigeria:
- Federal Hospitals - found in the larger cities with good facilities, and fee paying. They are specialist hospitals and usually require a referral letter.
- General Hospitals – In big towns. Free service.
- Comprehensive Health Centre.
- Primary Health Centre.
- Private Clinic. Various levels of trained, competent staff. Fee paying.
- Religious-based "Mission" medical facilities. Usually pretty well equipped. Basic fees charged.

Here we have to once again provide a big disclaimer for the information found in this section. Medical assistance is an extremely personal matter. One person may find a doctor and facility to meet his/her needs while someone else may find it grossly inadequate. The same doctor may make a proper diagnosis for one patient and may misdiagnose another.

The biggest and best government-run hospital near Abuja is

Gwagwalada Specialist Hospital with 300 bed spaces and modern facilities for surgery and research. As a Federal Specialist Hospital, it charges fees and patients usually need a referral.

The hospitals and facilities listed below have been used by nationals and foreigners and are included on the United Nations list of clinics for their staff in Abuja or on VSO's list of approved medical facilities for their volunteers. They are private hospitals for which there is an initial registration fee. Consultation fees are decided at the discretion of the physician. Most of the hospitals/clinics have their own pharmacies and medical laboratories capable of providing urinalysis, biochemistry, haematology/serology and ultrasound services.

National Hospital ♥

Dr D. Etti, Chief Medical Director
Plot 132 Central District
P O Box 425
Garki, Abuja
☎09 234-2686-9, 234 1244, 2341328, 234 7241, 234 2686-9
General Practitioner Prof Abengowe ♥

Cardiologist Prof Abengowe (residence Kaduna – visits Abuja Thursdays)
Dr. (Mrs.) Osunkwo ♥
Paediatrics Dr Mrs. P. Ahmed ♥
HIV/AIDS   Dr Antei
Gynaecology   Dr Wokocha
Physiotherapist   Mrs O.A. Ladipo
Ophthalmologist   Dr E. A. Akabe
Laboratory ♥

Abuja Clinics

Location 1 — Garki:
Plot 1014
Area 3, Garki
☎09 234-2199; 234-2299; 523-1843

Location 2 — Maitama:
Dr Patrick Onyechi, Consultant Surgeon
(Trained in Europe and the United States)
Plot 1261 Amazon Street
Maitama, Abuja
☎ 09 413-7020-6, ext.6000
☎ 0804-418-4570

General Practitioner	Dr Onyechi ♥
Surgery	Dr Onyechi
Paediatrician	Dr A.U. Awogu
ENT	Dr Ogbuje
Gynaecologist	Dr C. Ugonna
Orthopaedic & Trauma	Dr F Maduekwe

Zankli Medical Centre
Dr Lovett Lawson, Medical Director
Plot 1021 B5 Shehu Yar'Adua Way
Opposite Federal Ministry of Works
Utako District
P O Box 7745, Abuja
☎ 09 523-6854; 563-9570; 523-9570; 670-7273-5
☎ 0803-701-2487

General Practitioner	Dr Lovett Lawson	📱 0803-701-2487
ENT	Dr Okujaiye	📱 0803 311 3738
Paediatrics	Dr Mrs F. Lawson ♥	
	Dr Ategbole	
Dental	Dr Badi Amer	
Orthopaedic	Dr P. Deshi	
Laboratory ♥		

Al-Hassan Hospital
Plot 2181 IBB Way
Wuse, Zone 4
☎ 09 523-5502-4

Amana Medical Centre, Abuja
    Dr E.C. Menakaya, Medical Director
    Plot 819 Uyo Close
    Garki Area 11, Abuja
☎ 09 234-9511; fax 234-8567

Arewa Specialist Hospital and Diagnostic Centre
    Dr F.A. Fashina, Medical Director ♥
(Trained at George Washington University, Washington D.C. — Obstetrics and Gynaecology with team of different consultants)
This is a temporary address and location
#25 Awka Crescent
Off Akure Street
Gwarinpa War College Junction
☎   09 671-5493
📱   0804-418-2221
Email:arewahmo@yahoo.com; drfash@yahoo.com

General Practitioner	Dr F. A. Fashina
Gynaecology	Dr F. A. Fashina ♥
Obstetrics	Dr F. A. Fashina
Pulmonologist	Dr A. Dosumu

Bio-Royal Hospital & Maternity Ltd.
    Dr Omo Odafen, Medical Director
    Plot 190 Okene/Jebba Close
    Area 2, Section 2 Garki
    P.O. Box 6450, Garki, Abuja
☎ 09 234-2440; fax 234-2458

Fereprod Medical Centre
    Dr F.F. Achem
    (Obstetrics and Gynaecology with team of different consultants)
    Uke Crescent
    Off Ahmadu Bello Way
    Garki 2, Abuja
☎ 09 314-2559

General Practitioner   Dr F.F. Achem
Orthopaedician   Dr Salawu 📱 0803 34 4451
Gynaecologist   Dr F.F. Achem
Obstetrician   Dr F.F. Achem
Laboratory

Nisa Premier Hospital
   Dr Ibrahim Wada
   (Obstetrics and Gynaecology with a team of different consultants)
   618 Alex Ekwueme Way
   Jabi, Abuja
☎ 09 413-3684; 521-2322-4; 521-0247
General Practitioner   Dr Ibrahim Wada
Obstetrician   Dr Ibrahim Wada
Gynaecologist   Dr Ibrahim Wada
Surgeon   Dr Miner

Pyramid Medical Centre
   Dr (Mrs.) Nadia Nasidi, Medical Director ♥
   Plot 1438 Nnamdi Azikiwe Express Way
   Cadastral Zone A3
   Garki, Abuja
☎ 09 670-1666; 413-8931
📱 0803-313-9975

St Francois Medical Centre
   Plot 501 Bangui Street
   Wuse II, Abuja
☎ 09 523-6282
Paediatrician Dr (Mrs) Semaan ♥
Laboratory

Dental Care

Smile Dental Practice ♥
   Dr D.S. Labo, Dental Surgeon
   (Trained in the United Kingdom)

Plot 1201 Yakubu Gowon Way
Asokoro, Abuja
☎ 09 314-2670 [manned 24 hours a day for emergencies]
🕘 M-F: 0900 – 1700
Sat: 1000 – 1500

Largent Dental Clinic
Nicon Hilton Hotel
(Aguiyi Ironsi and Shehu Shagari Way)
Floor 02
☎ 09-413-1811 ext. 6417; 413-7899
🕘M-F: 0900-1700
Saturday:1000-1500

There is also an orthodontist that practises out of this office.

Zankli Medical Centre
Dr Badi Amer, Dental Surgeon
(See above for contact information and phone numbers for Zankli)
🕘 09 6700248
📱 0803-787-3870

Laboratories

Echo-Scan Services Limited (most results the next day)
Plot 643, Gimbiya Street
Garki
Abuja
☎ 09 3149224
📱 0804 4115848
🕘M-Sat: 0800-1800

St Francois Medical Centre
Plot 501, Bangui Street
Wuse II, Abuja
☎ 09 523-6282

Zankli Medical Centre
Plot 1021 B5 Shehu Yar'Adua Way
Opposite Federal Ministry of Works
Utako District
P.O. Box 7745, Abuja
☎ 09 523-6854; 563-9570; 523-9570; 670-7273-5

Pharmacies

We hesitate to recommend a specific source because of the existence of counterfeit drugs. Sometime, the pharmacies themselves do not know that their drugs are counterfeit.

King Newland Pharmacy
Nicon Hilton Hotel
(Aguiyi Ironsi and Shehu Shagari Way)
☎ 09 523-1811

Lawcas Pharmacy
Adetokunbo Ademola Crescent
Before Amigo Supermarket
Wuse 2
Abuja
☎ 09 523-8990

Rhosaq Pharmacy
Zone 4 Shopping Complex
Opposite Sheraton Hotel
Abuja
☎ 09 523-2262, 523-2268

Tonia Pharmacy ♥
Landmark Plaza
Plot 3124 IBB Way
(Under Great Wall of China)
Maitama, Abuja
☎ 09 413-6248

Zagbayi Pharmacy Ltd.
Shop No 2 Addis Ababa Crescent
Wuse Zone 4
Sheraton Hotel
Abuja
☎ 09 523-5708

Keeping Your Pets Healthy

Food and Supplies
Pet foods and supplies (such as kitty litter) are sometimes found in the larger supermarkets such as Grand Square and Park 'n Shop. They may not always be available however.
Yearly rabies injections are necessary.

Kennels
Dr A.B. Muhammed
Vet World Limited
Ber 1, Banex Plaza Ext.
Plot 750, Aminu Kano Crest.
Wuse II, Abuja
☎ 09-413-8672
email: bala_bubkar2000@yahoo.com or
Plot 21, Vet World Street
Off Hamza Abdullahi Road
Near Byzahi Junction
Kubwa - Abuja
☎ 0803-307-0278 (GSM)

Doggee World
Plot 185
Deeper Life Street
Asokoro,
☎ 09-670-3347 (ask for Jude)

Training

Continental Dog Club
FHA Qtrs, Block 16, Suite 17
(Next to Tocim Supermarket)
Asokoro, Abuja
☎ 09 670-4447; 0803-452-7679
Email: marvinade@yahoo.com
This is a company that specialises in dog training and pet supplies. The parent company is K9 Rules Dog Training Academy (which has branches in the U.S., Lagos, Port Harcourt and Ado-Ekiti.) They provide courses in obedience, provide dog sports and occasional boarding and dog walking.

Veterinary Services

El-Mond Veterinary Services
Dr Monday Ojeamiren
(Especially good with horses)
Plot 53 Site 5
Opposite the Anglican Church
Kubwa, Abuja
☎ 08033026534

Resol Vet. Centre
Dr Philimon Nwale
Wuse, Zone 7, Abuja
☎ 0802-324-8201

Time Vet Clinic
Dr Kola Olowoeyo
No 8 Zumunta Road
Karu-Abuja
◐ M-F: 804-412-6917
◐ M-Sat: 0800 - 1800

Vet World
For animal health services and products

Town Office:
Dr A.B. Mohammed
(Makes house calls)
Ber, 1 Banex Plaza Extension
Plot 750, Aminu Kano Crescent,
Wuse II, Abuja
☎ 09 413-8672

Location 2:
Plot 21 Vet World Street
Off Hamza Abdullahi Road
Near Byazhi Junction
Kubwa, Abuja
Dr Victor Ughaerumba
☎ 08037025042

CHAPTER 14

Staying Safe

Start looking for a black goat before dusk.
(Nigerian Proverb)

Yi taka tsantsan da duniya.
(Hausa Proverb)
Tread the world carefully.

Know the Situation

Foreigners are advised to check with their foreign ministries for the latest travel advice on Nigeria. Bear in mind, however, that those reports mostly relate to the situation in Lagos and are written to cover themselves for "worst case scenarios." Some websites for travel advisories are included in the "Additional Resources" section of the book.

Although Abuja is much safer than Lagos, as with any city, caution and common sense should still be exercised. For travellers, armed thieves and car hijacking are risks. Try to avoid driving after dark. Also, avoid taxis where there is a second person riding along for an unknown reason.

Occasional social, religious and/or ethnic unrest can present a security threat. Political gatherings, street demonstrations and workers' protests also have the potential to turn violent.

If you are a victim of a crime in Abuja, report it to the local police. Foreigners should also contact their local Embassy, High Commission or Consulate for assistance. They should be able to help in finding medical care, in contacting family members or friends and in wiring funds (if needed). They should also be able to explain how the investigation and prosecution are likely to proceed. Unfortunately, the penal system moves very slowly in Nigeria and the police lack the necessary training and equipment to investigate and prosecute most crimes.

Driving in Abuja

Compared to other parts of Africa, Abuja's road conditions are fairly good. Major streets are wide and well maintained. Unpaved side streets can however be difficult to manoeuvre.

What makes driving in Abuja a challenge is the lack of skill of the other drivers, the condition of many of the vehicles and the unreliability of the traffic lights and signs. The traffic rules are only loosely followed and the plethora of motorcycle okadas criss-crossing the road "at will" sometimes makes drivers feel they are playing a video arcade game. The name "okada" was coined after the reputation of a domestic airline – Okada Air. Like their namesake, no sooner do the passengers get on, than the okadas take off.

Night driving should be minimised for several reasons:
- Many cars do not have working headlights.
- Non-functioning traffic lights and streetlights are extremely dangerous when combined with vehicles without headlights.
- Even when the headlights work, quite a lot of Nigerians do not

use them because of a belief that they run down the battery or use more gas to operate.
- The risk of vehicle hijacking or robbery is greater.
- Police checks set up on some roads at night are not easily seen as the police are dressed in black and do not have bright torches.

To stay as safe as possible:
- Ensure that the vehicle is in good working order.
- Carry a first aid kit, a fire extinguisher and an emergency triangle (the latter two are required by law).
- Wear seat belts (by law front passengers must also wear seat belts).
- Avoid unnecessary driving after dark.
- Leave a space between the vehicle in which you are travelling and the vehicle (or object) in front (e.g., your house gate) in case you need to move in a hurry to prevent being trapped.
- Drive defensively — constantly expecting sudden lane changes (without the use of an indicator) and sudden stopping (without the forewarning of brake lights).
- Use headlights to "flash" other drivers frequently to let them know you are coming through an intersection and use the horn as an additional warning device.
- Avoid driving beyond the city limits at night or embarking on long road trips that will entail arriving after dark.
- Avoid isolated or overly crowded areas, especially at night.
- Always drive with doors locked and windows closed.

Because of the aforementioned issues, pedestrians and cyclists are particularly at risk and do not have "the right-of-way" in Nigeria.

If there is an accident, a large group of people may gather. Sometimes those groups can turn into a mob crowd. If it looks as if this is about to happen, drive (or take a taxi if the car is immobilised) immediately to the nearest police post and report the accident.

Driving Outside of Abuja

Driving outside Abuja with non-CD plates can be quite a nerve-racking experience for foreigners. There are numerous police and army checks on the road, but also many other types of gauntlets to pass. One is Local Government Revenue-excise officials who surround the car, put nailed planks under the wheels and demand to see your permit for advertising on the side of the car. This will cost around ₦5000 and is 'valid' for one year. It can be shown anywhere in the country, so to that extent it is worth paying, even though it is not exactly legal. Another is Road Safety teams that will flag you down and check your car for sins such as lack of warning triangle or 'wrong type of fire extinguisher'. It is best to provide copies of the car papers — not the originals — or it may be expensive to have them returned. The best way round this is to carry an official letter from a government or international body saying who you are and who to contact in case of any query. This is usually sufficient.

The "Dash"

While the government has authorised vehicle checkpoints to reduce crime, unauthorised checkpoints to extort money continue to be a problem. They are most common after about 9.00 p.m. Foreign drivers should have a copy of their passport and visa in case it is needed to verify legal status and to avoid having to pay a "dash" when stopped.

When approached for a dash, maintain a calm exterior and keep your voice even. Alex Newton in *The Lonely Planet* put it well, "Be aware that confrontations with police are a game and you are a player". If you are walking along minding your own business and a police officer queries, 'What have you for me master?' You are not obligated to "dash", i.e. give a bribe. A case in point: at the airport a customs official asked me that same question. I replied, 'A firm handshake and a smile.' He broke into a grin and wished me a safe journey".

Fraud and Scams — 419

Unfortunately, one of the things for which Nigerians have made themselves famous is their involvement in scams. They are affectionately referred to as "419s", after the law passed to prosecute those engaged in this activity. There are many different types and variations but the most common are listed below:

1. A letter is faxed or emailed to a foreigner, telling him that he can make a large profit in exchange for the use of his bank account. That letter and/or a subsequent letter will explain that a prominent Nigerian official has, perhaps $30 million that he would like to remove from the country and needs a way to do so. In exchange for the use of the bank account, the investor might receive 10%. Obviously, what happens instead is that once the bank account number is known, the con artists attempt to make a withdrawal from the account.
2. Similarly, another scam involves sending foreigners emails saying they are from former politicians who are seeking donations to be able to conduct various types of transactions. They ask for the money to be wired and again, once the banking information is known, they try to make their own withdrawal from the account.
3. Yet another variation involves a request for a small donation to assist with a project or social programme. If successful, they may ask for a larger donation in the future. The organisation is bogus.
4. One Nigerian-based scam (operating mostly out of Lagos) involves inviting business people to Nigeria and telling them they do not need a visa. They are met at the plane and do not proceed through immigration or customs. They are wined and dined and then asked to transfer a large sum of money toward the business venture. If they refuse, they soon find out that they are illegally on Nigerian soil.
5. Those seeking real estate also need to be wary as another popular scam is for someone to present him/herself as the owner of the property in question, make a deal with the customer and take off with the money. (This has also been attempted with property back in the UK.) Since most real estate deals occur in

cash, it is extremely important to request official documentation of the property and ensure that when it comes to handing over the cash, you are dealing with the owner.
6. Warn family, friends and banks at home to beware. Your personal information may be used in scams. For example, if your family/friends receive notice that emergency medical treatment is needed for you, they should always verify before sending any funds (through your embassy or workplace).

Some Stay Safe Rules in Nigeria

- Never provide banking information or credit card number to anyone.
- No bank information should be sent by post; couriers and even diplomatic pouches are not 100% reliable. Do not write out-of-country cheques or use credit cards.
- Ensure your bank does not release any funds without special security clearance (a pin or security code) which should be agreed before leaving your country of origin.
- Do not send account details by fax or email; and always assume someone is listening to the phone calls. Be careful not to give personal details to 'wrong numbers'.
- After their use, shred documents that include personal information — credit card numbers, banking information, address outside of Nigeria, national I.D. number (e.g., U.S. Social Security number). Remember that rubbish will be sifted through by local 'recyclers'.
- Keep personal documents such as those listed above and tax information and real estate documents locked in a secure place. Do not assume that a locked drawer in a cupboard is sufficient. These documents should be in a safe or inside several levels of security. e.g., locked inside a bag, inside of a suitcase, etc.
- Unsolicited contact from Nigerian companies or business people should be thoroughly checked out with the U.S Commerce Department, the British Foreign Trade Office, the Nigerian Embassy or Chamber of Commerce.
- Advise friends and relatives at home to be careful as well, as your name and details may be used to initiate fraudulent contacts.

- If it is necessary to manage overseas accounts, internet banking is as secure here as anywhere in the world. It is not advised, however, to use internet cafes or hotels for this purpose as those details can be tracked through the computer.
- Otherwise, consider asking someone back home to handle monetary affairs, keep all bank details and credit cards carefully locked away and ask other foreigners to hand-carry confidential documents in and out of the country.
- Do not carry large sums of cash.
- When going to the market or other crowded places, men should put wallets in front pockets and women should hold bags tightly to their bodies or carry the money in a different manner.
- Possessions are replaceable. Your life is not. If you are approached for your car, your possessions or your money, the safest course of action is to co-operate.
- At home you will likely have security guards attending the gate and razor wire fences are quite common.
- Grilled or bulletproof doors are recommended for the entrance and 'keep' or secure area (usually the master bedroom, or the sleeping area might be separated from the rest of the house by a secure door).
- Many houses have panic buttons and every window should have burglar bars.
- Also, consider safe ways to get out of your house in an emergency.
- Have a phone and emergency light or torch in the bedroom.

In Case of Emergency.

(See appendix for emergency number on page 323)

As a Foreigners, contact your Embassy or High Commission listed in the "Hints to Foreigners" section of this book for advice on the situation. They should be able to assist.

Police Checkpoint and Traffic Light Enhance Security on the Road

Ambulance

There are two relatively new emergency medical services in Abuja. In order for them to respond to a call, you first have to be registered with them.

Critical Rescue International (CRI)

Plot 142
Cadastral, Off Adetokunbo Ademola Crescent
Wuse 2, Abuja
☎ 0802 463 4000
    08028880000

South African trained staff, with call centre in Lagos and clinics in many cities across Nigeria. You can register with their UNIC Health insurance plan. They will assist in emergency evacuations for a fee if you are not a member of their programme.

EMC
UNIC Insurance Building
Dr Norbert Etchandy
☎ 0803 669 3685
Abigail Simon-Hart
☎ 0803-303-9660;
Email: emcphc_marketing@yahoo.fr

Fire

Fire Brigade
☎ 09 234-1299

Be prepared for they may not come immediately or have sufficient water in their vehicle to extinguish the fire.

CHAPTER 15

Staying Fit and Beautiful

Health is a state of complete physical, mental and social well-being and not merely the absence of disease or infirmity.

(The World Health Organisation)

Sports and Recreation Centres

Energym Fitness
Nwaora Plaza
Plot 1103 Aminu Kano Crescent
Wuse II, Abuja
☎ 08034530070
⏱M-Sat: 0700-2200 hours
Sun: 1300-1800

Faridah
No 30 Maitama Sule Street
Opposite OAU Quarters
Asokoro, Abuja.
☎ 09 314 9244, 08044103254
🕒 M-Sat: 0630-2200

Abuja Horse and Country Club
(Owned and managed by Julius Berger)
Jobi District, Abuja
☎ 09 521-0942; 0978
(Berger Switchboard. Ask for the President of the AHCC)

This is a membership-based club, but it is not restricted to employees of Julius Berger only. Members may stable their horses at the club and make use of the facilities. There is a large open area for riding. It is not possible to rent horses or take riding lessons without owning a horse. However, there is a relatively frequent turnover of members selling their horses.

Area 1 Shopping Centre
Opposite Abuja Council for Arts and Culture
Basketball, handball, lawn tennis and volleyball playing fields. No fee required.

Hilton Fitness Club ♥
Nicon Hilton Hotel
(Aguiyi Ironsi and Shehu Shagari Way)
Floor 02
☎ 09 4131811- 40 ext. 6423

Members have free access to the various fitness options. Visitors can also pay a day fee for the use of the pool. Inside: weights, treadmills, stationary bicycles, aerobics classes, table tennis, saunas and massage. Outside: tennis, squash, badminton, basketball courts, swimming pool, playground, snooker and mini golf. Lessons and personal fitness trainers available. Non-members can also pay for a massage there.

IBB International Golf and Country Club ♥
Udi Street, near the French Embassy
P.O. Box 6935
Wuse, Abuja
☎ 09 523-2015; 523-4139
Fax: 09 523-2014
🕒 Daylight to dark

Members only; international standard 18-hole golf course. Beautifully maintained with Aso Rock at the background, this course has hosted many national and international tournaments. The clubhouse has a reasonably priced restaurant. Exchange membership privileges with certain other golf clubs. There are also lawn tennis courts. There is also a nice walking path around most of the golf course. Visitors with a member can pay a fee and play a game of tennis or a round of golf (weekdays ₦2250; weekends ₦2750).

Old Parade Ground
Festival Road
Trade Fair Complex
Garki
Open lawn tennis courts.

Sheraton Fitness Club
Ladi Kwali Way
Wuse II, Abuja
☎ 523-0225-244; 523-8101-131
Fax: 523-1570-1

Members have free access to the use of the club. Visitors can pay a day fee to use the pool. Inside: table tennis, gym, steam room, sauna, massage rooms (separate fee), darts and two squash courts. Outside: swimming pool, four tennis courts. Non-members can also get massages there.

Walking and Jogging

Some foreigners enjoy jogging or walking along the street. Early morning or evening is preferred as the sun can get very hot. Avoid deserted or overcrowded streets. Watch out for traffic as pedestrians do not have right of way and cars and motorcycles often drive on the walking paths. People will be happy to greet you as they go about their business of the day. Women should be aware that some locals may be offended by skimpy attire.

Places that are good for walking include around your neighbourhood, the golf course, Millennium Park, or join the Hash Harriers which meet around 3.00 p.m at the Hilton on designated Saturdays each month.

Yoga Instruction

Patrick N.C. Fom
23 years experience as a Yogi, Basic Hatha Yoga; Asanas (Yoga positions); pranayama (breathing exercises) and low and moderately high impact aerobic warm-ups. Sessions take place the last weekend of every other month in Jos Plateau, at Kuru Village, Jos south, Lo Judah Palace Place (family compound) near the Chief's Palace (20 minutes outside of Jos). Hiking, sight-seeing, etc. Lodging at Plateau Hotel.
☎ 0802-357-8514

Tae Kwon Do

Instructor Tony Anafulu
☎ 08055250121, 08033201071
Head coach of the FCT Tae Kwon Do Association, coaches several of the schools' after school clubs and can be hired for private or group sessions.

Salons

Amigo Salon
No. 15 Ademola Adetokunbo Crescent
Wuse II, Abuja
☎   09 523-4067; 523-8624
⏰ M-Sat: 0900-1800
Unisex hairstyling, manicure, pedicure, waxing, eye brow plucking.

Fabio's Salon ♥
First location:
Plot 687
Crystal Palace Hotel
Port Harcourt Crescent (near Legends)
Area 11, Abuja
☎ 09 314-0035
🕘 M-Sat: 0900 - 1800

Second location:
Nwaora Plaza
Plot 1103 Aminu Kano Crescent
Wuse II
☎ 0803 471 3832

Offers body massage, manicure, pedicure, unisex hairdressing and facial treatment. A favourite of the foreign community.

Insight
3 Freetown, beside Rockview Hotel
☎ 0803-330-0882
Hair care, massage, beauty treatments, waxing, skin lightening and facials.

Lactina-Pride Unisex Saloon
Plot 3124 IBB Way
Landmark Plaza
Maitama, Abuja
☎ 09 413-1772-4; 413-1710; 0803-452-9833
🕘 M-Sat: 1000-1800
Email: www.kivilac.com

Weaves and braids, Senegalese weaving, removal of facial wrinkles, manicure, pedicure, nail repair, haircutting for men, hair colouring and hair treatment of all kinds.

Metro Studio Salon (Unisex)
Metro Plaza, 2nd Floor, 4th Avenue
Central Business District, Abuja.
African, European and Asian hairdressing, hair loss, bumps, dyeing, skin lightening treatment, professional slimming, manicure, pedicure, dryness of feet and hands, weak nails and facial treatments.

Nicon Hilton Hotel
BMG Beauty Centre
(Aguiyi Ironsi and Shehu Shagari Way)
Floor 02, Wing C
☎ 413-1811, ext. 6416
M-Sat: 1000-1800
Email: bmgbeautycentre@yahoo.com

Offers manicure, pedicure and hairdressing. The barber shop in the back is popular with foreign males and middle-upper class Nigerians.

Pretty Woman Beauty Salon
Cairo Street
Opposite NEPA office,
Off Adetokunbo Ademola Crescent
Wuse II, Abuja
☎ 0803-312-0848; 0803-305-7553

Offers body massage, manicure, pedicure, hairdressing and facial treatment.

Sheraton Hotel Salon
Ladi Kwali Way, Salon is near the pool
Wuse II, Abuja
☎ 523-0225-244; 523-8101-131
Fax: 523-1570-1
M-Sat: 700-2200

B-Natural Salon & Day Spa.
Asokoro Shopping Mall,
Off T.Y. Danjuma Street, Asokoro.
☎ 09/3149026 or 7, or 0803/317-3355

Unisex hairdressing, manicures and pedicures.

Clothing and Shoes
Most clothing should be light, porous and washable. Pure cotton is the most comfortable. Tropical weight clothing is worn all year round. A light sweater can be useful in air conditioned rooms, for trips to Jos and the North, and for cool winter nights. Unless, you buy the material and have it made yourself, the imported clothing sold in Abuja is expensive — particularly children's clothes. Sometimes bargains can be found in Wuse market. See the "Enjoying the Culture" section for vendors of traditional clothing.

Reputable dry cleaning is available at the Hilton, Sheraton and Rockview hotels. However, it is recommended that as much washable clothing as possible is brought.

Dressmakers/Tailors

Any Wear
Leisure Castle Complex
No. 4 Gana Street
Maitama, Abuja
☎ 0803-332-0671; 0803-787-1225
⊕M-Sat: 1300-2000;
Sundays: 1500-1800

Fabrik Shoppe
Emab Plaza
Shop D 16
⊕M-Sat: 0930-1800
Woodin fabric from Cote d'Ivoire and tailor.

Mitai Creations ♥
Mitai S. Oraegbu — Designer

Garki Model Market
Shop 44 Kogi Street, Garki, Abuja
☎ 0803-705-1729
Email: mitaicreations@yahoo.com

African clothing; European styles with African cloth, African jewellery, bride and bridal outfits, wedding cards, tailoring services (home service available), bags, corporate gifts, uniforms, wedding cakes, hall decorations.

MO Style/Fabric,
Shop #19, Kasim Ahmed Line
Garki Model Market,
Off Samuel Ladoke Akintola Boulevard
Garki II
☎ 234-3824, 0803/314-0444, 0804/411-7177

Modupe Aligasim makes wonderful Western and African-style clothes with your cloth or hers. She also has ready-made clothes, and she'll do house calls.

Senegalese Tailors
#7 Ontario Crescent
Off Mississippi Street
Maitama

Designs for males and females, can purchase material there or bring your own.

Violet's Lingerie
Suite F1&2 Emab Plaza
Aminu Kano Crescent,
Wuse II
⏰ M-Sat: 0900-1900

Lingerie, swimsuits, women's accessories, etc. Sells Victoria Secret, Marks & Spencers and other European brands.

Dry Cleaners

Hilton, Sheraton and Rockview Hotels

Ambassador Dry Cleaners
10 Usuma Street
Maitama, Abuja
☎ 0802-333-7628

CHAPTER 16

Staying Active

Laziness spreads the mat for hunger to lie on.
(Nigerian Proverb)

Videos and Video CDs

There are a number of video shops where video tapes can be purchased or rented. A number of the videos are bootlegged and are not good quality. A couple of places that our readers recommend for good quality videos, DVDs and video CDs are:

Movie Mania
Shop E1 & E2, Sheriff Plaza
Aminu Kano Crescent, Wuse II
☎　　　0803-450-8567
Email:　　moviemania_abj@yahoo.com

9-11 Video Shop
Superstores
Maitama, Plot No 635
Usuma Street
Abuja
☎ 09 413-0441
🕓 0900 –2300

Sheraton Video Shop
Sheraton Hotel
Ladi Kwali Way
Wuse II

Videos and video CDs of varying quality can also be purchased on the street, at Wuse Market or at a number of other stores.

Churches

The main denominations including Catholic, Anglican, Methodist, Presbyterian, Baptist and Mormon have churches in Abuja.

Capital Assembly
Ladi Kwali Hall, Sheraton
Every Sunday: 0700-1000; 1000-1400

Christ Embassy, Abuja
Berger Round about
Every Sunday: 0900

Family Worship Centre
Idris Gidado Street
Off Nnamdi Azikiwe Expressway
3 Sunday services at 0700, 0900, and 1130 hours

House on the Rock
Congress Hall, Hilton
Every Sunday: 0815; 1115

International Church
Meets at the Model School, adjacent to the American International School, off IBB Way in Maitama.
Every Sunday: 1000

LDS (Mormon) Church
Plot 1929 Accra Street
Wuse, Zone 5
Every Sunday: 0900
Hilary Eko   0803-311-3924

PW Life Camp (Catholic)
Service held in meeting room of the Club House; complementary lunch served following the service.
Every Sunday: 1330

Apostolic Nunciature (Catholic)
Plot 3133 Pope John Paul II Crescent
Off Gana Street
Maitama
Every Day: 0730
Every Saturday: 0630 (French language)
Every Sunday: 0900 and 1030

Summit Bible Church
National Centre for Women Development
Better Life Street
5th Street
Central Area, Abuja.

Holy Trinity Catholic Church
Aguiyi Ironsi, Road
Maitama, Abuja
Mass Daily: 0600; 0800; 1000

Charitable Organisations (volunteer opportunities)

Doctors Without Borders
7 Ganges Street
Off Alvan Ikoku Way
Ministers Hill, Maitama, Abuja
☎ 09 413-8084-6; fax 413-8087
Email: msfabuja@premiernet.net.ng

Family Care International
P.O. Box 8015
Wuse Zone 3
FCT Abuja
☎ 08042127942, 08044130204
Email: abu_famcare@yahoo.com

Habitat for Humanity
IBB Way
Wuse II
www.habitat.org

UNICEF
UN House
Central Business District
Off Independence Avenue
Near National Hospital
Human Resources Department

Cultural Activities

Concerts, exhibits, plays and the like are often sponsored by different organisations, either in their own venues or at one of the large hotels or conference centres. Below are organisations that regularly host events.

The British Council
Plot 2935 IBB Way
Maitama, Abuja
☎ 09 413-7870-9; 413-4559-64; fax 413-7883; 413-0902
Email: abuja.info@ng.britishcouncil.org

The Abuja office of the British Council opened in 2001 and is located at the Maitama roundabout. Membership is based upon the recommendation of an existing member. There is a fee of ₦10,000 for an annual membership. Members are entitled to attend cultural events, borrow books and periodicals. A fee is charged for the late return of materials. Free 1-hour per day internet access is also available. British Council also facilitates information exchange regarding scholarships and admission to British Universities. The Roof Top Café is also located on the premises.

The British Council also has regular music, dance and theatre events. For more information on the British Council, see Chapter 12 " Staying in Touch" under Libraries.

French Cultural Centre
9A Udi Street
Off Aso Drive,
Maitama, Abuja
☎ 09 5241116
🕐 Info Desk 0900-1700

The centre is part of the French Embassy and serves as a place for French lessons and cultural events. French lessons are taught for persons 15 years and older. The lessons take place in the mornings, afternoons or evenings, from Monday to Friday (also on Saturday morning), usually for 4.5h/week. There are also more intensive classes (6h/week). They are planning to conduct French language classes for children, but currently are more focused on training adults. There are a total of about 300 students. The academic year runs from July to June. Fees for 2004 = 161 Naira per hour.

The French Cultural Centre also has a public library with 1200 French books. It organises exhibitions, concerts and a weekly film (French films with English subtitles).

Abuja Council for Arts and Culture
Area 10
Garki, Abuja
Venue for travelling plays and cultural events, also has a museum and various artists selling their crafts.

Sports

The Hash
This is an international club started by the British in Kuala Lumpur (Malaysia) in the 1940's at the Royal Salangor — "Hash House." Its purpose is to enjoy the great outdoors while having a good time socialising with friends. The group meets every other Saturday at the Hilton parking lot. Times vary (usually 3:00 p.m.) so check around. A different group organises and sponsors the run/walk each time. Sometimes the runs/walks are rural and other times urban. An optional dinner follows the trek for those so inclined. The Hash is open to all members of the family. Hash clubs exist in countries throughout the world.

Aso Rock
Special permission from the Nigerian military is needed to climb this commanding rock. Foreign missions usually organise climbs a couple of times a year. It takes about 2.5 hours to reach the top and descend depending upon how far the car is driven. The final climb is steep and the descent can be difficult. Wear shoes with a good grip and take plenty of water.

Golf Club
See "Staying Fit and Beautiful" and the Outing sections of "Minding the Children".

Abuja Stadium and Sports Village
Watch for events.

The Dome
N-Glory Centre,
Plot 432,
Cadastral

Central Business District
Abuja
☎ 09 6715587, 0804 2125 644, 08055083614
Email: info@thedome-ng.com, www.thedome-ng.com
Bowling, dancing, gardens, nite club, restaurant, pool.

International Women's Club of Abuja

Established in September 1998, the IWCA is a non-political, non-religious charitable organisation that also provides a social meeting point for women of any race, colour, creed or nationality. The membership fee is ₦2000. The club meets monthly and offers a variety of activities and classes (cooking, fitness, handicrafts, English, etc.), coffee mornings, family events, bookclubs and French and Spanish conversation groups. The level of activities of the club depends upon the membership.

Life Camps

There are a number of companies, mainly constructions firms, which have built their own staff living quarters on the edges of Abuja. These are called life camps and are fairly self-contained villages. They provide housing and amenities such as sports facilities, schools (the Berger German School and Bouygues French School), shops, playground and swimming pools. These services are usually restricted to their own staff, but occasionally events are open to the wider population of Abuja (look out for the Berger *Weihnachtsmarkt* or Christmas Market at the end of November). Sometimes housing is available for outsiders to rent.

Annual International Social Events

Listed below are some annual social events. The exact dates and locations can be found through the Embassies or schools as appropriate. See the "Enjoying the Culture" section for annual Nigerian festivals.

October	–*Oktober Fest –	German harvest festival usually celebrated at the Julius Berger Life Camp
	– Thai Festival –	Annual festival of thanksgiving, location varies
November	–*Christmas Bazaar –	*Weihnachtsmarkt* or Christmas Market. Julius Berger Life camp is brightly decorated and food and gifts are sold
	–Anniversary Hash –	Large anniversary celebration with raffle for large prizes (e.g., airline tickets, appliances, etc.)

Also be on the lookout for Spring and Winter Bazaars at the various private schools and art and jewellery showings at private homes and Embassies.

---

*By invitation only

CHAPTER 17

Enjoying the Culture

A coconut shell full of water is like an ocean to a small ant.
(Nigerian Proverb)

The tortoise cannot make any progress until it sticks its neck out.
(Nigerian Proverb)

Annual Festivals

During the Muslim *Id-el-fitri* and *Id-el-Kabir* holidays, traditional Durbar celebrations are held in the main squares of many major northern towns. Villagers from a large area join in the one to two day celebrations consisting of colourful parades, charges by brightly adorned-armed horsemen, dancing and entertainment. The Durbar festival at Katsina is one of the most spectacular. Sokoto, Maiduguri, Zaria and Kano are also known for their Durbars.

During *Sallah*, the requirement to fast makes people weak as no food or water is taken during daylight hours. Office hours are subject to changes and events should be carefully scheduled to avoid lunch/food events during daylight hours.

As at Christmas time for Christians, cards are exchanged during *Eid* and gifts and new clothes are given. Acknowledgement of the holiday season by asking, "How is the fasting?" is appreciated. Also, in hosting Muslim friends when it is time to "break fast," something sweet and light like fresh fruit or porridge is appropriate to offer.

The dates for the Muslim festivals vary greatly depending upon the movement of the moon. They are listed in the table below.

Muslim Holidays

Name	State	Description
Id-el-Fitr	National Holiday	National Holiday.
Kunshi Festival	Bauchi	Kunshi Festival at Bauchi (the seventh day of Ramadan)
Durbar Festivals	Northern States	Durbar Festivals in most Northern cities in Nigeria to celebrate the end of Ramadan. Kano and Katsina host larger *Sallah* celebrations.
Id-el-Kabir	National Holiday	National Holiday. *Id-el-Kabir* to celebrates Ibrahim's acceptance of the sacrificing of his son Ishmael and the return of the pilgrims to visit Mecca. On this occasion Muslims slaughter rams.
Durbar Festivals	Northern States	These Durbar Festivals are usually larger than Ramadan and are held in most cities in Northern Nigeria. Again Kano and Katsina host larger celebrations.
Id-el-Maulud	National Holiday	National Holiday. This celebrates the birth of the Muslim Prophet Muhammad. Durbars are held in some cities.

The dates for secular and Christian festivals and national public holidays are listed in the table below.

Public Holidays and National Festivals

Month	Date	State	Description
January	1	National Holiday	New Year's Day (holiday)
	1	Kwoi/Kafauchau	Masquerade -- South of Kaduna
	TBA*	Edo	*Ukpeze* Festival -- Yam Festival celebrated by the people of Ewohimi
February	TBA*	Yobe	Fishing and Cultural Festival at Gorgoram near Hadejia – Jigawa/Yobe State.
	TBA*	Sokoto/Kebbi	*Argungu* Fishing Festival is a spectacular fishing competition held on the banks of the Sokoto River in Argungu. Visitors come from around the world for this three-day festival. Caution as it is not held every year.
	TBA*	Plateau	*Ogona* Festival at Umaisha
March/April	TBA*	National Holiday	Good Friday Easter Monday
April	TBA*	Plateau Fishing	Festivals in Dorok, Din and Shendam.
May	1	National Holiday	May Day
	29	National Holiday	Nigerian Democracy Day
July	TBA*	Bauchi	*Gere* Masquerade -- celebrated by the Gerawa people in the seventh month of each year.

*TBA – To be announced

August	Last Friday in August	Osun	Osun River Festival held in Oshogbo (Osogbo) to honour the goddess of Osun whose spirit is believed to dwell under the Osun River. Music, dances and sacrifices to Osun help restore the bond between the goddess and the people of Oshogbo.
	TBA*	Pategi	The *Pategi Regatta* is one of the most photographed festivals on the Niger River between Ibadan and Kaduna. There's swimming, traditional dancing, acrobatic displays and fishing in addition to the rowing competition.
October	1	National Holiday	Nigerian National Day (Independence Day)
Oct.-Dec.	TBA*	Plateau	Millet harvest festivals
December	25	National Holiday	Christmas Day
	26	National Holiday	Boxing Day
	TBA*	Benin City	*Igue* Festival is a week-long celebration in Benin City with traditional dancing and food.
	TBA*	Enugu	The week-long *Mnonwu* Festival includes spectacular mask parades.

Several festivals have become local government events with the attendant speeches and protocol. Ask before making plans to attend.

---

*TBA – To be announced

Music

One of the most popular singers in Nigeria (and Africa in general) was **Fela Anikulapo Kuti**. Fela's music was influenced by the Black consciousness movement in the United States in the 1960s (he met Malcom X in 1964) and the soul sounds of James Brown. Fela is no longer alive, but he created and performed an Afro-beat style fused with American blues, jazz, funk, soul and traditional Yoruba music. His lyrics often contained political messages.

King Sunny Ade, who still performs, is another popular singer. He is the king and creator of a popular style of music called "juju," which uses a combination of guitars, traditional drums and vocals. One of his most popular albums is "Juju Music" (1982).

Femi Anikulapo-Kuti (son of Fela) performs modern jazz and "afro blues." **Bobby Benson** performs a mixture of traditional African music with up-tempo trumpets. "Taxi Driver" is a famous song about the traffic jams "go slows" in Lagos. **Sunny Okosun** plays a funk/highlife/Afro pop music genre called Afro-Soul. **Ebenezer Obey** plays an older form of highlife. Other popular groups are style plus and the **Ghetto Blasters**. "Age" (Age Beeka) is a very highly talented Abuja-based singer-songwriter who performs contemporary music and is quite popular with the international residents in Abuja.

There are several places that music can be purchased including video shops (e.g., 9-11), supermarkets and street vendors. A couple of record stores recommended by our readers are:

The Studio
Emab Plaza C17
Aminu Kano Crescent
Wuse II, Abuja

Grand Square Record Shop
Buhari Way
Central Area, Abuja

Literature

Nigeria has produced some of the most acclaimed and prolific writers in the world. **Wole Soyinka** who was the first African to win the Nobel Prize in Literature (1986) is well known as a playwright, poet, novelist and critic. The political nature of some of his writings landed him in jail during the military regime. Among his writings are *The Man Died, Trial of Brother Jero, The Lion and the Jewel* (1959) and *The Road* (1965). **Chinua Achebe** is another renowned novelist. Among his works are *Things Fall Apart* (1958), Anthills *of the Savannah* (1987) and the children's book, *How the Leopard Got His Claws* (1973).

Nigeria lost a wonderful writer in Kenule (Ken) Saro-Wiwa, who was executed by the military regime for his political writings. **Flora Nwapa** is well known for re-creating Igbo life from a woman's viewpoint. *Never Again* (1975) and *Cassava Song and Rice Song* (1986) are some of her most famous books. **Amos Tutuola** is best known for his novel *The Palm-Wine Drinkard* and *His Dead Palm-Wine Tapster in the Deads' Town* **(1962).** Other accomplished writers include **Ben Okri, Buchi Emecheta** and **Cyprian Ekwensi**. See "Staying in Touch" for bookstores where these and other good literature can be purchased.

Clothing

Nigerian dress is not dull. There is a wonderful array of fabrics, colours and styles available to both men and women. The traditional "wrapper" worn by the women is a useful item that travels and washes well. It serves as a skirt, shawl, umbrella, blanket, tying cloth to 'back' babies, towel, picnic blanket and a corner of it often serves as a purse. Several areas of Wuse Market have 'ready made' clothes. However, don't be confused by the tailors that are displaying things sewn for other people. There are many tailors found in the market, in their own shops, or carrying their sewing machines around the city on their shoulders ready to mend things at your door. Most are good at copying items of clothing that already fit you. There are also a number of designers. Some are willing to come to your house. Finding one that does good work, on time and for a good price is a bit more difficult. If they are very good they tend to be very busy and it can take a long time to get your work done. Try the following:

Bunmi Sofolahan
Trendy Collections
Garki Model Market
☎ 413-7064; 0803-305-8054

Fanic Design Ltd.
Fatima Ibrahim
☎ 0803-314-0709

Hawa's Senegalese Designer Tailor Shop
House No 7 Ontario Crescent
(Off Mississippi Street)
Maitama, Abuja
☎ 09 413-2137; 0803-590-1679
Unisex clothing available

Mitai Creations
Garki Model Market
☎ 0803-705-1729

Art and Crafts Work

Handicrafts can be purchased at the airport, hotels and markets and may include: sculpted wood objects, masks, Yoruba statuettes, calabashes, leather goods, crocodile and snake skins, horns, pottery, cloth (batik, *adire, Aso-Oke*), jewellery (coral, malachite, ivory), wickerwork (baskets) and musical instruments. Remember that buying crocodile, ivory and other animal goods encourages killing. Importing some of these items to other countries is illegal without special permit, which may result in heavy fines in Europe and the United States.

Alternative Trade Network of Nigeria (ATNN)
1 Museum Street
(Behind Union Bank)
P.O. Box 1004, Jos, Plateau State
☎   073450178
Email: natn@hisen.org
🕐M-F: 0800-1700
Saturday: 1000-1800
Non-profit fair trade association established in 1994

Cabana Art Gallery
RH 7, Abuja Council for Arts & Culture
Area 7, Box 847
Garki,
Abuja

Chess Board Galleries
Suite 37/38 McLewis Plaza
(Near Al-Nur Filling Station)
Wuse II, Abuja

Shop 9 Crafts Village
Nicon Hilton Hotel
(Aguiyi Ironsi and Shehu Shagari Way)
Wuse II, Abuja
☎ 0803-332-8901
African art, furniture and frames

Colours of Africa
470 Aminu Kano Crescent
Wuse II, Abuja
Art, furniture, clothes, accessories, souvenirs, cards and jewellery.

Hilton Handicraft Village
Nicon Hilton Hotel
(Aguiyi Ironsi and Shehu Shagari Way)
Behind swimming pool area
Stocks authentic African artworks including pottery, weaving, fabric,

thorn carvings, ebony works and paintings. Pottery maker associated with Maraba Pottery from Kaduna will provide a demonstration and classes for a small fee.

Kehinde and Taïwo (Kenny and Taye) Oyedeji ♥
Twin brothers who paint typical Nigerian scenes on rice paper and other media. They painted the mural on IBB between Adetokunbo Ademola Crescent and Olusegun Obasanjo Crescent.

Graduates of Ibadan Polytechnic. They are extremely kind and delightful people.
☎ 0803-313-9703
Email: kennytay2@yahoo.com

Life Strokes Art Gallery
Suite 23A Mc Lewis Plaza
Blantyre Street
Off Adetokunbo Ademola Crescent
Wuse II, Abuja
Original artwork, prints, jewellery, furniture, framing.

Nike Centre for Art and Culture (Workshop)
Piwoi Village
7.5 Kilometres from Abuja on the Airport Road
On the right hand side coming from Abuja
Just after the new petrol station
☎ 0804096656, 08023131067
They sometimes have artists working on site.

Nike Art Gallery
Block 32 Flat 7 Gaborone Road
Wuse Zone II
Abuja
☎ 0804-2109380; 0802-313-1067; 0803-303-6969
💻 www.nikeart.com; ronike@21ctl.com

The centre and the gallery have a wide variety of traditional arts and crafts including adire (indigo pattern dying), cloth and clothing, quilts, carvings, masks, jewellery and much more. Chief (Mrs) Nike Davies-

Okundaye also has a Centre for Art and Culture in Oshogbo (Osun State) and at Ogigi (Kogi State), an art gallery at Lekki Extension in Victoria Island, Lagos and the "Nike Centre" mentioned above.

Out of Africa - Sheraton
Sheraton Hotel
Ladi Kwali Way
P.O. Box 143, Wuse, Abuja

Clothing for adults and children, toys made with batik (Nigerian fabric), art, crafts, souvenirs, etc. There are also other stores and crafts tables set up at the Sheraton selling necklaces, leather bags, stone boxes and other crafts.

Renaissance
Samuel Onyilo U.
☎ 09 521-2129
Art and iron furniture.

Roda
Jos Plateau State
☎ 0803-701-8923
Original water colour paintings

Signatures
Plot 654 Aminu Kano Crescent
Wuse II, Abuja
☎ 09 6712210
◐M-Sat: 0830-1800
🖳 signature.gallery@hyperia.com

Collection of contemporary African art and crafts. Originals and prints, interior design. Moving in 2004 to a new address on Adetokunbo Ademola, down from Peniel Apartments.

Tourist Spots Around Abuja

Markets in Outlying Villages

There are a number of small village markets and pottery workshops outside Abuja. Some specialise in certain crafts and some will be found only on the day of the week noted as their market day.

A.B.U.

On Fridays there is a small village market with local fruit and vegetables and wooden pounding bowls. A.B.U. is on the left side of airport road before the airport turn off travelling from Abuja.

Bwari

On Tuesdays and Saturdays there is a Fulani local market. To get there, go out on Kaduna road, follow signs to Usman Dam, turn left before the Usman Dam gates, past Ushafa village (where there is a good pottery village) and follow the road to Bwari. The roads in this area can get rather difficult in the rainy season..

Dikko

On Saturdays one of the best Fulani markets is held here with calabash, hats, knives, material, beads, fruit, vegetables, chicken, etc. It is out on the Kaduna road, past Zuma rock. Before the toll gate take the turning for Bida and Minna. The market is on the left hand side.

Kuje

This market is held on Saturdays. It is located 16 kilometres from Abuja, off airport road.

Madala

On Thursdays, there is a large market that sells everything including woven baskets, calabashes, enamel pots, etc.

Papa

On Fridays there is a village market with local fruit and vegetables, beads and pots. There is a pottery village with good pots for planters located here as well. It is near Abuja on the Kaduna road, just before the Quarry.

Pottery
There are a number of pottery places near Usman Dam (on the way to Kaduna) at Ushafa and Bwari, as well as one selling big vases and pots near the airport.

Ushafa (Now often called "Bill Clinton Village")
Ushafa Village is about 30 kilometres from Abuja on the road from Dutse to Usuma and Bwari. To get there, go out on Kaduna road, follow signs to Usman Dam, instead of turning right to the Usman Dam gates, follow the road left to the junction. There is road construction in that area at the moment so ask traders in the area for the pottery workshop - pottery and terra cotta items.

Bwari Village
Bwari village is another 20 minutes past Ushafa and can be reached by going left at the junction that will take you to Ushafa village. Follow the road to Bwari and at the 'T' junction by the traffic controller ('Yellow Fever') turn left, and go past the Law School. Look for the thatched roofs on the right side of the road. The roads in this area can get rather difficult in the rainy season. You can call ahead to Stephen Mbya 09 0809529. He can organise a tour and demonstration as well as pottery activities for kids. There is also a nice place for BBQs and picnics.

Maraba Pottery
About 20 minutes outside of Kaduna on the Jos Road.

Guided Tours
Check out the following for guided tours in Abuja. They can also organise special educational tours for students to the outlying villages.

Cazogie: Travels & Tours
Metro Plaza, Suite 22
Plot 991/992
4th Avenue
Opposite War College
Central Area, Abuja
☎ 0803-705-1793

First Adventure Tours
Suite 3, Mangal Plaza
Wuse Zone 1
P.O. Box 12786
☎ 290 2834, 0802807 6252, 080323076252
Email: info@adventureparadise.com
www.adventureparadise.com

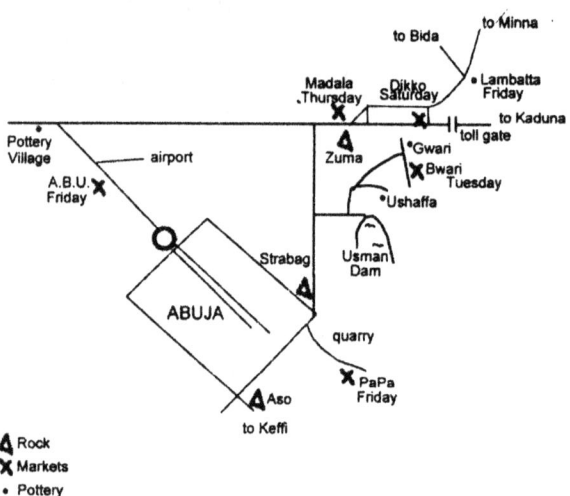

Markets and Pottery Outside Abuja

A.B.U
small village market
local fruit and veg
wooden pounding bowls

Dikko
one of the best Fulani markets
in the area
calabash hats knives
materials beads etc.

Madala
large market sells everything
woven baskets calabash enamel pots

Papa
village market
local fruit and veg beads pots

Pottery village
pots of every size
good for plants

Ushaffa
turn right at village, follow church
signs a pink building

Gwari
look out for large straw
and mud houses which are unusual

Ego-coty: Car-Hire Services
Peniel Apartments
Plot 137 IBB Way
Wuse II,
Abuja
☎ 08033275108
Car hire for single drops, two hour tours around Abuja, set prices for trips outside Abuja and to other towns.

Further Afield
Mileage Guide
The following chart lists the distances from Abuja to the State Capitals travelling by car on major roads. *Spectrum Road Map of Nigeria* is an excellent guide.

State Capitals	Distance from Abuja (Km)
Abakaliki	477
Abeokuta	740
Ado Ekiti	480
Akure	420
Asaba	404
Awka	440
Bauchi	445
Benin City	450
Birnin/Kebbi	573
Calabar	729
Damaturu	957
Dutse	512
Enugu	393
Gombe	606
Gusau	490
Ibadan	645
Ikeja	761
Ilorin	482
Jalingo	691
Jos	313 (3.5 hrs by road)
Kaduna	186 (2.5 hrs by road)

Kano	396 (4.5 hrs by road)
Katsina	570
Lagos	795 (8.5 hrs by road)
Latfia	180
Lokoja	193
Maiduguri	918
Makurdi	280
Minna	156
Oshogbo	428
Owerri	533
Port Harcourt	616
Sokoto	748
Umuahia	513
Uyo	593
Yenogoa	647
Yola	855

Kaduna

Kaduna was established as an administrative centre by Lord Lugard in 1913. The Polo grounds still host a polo tournament every October/November. The museum on Ali-Akilu Road with a crafts shop behind it is worth a visit. There is a small street of shops with Malian Batik and tie-dyeing near the polytechnic. The Arewa Centre has one of the better bookshops for Nigerian books and archives. Other spots of interest are Maraba Pottery Workshops, Havila Pottery Village (formerly Jacaranda), Matsirga Waterfalls, Kangimi Dam and Kagoro Hills. Check out the NAF (Nigerian Air Force) Club for good live music Friday and Saturday nights. The French Café is worth stopping at for bread, coffee and meals.

French Café
No 2 Ali Akilu Road
Kaduna
☎ 062 246151

Trappco Resort
Gwazaye Village
beside Kaduna International Airport
☎ 062 216050; 08027784647, 08037136121
trappcoranchi@yahoo.com
Suleman Abubakar, Managing Director

This is an actual tourist resort with quad bikes, horse-riding, pedal boating and a swimming pool. Food and rooms are also available.

Zaria
Zaria is one hour drive from Kaduna, an interesting old town to explore. Check out the beautifully painted Emir's palace, where an impressive Durbar festival is held every year. The Teejay Palace Hotel,
No 6 Western Way Close,
GRA Zaria.
(☎333303, 335640). It is a place to stay. There is a pottery nearby which is also worth a visit.

Minna
The name of the town comes from the Gwari words "Mi", meaning "to distribute" and "Na", meaning "fire". The city was originally situated on a hill surrounded by Gwari villages. One of the customs was for all the villages to put out all their fires and go in search of new fire in the town of Minna.

There are Fulani villages to visit, a very good boarding school, and Maizube farms. Shiroro International Hotel is one place to stay.

Assop Falls
A nice stop over for a picnic and a stretch on the way from Abuja to Jos. On the left hand side of the road, just after Gimi, you will see small signs for "tourist area".

Jos
Jos is one of the most easily accessible towns outside Abuja and provides a pleasant respite from the heat as it is located on a plateau, 12,000 metres above sea level. The drive is beautiful and takes

four hours. There is an excellent museum with replicas of different kinds of Nigerian architecture. There are several good restaurants. For good snacks and excellent home made cakes and ice cream, visit the Afri-One internet café on the main street. Fans of Dairyland products can sample their fresh milk, cheese and yoghurt and the Dairyland café. Excellent vegetables can be bought from local markets outside Jos. There are several mission guest-houses that will put people up for the night, or hotels (Hill Station, Plateau are the older ones). Other spots of interest are the zoo and the Jos Wildlife Park. The Shere Hills are less than an hours drive and provide a good spot to picnic and scramble on the boulders. Rayfield Lake is an old tin-mining site often used for swimming and boating. Kurra Falls, a NESCO (Nigeria Electrical Supply Corporation) hydro-electric water development of a series of dams set in the rolling countryside is a nice place to camp, swim in the lake and go for walks. Also worth mentioning are Kerang Volcanic Mountains and Wase Rock.

Kano

Nigeria's main northern city is not to be missed. Kano is architecturally and culturally different from the South and the East. Dating back more than a thousand years, it was for centuries one of the most active commercial centres in West Africa. Kurmi Market is still the site of one of the largest, and oldest, markets in Africa. Spots of interest are the museum, the old town and city walls, the Emir's palace, the central Mosque, the British Council building and the dye pits. The twice yearly Durban horse festival to celebrate Eid is very impressive. Tickets to view the procession from the Emir's Palace can be bought from the British Council. There is excellent (but expensive) accommodation at the Prince Hotel, Tamandu Road, Off Audu Bako Way, Nassarawa, Kano ☎064 629402, 633393, Fax: 064 635944) which has a pool, or La Locanda, 40 Sultan Road. Tel: 064648269), which has six guest rooms and is an Italian restaurant and guest-house.

Katsina

Just northwest of Kano, this 15th century town was a powerful centre of commerce and iron working. It has one of the biggest sallahs in the north with a long procession of horsemen and entertainers. The Liyafa Palace Hotel is recommended. Places of interest are the old market, dye pits, a museum (not open on weekends) and a minaret which is all that remains from the first mud mosque built in Katsina. You can walk up the outside for good views of the town.

Yankari Game Reserve (Bauchi State) (077 542174, 077 543671)

The Yankari Game Reserve is about 7.5 hour drive from Abuja and the only place to see wild animals in their natural habitat. The reserve has elephants, baboons, monkeys, various types of antelope, buffalo, warthog, hippopotami, crocodiles and lions. The best time to go is in the dry season from December to April when it is easier to travel on the roads and the game is more likely to gather at the Gaji River for water. Safari drives, in your own 4 wheel drive vehicle or an open top lorry, usually go out around 7.30 a.m and 4.00 p.m. Guides are provided by the reserve. Water and electricity supply vary. There are over 70 rooms available running from ₦1500 per night to ₦9500. A deposit for each night is required. Take your passports as you will have to sign in at the park gate and pay entrance fees for the vehicle and each person. A fee is charged for the cameras and swimming in the springs. The warm springs are clear and delightful to swim in day or night.

Take snack food and drinks as the restaurant is adequate but basic. Cooking is not allowed. Be careful of the baboons which will try to steal anything and can open unlocked doors. You are especially a target if walking about with food. Other items you might appreciate having are candles and bug spray (light coloured clothes are recommended against the tsetse fly which bites but carries no disease in this park). Mobile phones have no service in this area and there is no landline at the actual park either.

Lokoja

Lokoja is located at the meeting point of the Niger and Benue rivers. It was an important trade centre and a free zone for runaway slaves in the eighteen hundreds. In 1900, it was the capital for Northern Nigeria. The Confluence Hotel is a big conference centre and hotel on the river outside the town. Places of interest are the Emirs Palace; Holy Trinity Church with the first primary school in the North founded in 1865; First Bank of Northern Nigeria with only the strong room remaining; European cemetery; Tourist board/ Museum and Colonial History buildings in the former Senior Staff Quarters which were prefabricated in Britain and rebuilt with no nails or screws; Mount Patti for a view of the town and Niger plains, and an old tree with names from colonial times carved in it; the prison in the premises of the Kogi Hotel Ltd. – the smaller two-storey building is where prisoners were hung; and the governor's office.

The Ranch Resort (formerly called *Obudu Cattle Ranch*), Cross River State
☏ 08035506256, 087 2390001
gmranch@proteanigeria.com

Located in the north-east corner of Cross River State, close to the Cameroonian border, this Cattle Ranch is a popular travel destination. About 7 hours by road from Abuja via Makurdi, the ranch is located in the Obudu Plateau about 60 kilometres from Obudu itself. At over 1,524 metres, the climate is cool and pleasant. The landscape is lovely with rolling grasslands, deep wooded valleys and waterfalls. The chalet style hotel at the ranch has tennis, mini-golf and swimming in a natural rock pool and a 9-hole golf course. There are some short marked trails, a forest look-out and local guides who are eager to take groups on day hikes to explore the park. For those with more stamina, 3-6 day hikes can be arranged to track gorillas. The hotel is part of the Protea chain and has recently been renovated, is good quality and suitable for families. Charter flights and weekend deals are also possible.

International Institute of Tropical Agriculture (IITA), Ibadan

For those desiring to escape from Abuja to 'the oasis of Nigeria', the IITA is a tranquil setting, although not very Nigerian in ambiance. The easiest way to reach IITA is by Overland Airways direct to Ibadan or fly to Lagos and arrange transport to Ibadan (about 1 ½ hours). The IITA is set in several acres of tropical forest and has a good snack bar, excellent restaurant and good sports facilities including golf course, tennis, fishing lake, swimming pool, hiking trails and boule. The setting is beautiful and relaxing. There is a rainforest trail and lake within the grounds. There are single and double rooms and self-catering family suites, which are clean but simple, resembling a 1960 style UK university campus. Call Mrs Mary Akinlotan (02241 2626) to book a room or email: *iita-hotel@cgiar.org*

The University of Ibadan also has a good museum and cloth markets.

Oshogbo

For those interested in art and music, Oshogbo in Osun State is well worth a visit. Trips can be arranged via Mrs Nike Davies-Okundaye, from Nike's Gallery (0804 2109380, 0803 3036969) and include a visit to the sacred forest (to see sacred shrines of various Yoruba gods), time at Nike's Art School, viewing of Susan Wenger house and her impressive sculptures, and excellent dance and music performances by local artists. The trips are fairly pricey, but are all-inclusive, include good food and excellent accommodation. To get there, fly to Lagos and Nike will arrange transport to Oshogbo (4 hours). The colourful Osun festival takes place on the last Friday in August.

CHAPTER 18

Additional Resources

Beauty isn't worth thinking about; what's important is your mind. You don't want a fifty-dollar haircut on a fifty-cent head.
(Garrison Keillor)

Never be afraid to sit awhile and think.
(Lorraine Hansberry)

Abuja Specific Resources

Tour Nigeria ... the Complete Culture and Tourism Magazine. Issue 1, 2001, published by the Federal Ministry of Culture and Tourism. The Federal Secretariat, Shehu Shagari Way, Phase II, P.M.B. 473, Abuja, Nigeria 09 234-8297.

Tourist Attractions in Abuja – Nigeria and Nearby Destinations. Nigerian Tourism Development Corporation. Block 2 Sefadu Street, P.M.B. 167, Zone 4 Wuse - Abuja, 09 523-0418-20; 523-3191-3; Fax 523-0962

Other Non-Fiction

The Crippled Giant. Important work. Takes some getting into.

Drewal, Henry John and Pemberton, John. *Yoruba: Nine Centuries of African Art and Thought,* 1990. Abrams. New York. With excellent photos, this book covers the art of the Nigerian people in detail, and is a must for the art enthusiast.

Enahoro, Peter. *How to be a Nigerian.* Spectrum Books Ltd. A tongue and cheek look at the life and customs of Nigerians, written by a Nigerian. A must read for anyone planning on living and working in Nigeria for any length of time.

Idrees, Aliyu A. and Yakubu A. Ochefu. *Studies in the History of Central Nigeria Area.* Volume 1.

Isaac, Sharon, ed. *Lagos: Easy Access.* American Women's Club of Lagos. March 1998. Printed by Simon Printers Ltd. First edition. Both this and the second edition are extremely useful to anyone travelling to Lagos. Includes an extremely thorough "Recommended Reading" section at the back of the book.

Madauci, Ibrahim, Yahaya Isa and Bello Daura. *Hausa Customs.* Northern Nigerian Publishing Company.

Maier, Carl. *This House Has Fallen,* 2000. Penguin Books. Good basic introduction to modern Nigerian politics. Well-researched and written by an expatriate journalist.

Nason, Ian, *Enjoy Nigeria.* Spectrum Books Limited (Ibadan, Owerri, Kaduna, Lagos). Revised edition 1993. Good information on less-travelled roads and little-known towns. New edition 2005.

Newton, Alex. *Lonely Planet: West Africa.* 1995. Lonely Planet Publications, Singapore. Provides a good summary of the history and culture in Nigeria. Does a good job of explaining options for the budget traveller in Nigeria. Updated in 1999 by David Else and Mary Fitzpatrick.

Orji, Orji, *Inside Aso Rock*, 2003. Spectrum Books Ltd. Describes life in the Villa, the seat of government.

Omotoso, Kole, *Just Before Dawn*, 1988. Spectrum Books Ltd. Dramatises the first one hundred years of Nigeria.

Ogbe Hilda, *The Crumbs Off the Wife's Table*, 2002. Spectrum Books Ltd. Narrates a mixed marriage.

Omolewa, Michael. *Certificate History of Nigeria.* Longman Press.

Embassy of France, *Nigeria: Tourist Guide* printed by Academy Press Ltd., Lagos. Includes good concise information on the history of Nigeria, art, architecture, geography, music, the press, commonly used phrases in Igbo, Hausa, Yoruba and suggested itineraries of places to visit. Does not include a date of publication but must have been sometime between 1986-89.

Spectrum Road Map of Nigeria 13th Revised Edition, 2002. This map is the most authoritative up-to-date road map covering the federation including Federal Capital Territory, Abuja.

Seuil, Ed. *Valleys of the Niger.* Published by the Elf Foundation. A beautiful book of art and natural beauty.

Red Book of West Africa, Spectrum Books Limited. A book of Who is Who in West Africa, first published in 1910.

Fiction
Achebe, Chinua. *Things Fall Apart,* 1958. This story is about the

impact of colonialism and religion on a traditional Igbo village in the early 1900s.

Okri, Ben. *The Famished Road*, 1991. Spectrum Books Ltd. Okri is the winner of the Booker Prize for Fiction. In this tale, modern Nigeria is seen through the eyes of a young boy.

Skinner, Neil, editor and translator. *Hausa Tales and Traditions*, 1969. Published by Frank Cass and Co Ltd.

Soyinka, Wole. *Ake, the Year of Childhood*, 1981. Spectrum Books Ltd. Ibadan. Account of a childhood in Abeokuta. Winner of the 1986 Nobel Prize in Literature.

Quotes
Lady Ademola, *More African Proverbs*, 2002. Pocket Gifts, Ibadan, Nigeria.

Travel Books
The following travel guide books are good resources for those interested in exploring other parts of Africa while in Abuja.

- Eyewitness Guide
- Fodor's
- Frommer's
- Lonely Planet
- Michelin
- Rough Guide

Websites

General Information on Abuja and/or Nigeria
www.abujayellowpages.com
Adetokunbo Ademola Crescent
Beside Saudi Embassy
☎0803-302-0610
www.afrione.com
www.cnenigeria.com

www.discovernigeria.com
www.e-nigeria.com
www.everything-nigeria.com
www.abujacity.com
www.motherlandnigeria.com
www.nigeria.com
www.nigerianet.com
www.allafrica.com/Nigeria
www.fosnigeria.com (federal government of Nigeria website)

Travel Websites

Adventure Center	www.adventurecenter.com
Cheap Flights	www.cheapflights.co.uk
Travel Select	www.travelselect.com
Travel Information	www.tiss.com

Security

Australian Department of Foreign Affairs and Trade
— www.dfat.gov.au/consular/advice

British Foreign & Commonwealth Office — www.fco.gov.uk/travel/countryadvice.asp

Canadian Department of Foreign Affairs and International Trade (DFAIT)
— http://voyage.dfait maeci.gc.ca/destinations/menu_e.html

Centres for Disease Control and Prevention
— http://www.cdc.gov/fraud

Federal Aviation Association (FAA)
— http://www.faa.gov/avr/iasa/

French Ministry of Foreign Affairs
— www.dfae.diplomatie.fr/voyageurs/estrangers/avis/conseils/default/asp

German Foreign Ministry
— www.auswaertiges-amt.de

New Zealand Ministry of Foreign Affairs and Trade
— www.mfat.govt.nz/travel/report.html
U.S. State Department
— http://travel.state.gov/travel_warnings.html; n
www.usembassy.state.gov/nigeria

Appendix

Emergency Numbers

Command HQ Control room	198, 199
Airport Police Station	09 8100199
APO (Legislators Quarters)	09 6707711
Asokoro Police Station	09 3140161, 09 6709911
Federal Secretariat (Phase 1)	09 5234252
Federal Secretariat (Phase 2)	09 2348281
Garki Police Station	09 2349457, 09 2349167
Gwagwalada Police Station	09 8821296, 09 8821199
Gwarinpa Police Station	09 6706611
Kubwa Police Station	09 6700709
Life Camp Police Station	09 5212199, 09 5211199
Maitama Police Station	09 4134683, 09 6708811
National Assembly	09 2340241
Nyanya/Karu	09 6702211
Wuse Police Station	09 5232472, 5231199, 5231503

Others

Abuja Area Command	09 4134682
Bomb Disposal Unit	09 2347212
Criminal Investigation Dept. (C.I.D.)	09 6703322
Operations Department	09 6703311
Public Relations Department	092341223, 09 6704411

www.ingramcontent.com/pod-product-compliance
Lightning Source LLC
Chambersburg PA
CBHW071152300426
44113CB00009B/1180